THE EUROPEAN UNION SERIES

General Editors: Neill Nugent, William E. Paterson, Vincent Wright

The European Union series is designed to provide an authoritative library on the European Union, ranging from general introductory texts to definitive assessments of key institutions and actors, policies and policy processes, and the role of member-states.

Books in the series are written by leading scholars in their fields and reflect the most up-to-date research and debate. Particular attention is paid to accessibility and clear presentation for a wide audience of students, practitioners and interested general readers.

The series consists of four major strands:

- General textbooks
- The major institutions and actors

- The main areas of policy
- The member-states and the Union

The series editors are **Neill Nugent**, Professor of Politics and Jean Monnet Professor of European Integration, Manchester Metropolitan University, and **William E. Paterson**, Director of the Institute of German Studies, University of Birmingham. Their co-editor until his death in July 1999, **Vincent Wright**, was a Fellow of Nuffield College, Oxford University. He played an immensely valuable role in the founding and development of the European Union Series and is greatly missed.

Feedback on the series and book proposals are always welcome and should be sent to Steven Kennedy, Palgrave, Houndmills, Basingstoke, Hampshire RG21 6XS, UK or by e-mail to s.kennedy@macmillan.co.uk

General textbooks

Published

Desmond Dinan **Ever Closer Union: An Introduction to European Integration** (2nd edn) (Rights: World excluding North and South America, Philippines and Japan)

Desmond Dinan **Encyclopedia of the European Union** (Rights: Europe only)

Simon Hix **The Political System of the European Union**

John McCormick **Understanding the European Union: A Concise Introduction**

Neill Nugent **The Government and Politics of the European Union** (4th edn) (Rights: World excluding USA and dependencies and Canada)

John Peterson and Elizabeth Bomberg **Decision-Making in the European Union**

Ben Rosamond **Theories of European Integration**

Forthcoming

Simon Bulmer and Andrew Scott **European Union: Economics, Policy and Politics**

Andrew Scott **The Political Economy of the European Union**

Richard Sinnott **Understanding European Integration**

Also planned

The History of the European Union
The European Union Source Book
The European Union Reader

The major institutions and actors

Published

Renaud Dehousse **The European Court of Justice**

Justin Greenwood **Representing Interests in the European Union**

Fiona Hayes-Renshaw and Helen Wallace **The Council of Ministers**
(continued overleaf)

Brussels Bureaucrats?

The Administration of the European Union

Anne Stevens
with Handley Stevens

First published 2001 by
PALGRAVE
Houndmills, Basingstoke, Hampshire RG21 6XS and
175 Fifth Avenue, New York, N.Y. 10010
Companies and representatives throughout the world

PALGRAVE is the new global academic imprint of St. Martin's Press LLC
Scholarly and Reference Division and Palgrave Publishers Ltd (formerly
Macmillan Press Ltd).

ISBN 0-333-60489-X hardback
ISBN 0-333-60490-3 paperback

This book is printed on paper suitable for recycling and
made from fully managed and sustained forest sources.

A catalogue record for this book is available
from the British Library.

Library of Congress Cataloging-in-Publication Data
Stevens, Anne, 1942–
    Brussels bureaucrats? : the administration of the European Union /
Anne Stevens with Handley Stevens.
        p. cm. – (European Union series)
    Includes bibliographical references and index.
    ISBN 0-333-60489-X
        1. European Union–Officials and employees. I. Stevens, Handley.
II. Title. III. Series.

JN35 .S74 2000
351.4–dc21
                                                                    00-059126

10   9   8   7   6   5   4   3   2   1
10   09   08   07   06   05   04   03   02   01

Copy-edited and typeset by Povey–Edmondson
Tavistock and Rochdale, England

Printed in China

For
Vincent Wright
(1937–99)
with my love

Contents

List of Figures, Tables and Exhibits

Figures

Tables

Exhibits

Preface and Acknowledgements

A big idea is not enough. The aspiration towards an integration of Europe that would make future European civil wars highly improbable if not impossible is perhaps the biggest idea that has been around in Europe since the middle of the twentieth century. But turning any idea into something that actually happens requires energy, effort and organisation. My interest in the details of the process – what people actually do from day to day to make it work – was one of my motives, over a quarter of a century ago, for choosing a postgraduate course in European Studies when I was looking for a way of reflecting on my working experience as a civil servant in a more academic framework. That led on to work on the French administration, as well as on the British civil service, to which I am connected by descent and marriage as well as by my early career. All these interests and experiences suggested that a study of the administration of the European Union would knit together many strands of understanding and interest.

The nomenclature is complex. The term 'European Union' (EU) refers to the whole structure, which was created at the coming into force of the Maastricht Treaty in 1993. What existed prior to that should be referred to as the European Community (EC), which continues as the largest 'pillar' in the complex architecture of the EU. The EC is, broadly speaking, the only element which is competent to make laws. It therefore continues to be appropriate to refer to European Community legislation and policies. The institutions, services and officials with which this study is concerned are mainly, but not entirely, those of the European Community. However, common usage has increasingly cut through the complexities and uses EU as a general term, even when it may technically be anachronistic or inexact. This book therefore generally employs the term European Union except where the specificity of the reference makes this particularly inappropriate. Within the European Commission President Prodi ruled in 1999 that its reorganised component parts – the Directorates General (DGs) – must abandon the longstanding habit of labelling themselves by roman numerals (for example, DG VI, DG X) and use instead names that describe their work (Agriculture, Education and Culture: see Table 1.1). We have generally tried to use both numbers and descriptors when referring to any period before 1999.

In undertaking this work I have incurred many debts of gratitude. My parents, Margaret and Bob Ross, with great kindness, took in a temporarily homeless couple and several chapters were completed under their hospitable roof. Bob Ross read the proofs with speed and meticulous care. Above all my debt is to my husband, Handley Stevens. His contact with the administration of the European Union began when his first posting in the Diplomatic Service took him to the 'third room' in the European Economic Organisations Department of the Foreign Office (as it then was) where he assisted the one desk officer responsible for the UK's relations with the European Economic Community at their nadir, when Harold Macmillan's application for membership had just been vetoed by French President Charles de Gaulle. Soon after British entry a decade later, at about the time I returned to academia, he was shuttling to and fro to Brussels as an official of the Department of Trade and Industry and later as the head of International Aviation at the Department of Transport during the negotiations which established EU policy in air transport. He took part in various groups convened by the European Commission or the Council of Ministers, and supported British ministers at Council meetings. These contacts and activities provided much matter for conversation and reflection and fed a shared fascination with the administration of the EU. Nevertheless, the decision that one of the aims of early retirement would be 'to help with the book', which would become a much more joint endeavour, required a considerable leap of faith on both our parts. The European Institute of the London School of Economics provided him with a welcoming base from which to do so and support for work on the recruitment and training of EU civil servants within the framework of a research project directed by Dr Moshe Maor and on the basis of work done by Olivier Sterckx (Maor and Stevens, 1996). We are both grateful to them, and also to Dr Howard Machin, then the Director of the Institute, for kindness and encouragement over many years. How closely Handley and I have worked together is reflected in the attribution of the book. We have discovered how much easier interviewing is with the moral and practical support of a partner. He has dug around in dusty papers, contributing in particular his experience of public sector personnel and financial management, while I have searched the Internet. We have criticised each other's style, reshaped each other's arguments, and he has above all taken a rather unformed text and fashioned and cut it into a much tauter and shapelier study. After a book and some three and a half decades of marriage we can still happily affirm that partnership flourishes.

We undertook over 40 interviews in 1995 and 1999. We are very grateful to all those who were so generous with their time and information. David Spence, academic and official, gave us valuable help and insights. We are also indebted to the Brussels Office of the County and University of Kent, to Sandra Penning, then its director, and to successive student *stagiaires*, especially Rachael Taylor and Sarah Weeks. I am grateful also to Aston University, and especially my colleagues in the School of Languages and European Studies, for allowing me time to take the book forward immediately after my arrival and tolerating their head of school's lapses when she proffered the excuse that 'I must get on with the book.' My understanding of both the evolution of administrative services and of the European Union has benefited greatly over many years from the help and advice of my friend and colleague Professor Clive Church, one of the rare people who share both aspects of my academic interests. He very kindly read the first draft of the full manuscript, as did a serving British civil servant with a close knowledge of the EU's services. Our thanks to them both, and to series editor Professor Neill Nugent, for their comments. I am particularly grateful to Dr Liesbet Hooghe of the University of Toronto for sharing the work in progress stemming from her extensive interviewing in the European Commission between 1995 and 1997 (Hooghe, 1999a, 1999b, 1999c, forthcoming). I also gratefully acknowledge permission to reproduce copyright material as follows:

Tables 1.3, 5.1, 7.1 and Figure 8.1 are copyright European Communities 1995–2000. We are grateful to Macmillan Press Ltd for permission to reproduce Figure 1.3. Table 4.1 is reproduced from Edward Page, *People who Run Europe*, Oxford

University Press 1997 © Edward C. Page by permission of Oxford University Press. Exhibit 9.1 is taken from Claudio Radaelli, *Technocracy in the European Union* © Pearson Education Limited 1999, Reprinted by permission of Pearson Education Limited. Exhibit 6.1 is translated from Marc Abélès, *La Vie Quotidienne au Parlement Européenne*, Hachette 1992 © Hachette 1992. Every effort has been made to contact all the copyright-holders, but if any have been inadvertently omitted the publishers will be pleased to make the necessary arrangement at the earliest opportunity.

Both Handley and I have had previous experience of Steven Kennedy's wise, supportive and patient help as a publisher. It goes from strength to strength and this book owes much to it. The encouragement and advice Vincent Wright gave at the inception of this project, which he did not live to see completed, was only a tiny part of the enormous role that he played in my life for a quarter of a century. The book is dedicated to him. For the weaknesses and errors which it contains I alone am responsible.

Birmingham and London   ANNE STEVENS

List of Abbreviations and acronyms

ACP	African, Caribbean and Pacific countries
BSE	bovine spongiform encephalopathy
CFI	Court of First Instance
CFSP	Common Foreign and Security Policy
CIE	Committee of Independent Experts
COREPER	Committee of Permanent Representatives
DG	Directorate General
DNE	Detached National Expert
DECODE	Designing Tomorrow's Commission
EC	European Community
ECHO	European Community Humanitarian Office
ECJ	European Court of Justice
Ecosoc	Economic and Social Committee
ECSC	European Coal and Steel Community
ECU	European Currency Unit
EDC	European Defence Community
EEC	European Economic Community
EP	European Parliament
EU	European Union
Euratom	European Atomic Energy Community
FFPE	Fédération de la Fonction Publique Européenne
GNP	Gross National Product
JICS	Joint Interpreting and Conference Service
MAP	Modernisation of Administration and Personnel Policy
NATO	North Atlantic Treaty Organisation
OLAF	Fraud Prevention Office
SEM	Sound and Efficient Management

SGCI   Secrétariat général du Comité interministériel
             pour les questions de coopération économique
             européenne
TEU   Treaty of European Union
UCLAF   Unit for the co-ordination of fraud prevention
VAT   Value Added Tax
WTO   World Trade Organisation

Introduction

Administration matters. Without it vision founders or evaporates. Administration cannot be an end in itself, as the derivation of the word from a concept of service indicates. If it is well done and harnessed to good purposes it enables the ends which are desired to be smoothly and sometimes speedily accomplished, while poor administration results in confusion and waste. In the early twentieth century the theorist Max Weber recognised that modern states which operate on the basis of rational and legal norms require a specialised administration. His famous definition of a state characterises it not only as enjoying a monopoly over the legitimate use of force within its territory, but also, importantly, as a political undertaking whose administrative staff exercise its powers. The existence of an administration was, in his formulation, essential to a modern state form.

Within the European Union (EU) the administration matters if only because without it the complex structure could not function. But the administration of the EU also has a particular and symbolic importance. Given the historical and theoretical role of the emergence of a specialised and professionalised administration in the development of modern states, some of those who wish to see the EU increasingly developing state-like characteristics have looked to its administration as a harbinger of closer union: the first sign and visible expression of the emergence of a European administration that might come to serve a European government.

This book does not argue that such a development has occurred, is occurring or is inevitable. It seeks to analyse the administration as it is now, and generally to eschew speculation about grand future developments, not least because we would argue that there is no clear or linear inevitability about the path which European integration will take in the twenty-first century. Instead we have chosen to focus upon the current state of an institution which is uniquely fascinating because it brings together people from the administrative traditions that have shaped and been shaped by the emergence of very different societies and governments, and requires them to find satisfactory ways of defining and carrying out the tasks that need to be done. It is a cliché of comment by polemicists, whether journalists, politicians, or lobbyists, that 'Brussels' is 'bureaucratic'. Those who operate the complex machinery that makes the European Union function are characterised as 'bureaucrats'. The word is almost always used in its pejorative sense, with all the accompanying connotations of rigidity, of a narrow minded penchant for over-regulation and unyielding application of the resultant legislation, of distance from the real concerns of everyday life, of attachment to well protected, indeed privileged, working conditions at the expense of the rest of the citizenry. As its title suggests this study seeks to look behind the image and to question the nature of the administration of the European Union. It is, it must be admitted, not solely concerned with Brussels as a geographical location. Just as, in the UK, all those who constitute 'Whitehall' are not found in the buildings along that road, so 'Brussels' encompasses staff in Luxembourg, elsewhere in the member states, and indeed in EU offices all over the world. Moreover, it argues that the administration of the EU needs to avoid bureaucracy in the sense ascribed to it above, but to cultivate and develop the positive characteristics which distinguish 'bureaucracy' as a modern and effective form of administration (see also Stevens, 1999).

Who are the Brussels bureaucrats, how much influence do they have over the outcome, and to whom are they accountable? How do they relate to one another and to national and local administrations within the complex network of EU institutions? Do they have an agenda of their own, and if so do they have the power and influence to carry it forward? Where do they come from, and what sort of ethos, administrative and cultural traditions do they bring with them? Is a collective European administrative culture emerging, and if so what is it like? Many of these questions have been addressed, at least in part, in the studies which have been published of the separate EU institutions, of the evolution of particular policies, or of the policy-making process. In seeking to explain how the EU administration works, this book draws on that literature, on some direct experience of policy-making at official level within the European Community and on more than 40 interviews conducted at the start and at the close of the Santer Commission's term of office.

That administration matters was dramatically illustrated by the downfall of the Santer Commission, which resigned on 15 March 1999, nine months before the end of their five-year term of office. The resignation followed publication, by the European Parliament's Committee of Independent Experts (CIE), of their first report on the allegations which had been made about fraud, mismanagement and nepotism in the European Commission (European Parliament, 1999a).

No single event has underlined more effectively the significance of the topic which this book seeks to address. The importance of 'Brussels' within the developing system of European multi-level governance is widely recognised, and there is extensive discussion of the major political issues such as proposals to extend the geographical coverage of the European Union or the range of functions subject to some degree of EU co-operation or control, but there is much less understanding of how the administration behind the scenes influences the shape and content of the regulations and expenditure programmes which emerge into the political arena and ultimately impinge on Europe's citizens.

It is our contention that the administrative system in all its fascinating multi-cultural complexity deserves to be studied not merely as an adjunct to the business of policy-making, but as a topic of substantial interest and importance in its own right. The events of 15 March 1999 demonstrated that if the faults and failings within the system are not remedied, it has the capacity to discredit and upset not merely its immediate masters but perhaps the whole process of European construction.

Although the Commissioners (but not Mme Edith Cresson) were cleared of most of the allegations which had been made against them at a personal level, they were found guilty of presiding over an administration which had turned a blind eye to mismanagement so deeply rooted in the culture of the organisation that it could be held to facilitate, even perhaps to encourage, fraud. These conclusions could be regarded as unfair, since the Santer Commission had done more than any of its predecessors to pursue a wide-ranging programme of management reform (see

Chapter 8), but the first reformers are often the victims of the processes which they unleash (Peterson, 1999a).

The report of the Committee of Independent Experts contained chapters dealing with the mismanagement of Community programmes in support of tourism, political and economic co-operation with countries of the southern Mediterranean, humanitarian aid (the European Community Humanitarian Office, or ECHO), vocational training (the so-called Leonardo da Vinci programme), the Security Office and nuclear safety. These were not new stories. Most of them concerned events which had taken place long before the Santer Commission took office in 1995 and some were already the object of enquiry by investigative journalists in Belgium, Germany and the UK. They surfaced simultaneously and with such damaging effect because Paul van Buitenen, an auditor in the Commission's financial control unit, who felt that his concerns about fraud and mismanagement were not receiving the attention they deserved from senior management in the Commission, filled his car with documents on all these programmes, drove to Luxembourg and eventually delivered them to Magda Aelvoet, a Green Party member of the European Parliament.

Even if the catalogue of fraud and mismanagement which emerged from the van Buitenen dossier and from the Committee's own inquiries was for the most part an assembly of old stories, the report which the Committee of Independent Experts produced in just two months was profoundly damaging because it painted a picture of a deeply flawed administration, accustomed to finding ways around its own rules, more concerned to spend than to look too closely at where the money was going, and desperately slow to take effective action when fraud was suspected. In a statement made in July 1998 to magistrates investigating the humanitarian aid programme, Claude Perry, a French national of Algerian extraction based in Luxembourg, who claimed to have made about £350 000 a year from a £10 million business based largely on Commission contracts, explained how his system worked in the following terms:

> The Commission wants a job done, and has no staff to do it, but they have an operating budget. So ... they hire a subcontractor like me. I submit an application and get a contract. Then the

Commission choose the staff, fix the salaries, tell the staff what to do. I am only a shadow boss, paying the salaries and expenses of these people the Commission calls 'submarines', because they operate out of sight. And I ask no questions.

If an official wants to holiday in Haiti or Madrid or somewhere within the framework of an aid programme for the Great Lakes region of Africa, I don't get involved. I just finance it, and bill it to that 'old whore', as we call the Commission. Everybody knows how it works, including the Commissioners. There are some 4000 of these submarine personnel working for the Commission. The system is still perfectly oiled and working. (Perry deposition quoted by Nicolas (1999, pp. 64–5) paraphrased in *The Guardian*, 15 March 1999).

Although Claude Perry's statement was made before a magistrate, it needs to be taken with a pinch of salt, bearing in mind that he will have been concerned to shift the blame for any fraudulent practices from himself as the contractor to the staff in the Commission who employed him. But the system he describes is broadly consistent with part of the picture which emerges from the CIE report. The Commission has taken on more work than it can manage with existing staff. It has solved the problem by getting outside contractors to run programmes on its behalf; however, the relationship between the Commission as client and the contractor, compounded by weaknesses in the Commission's financial control regime, has been too close to prevent the misappropriation of resources (see Chapter 3).

Although the most spectacular incidences and consequences of mismanagement and administrative failure occurred in the Commission, the services of some of the other institutions, including the Parliament and the Committee of the Regions, have given rise to court proceedings related to nepotism or misconduct. However, although scandal and mismanagement brought officials and administrative systems into the limelight, and although one of the themes of this book is the constant battle for reform, we do not want to suggest an overall and unmitigated picture of maladministration. Given the complexity of the tasks they face, and the limited resources available, many of the services perform remarkably well. We hope therefore to highlight strengths as well as weaknesses. As we examine this administration it will be appropriate to pay most attention to the Commission, which is by far the largest and the most complex of the EU institutions, but we have endeavoured to cover them all and to refer to them separately, particularly where there are important differences to note.

We begin by setting the administration within the institutional context which it is designed to serve (Chapter 1), and by outlining the different national and international administrative traditions which have contributed to the concept of a European public service (Chapter 2). In Chapter 3 we note how these traditions have found expression in a law-based system of administration based on a staff regulation and a financial regulation common to all the EU institutions which together provide the rather rigid framework within which the administration has to operate; and we show how this has failed to prevent irregularity and fraud on the scale identified by the Committee of Independent Experts. In Chapter 4 we observe how the rigidity of the system and its consequent vulnerability has resulted in a formal system of recruitment to a career service which has been widely supplanted and undermined by more informal modes of entry; and in Chapter 5 we observe a similar erosion of the principle of promotion on merit. We conclude our examination of the personnel policy dimension of EU administration by considering the factors which may make the EU a unique administration (Chapter 6). It has demonstrated a remarkable capacity to advance the European project over a period of more than 40 years through all sorts of vicissitudes, but has failed to respond adequately to the revolution in administrative cultures that has swept through the bureaucracies of the Western world in the closing decades of the twentieth century.

In the second half of our study we analyse the wide range of tasks which the EU administration is called upon to carry out (Chapter 7) and the hierarchical structures and procedures within which they operate (Chapter 8). We note that whereas the nature of the work to be done has changed over the years so that today there is a substantial role for management functions, as the Commission in particular has assumed increasing project and programme responsibilities on behalf of the Community, there is nevertheless a long history of failed attempts to bring about reform and a more active management culture within an organisation which still tends to focus primarily on its important and more glamorous policy-making role. In Chapter 9 we observe how conflicts are resolved both within and between the different institutions, and Chapter 10 explores the complex relationship between administration and policy-making. A final chapter seeks to measure the strengths and weaknesses of the EU administration, and to draw some conclusions about its place in the processes of European integration.

Chapter 1

The Structure and Resources of the European Union

Early moves in Western Europe towards the creation of 'European' institutions were influenced by three factors: growing ideological and political division between East and West; determination that the dire political, economic and social consequences of the 1930s depression should never be repeated; and rejection of the notion of competitive and assertive nationalism as a basis for relationships between states. At the end of the 1940s the desire to move towards greater economic and political integration, which was already quite clearly expressed within the French and Italian governments and administrations (Bossuat, 1995, p. 22), intersected with a quite specific economic and political problem: the future of the coal and steel industries. Jean Monnet, then the head of the French Government's economic planning agency, had devoted much of his fascinating life to work that promoted international co-operation. He was deeply convinced of the need for international integration. He also believed that groups of rational people, if brought together and confronted with a specific problem, could and would find rational answers that would serve the interests of all. He saw the solution of the immediate problem as the first step in a long process whereby the benefits of solving difficulties in this way would be borne in upon governments and their peoples so that union would result, and conflict, particularly Franco-German conflict, would disappear. Monnet enlisted the political enthusiasm of the French Foreign Minister, Robert Schuman, and the consequence was the Treaty of Paris, signed in 1951 between Belgium, France, Italy, Luxembourg, the Netherlands and West Germany. This came into force in July 1952 and established the European Coal and Steel Community (ECSC) which differed from previous

1

international organisations in one vital respect: the parties to the treaty agreed to be bound by the decisions reached within the ECSC framework even if they did not explicitly consent to them. They also agreed that the ECSC institutions – a decision-making High Authority, a supervisory Council of Ministers and a consultative Parliamentary Assembly – should be able to exercise their powers within the member states without requiring any further processes such as national legislation.

It did not prove possible, during the 1950s, to extend this supranational principle to the field of defence, for a proposed European Defence Community foundered. By the end of the decade, however, the six member states were able to move forward in two areas: the economic field, with a particular emphasis upon a common market; and atomic energy, which was at that time seen as perhaps the key area for future technological and economic advance. The Treaties establishing a European Economic Community (EEC) and a European Atomic Energy Community (Euratom) were signed in Rome in 1956 and came into force in 1958. There were significant differences between these treaties and the ECSC treaty but they all incorporated a broadly similar institutional framework, albeit with differences of emphasis. In 1967 the so-called Merger Treaty established a single set of institutions for what then became known as the European Communities. By then a common agricultural policy and a customs union had been achieved.

The two decades after 1967 witnessed the enlargement of the Communities to include the UK, Ireland and Denmark (1973), Greece (1981) and Spain and Portugal (1986). Although genuine economic and monetary union still seemed a distant prospect, the European monetary system was established, by political agreement, in 1979. The Regional Fund was launched, and by the end of the 1980s had been brought together with the European Social Fund and part of the agricultural policy to operate under a common framework as the EU Structural Funds, which deployed an increasing proportion of the EC budget. The judgments of the European Court began to have an important impact upon the policies of the member states.

The 1980s saw a renewed vitality in the process of integration, with the launch of the single market programme due for completion in 1992, and the Single European Act, which came into force

FIGURE 1.1   *The pillared structure of the EU*

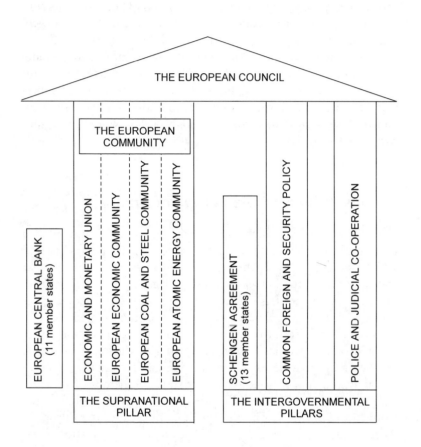

in 1987. It was a single act both in the sense that it amended all the three founding treaties that formed the bases of the ECSC, the EEC and Euratom, and in that it brought new policy areas into the treaty framework. Six years later, in November 1993, the Treaty of European Union (TEU, or the Maastricht Treaty) came into force. This Treaty created the European Union with its 'pillar' structure incorporating co-operation in a common foreign and security policy and in justice and home affairs (see Figure 1.1). The treaty contained a timetable for economic and monetary union. On 1 January 1995 the Union encompassed 15 member states, adding Austria, Finland and Sweden to its membership. Further treaty revisions were embodied in the Treaty of Amsterdam, signed towards the end of 1997, which came into force on 1 May 1999.

The institutions of the European Union

Under the treaties, which provide the European Union with a partial written constitution, the EU rests on three `pillars', two of which operate primarily through agreement between the member states, but since the EU as such has no legal right to sign treaties or pass binding legislation (Lintner and Church, forthcoming) its policies are largely embodied in legal acts of the EC which derive their legitimacy from the treaties, and their force from the political will of the peoples and governments of the member states. Policies may also be expressed through, for example, international agreements with non-member states or groups of states.

The institutions of the EU are the European Council, the Council of Ministers, The European Commission, the European Parliament, the Court of Auditors and the Court of Justice. Their role and working relationships are represented in Figure 1.2. *The European Council*, which meets at the level of heads of government, is the only institution of the EU (the others are all institutions of the EC). Its main role is to give overall political direction to the institutions of the Community, and to resolve at the highest level disputes which cannot be settled elsewhere. *The Commission* formulates policy and proposes the legislation and expenditure programmes required to carry it out (see Table 1.1).

FIGURE 1.2 *The role and working relationships of the EU institutions*

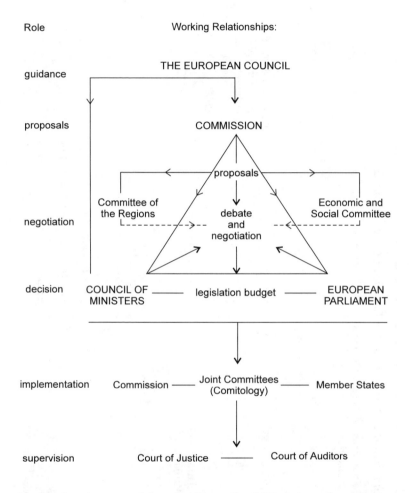

Legislation is enacted by *the Council of Ministers* after lengthy processes of consultation, debate and negotiation, primarily among the member states, but also increasingly with the *Parliament* (EP). *The Economic and Social Committee* (Ecosoc) and the more recently created *Committee of the Regions* also give their advice on the proposals which the Commission sends to Council and Parliament. The EP and Council together constitute the budgetary authority.

TABLE 1.1 *The Administrative Structure of the European Commission, 2000*

Responsible Commissioner	*Special areas of responsibility*	*General Services*	*Policy Directorates General*	*Internal Services*
President Romano Prodi		Press and Communication Service		Secretariat-General Legal Service
Vice-President Neil Kinnock	Reform			Personnel & Administration Inspectorate General Translation Service Joint Interpreting and Conference Service
Vice-President Loyola de Palacio	Relations with Parliament		Energy & Transport	
Michel Barnier			Regional Policy	
Frits Bolkestein			Internal Market Customs & Taxation	
Philippe Busquin			Research Joint Research Centre	
David Byrne			Health & Consumer Protection	
Anna Diamantopolou			Employment & Social Affairs	

Franz Fischler		Agriculture Fisheries
Pascal Lamy		Trade
Erkki Liikanen		Information Society Enterprise
Mario Monti		Competition
Poul Nielson		Development European Community Humanitarian Office
Chris Patten		External Relations Common Service for External Relations
Viviane Reding	Publications Office	Education & Culture
Michaele Schreyer		Budget Financial Control Fraud Prevention Office
Pedro Solbes Mira	Statistical Office	Economic & Financial Affairs
Gunther Verheugen		Enlargement Service
Antonio Vitorino		Justice & Home Affairs
Margot Wallström		Environment

Most of the implementation and enforcement of EU policy and legislation takes place at the level of the member states and through their national systems and institutions. In a few areas, however, such as competition law, agriculture or coal and steel, the Commission has important powers of secondary legislation and implementation. Frequently these powers are exercised through joint bodies representing member states and the Commission within committee structures whose differentiating features, reflecting fine distinctions in the balance of power between the parties, are so complex that the system has become known as 'comitology' (see Chapter 10). *The Court of Justice* (ECJ: see Figure 1.3) and the *Court of Auditors* have essentially supervisory roles. Through its interpretation of legislation the ECJ has at times played a major role in the development of the EC's scope and powers and the balance of the institutions. The Court of Auditors reports on value for money in Community expenditure, and especially on financial regularity and the pursuit of fraud. The administrative structures of the main EU institutions are set out in Figures 1.3–1.5 and Table 1.1.

The resources of the European Union

In pursuing its objectives under the treaties which form its constitution the European Union has three main resources upon which to draw. It has legal powers, it has money, and it has staff. It is with the last of these that the main bulk of this study is concerned, since the staff are the key to the administration of both the legal and financial resources. But it is important to understand the tools at their disposal and the constraints which the staff of all the EU institutions face in obtaining these resources and using them.

The legal powers of the European Union

Pillar I of the EU, the European Community, may make law. European Community law takes two main forms: regulations, which apply immediately and directly; and directives, which set out what is to be done, but leave to the member states the choice

FIGURE 1.3 *Abridged organisation chart of the European Court of Justice and the Court of First Instance*

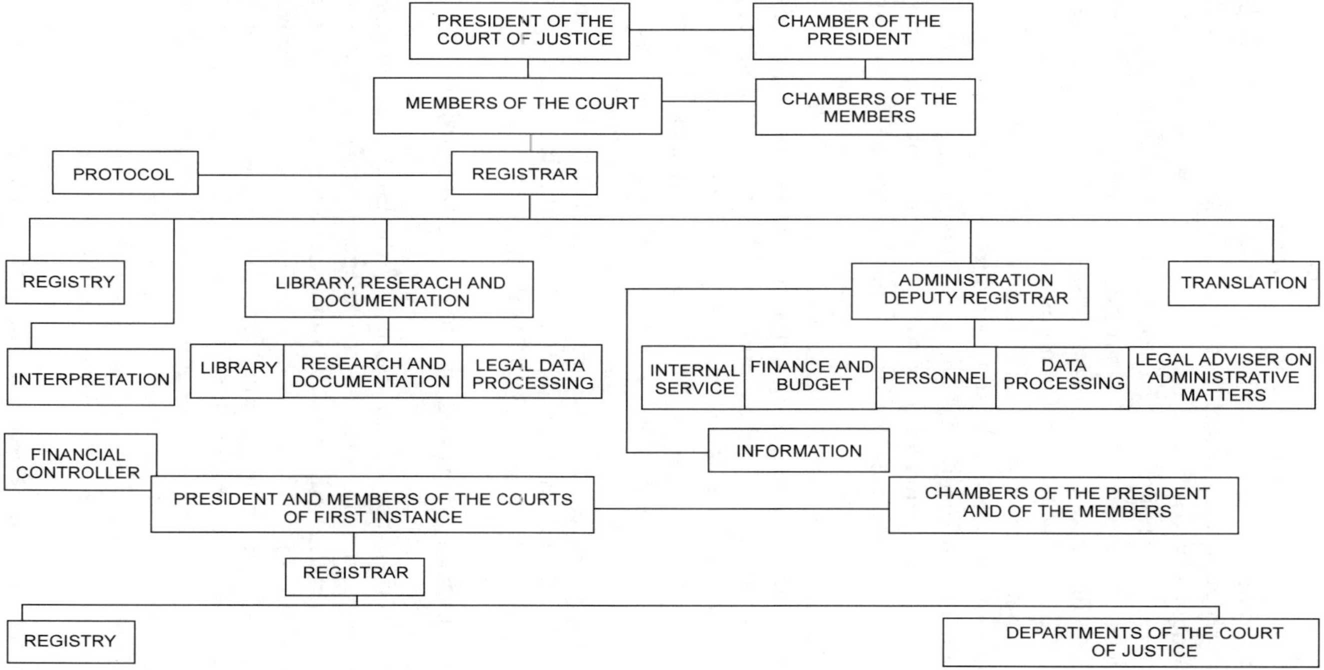

PRESIDENT OF THE COURT OF JUSTICE

CHAMBER OF THE PRESIDENT

CHAMBERS OF THE MEMBERS

MEMBERS OF THE COURT

REGISTRAR

PROTOCOL

REGISTRY

INTERPRETATION

LIBRARY, RESEARCH AND DOCUMENTATION

LIBRARY

RESEARCH AND DOCUMENTATION

LEGAL DATA PROCESSING

ADMINISTRATION DEPUTY REGISTRAR

INTERNAL SERVICE

FINANCE AND BUDGET

PERSONNEL

DATA PROCESSING

LEGAL ADVISER ON ADMINISTRATIVE MATTERS

INFORMATION

TRANSLATION

FINANCIAL CONTROLLER

PRESIDENT AND MEMBERS OF THE COURTS OF FIRST INSTANCE

CHAMBERS OF THE PRESIDENT AND OF THE MEMBERS

REGISTRAR

REGISTRY

DEPARTMENTS OF THE COURT OF JUSTICE

Source: Dehousse (1998) p. 11.

of the exact legislative measures required. (Note, however, that directives can confer rights directly on individuals.) In addition, the Community authorities may take decisions, which are legal measures applied to a single entity (a firm, for example). In 1998 the Council of Ministers, or the Council and the EP together, enacted 202 regulations, 53 directives and 196 decisions. Under its delegated powers the Commission also enacted 773 regulations 44 directives and 573 decisions.

The process by which a Community law is made involves, first, the formulation of a proposal for a law which is approved by the College of Commissioners and passed to the Council of Ministers and the EP (see Figures 1.4 and 1.5). There follows an extensive period of negotiation within and between the three law-making institutions (Commission, Council and Parliament) whose respective powers vary depending on the subject matter of the proposal (for a detailed analysis see Nugent, 1999, pp. 358–74). Most legislation – apart from agricultural, justice and home affairs, trade, fiscal harmonisation and Economic and Monetary Union issues – is now subject to co-decision. The procedural details are complex, but the key point is that if the EP is not satisfied with the Council's response to its proposed amendments, it can insist on the establishment of a conciliation committee which has to hammer out a compromise acceptable to a qualified majority within the Council and an absolute majority in the Parliament. If no such text can be found, the proposal falls.

The financial resources of the European Union

Money is the second main resource of the European Union. The original treaties provided for the financing of the Communities which they created. The 1965 merger treaty, which brought together the institutions of the three Communities, also provided for a single general budget. In 1970 a budgetary treaty made provision for the Community to be furnished, as foreseen in the Treaty of Rome, with its 'own resources': that is, with funds that would automatically accrue to it on the basis of set formulae so that it would not be dependent on periodic decisions by the member states. However, any changes in the formulae involve treaty amendments, which require national ratification so '[a]ny one member state can effectively block an increase in the Union's

FIGURE 1.4 *The administrative structure of the Council of Ministers of the EU*

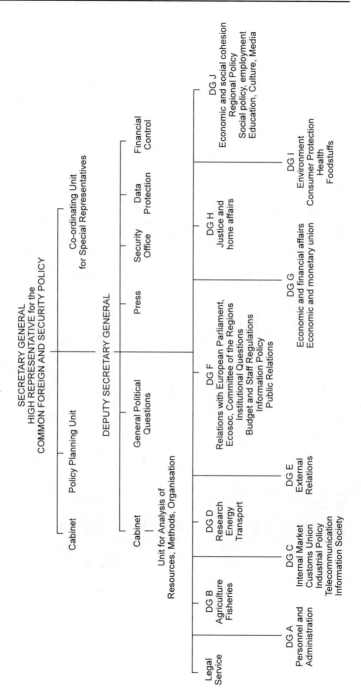

FIGURE 1.5   *The administrative structure of the European Parliament*

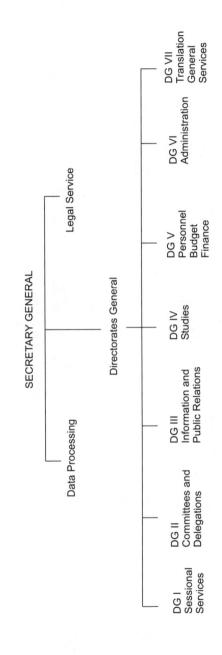

SECRETARY GENERAL

Data Processing

Legal Service

Directorates General

DG I
Sessional
Services

DG II
Committees and
Delegations

DG III
Information and
Public Relations

DG IV
Studies

DG V
Personnel
Budget
Finance

DG VI
Administration

DG VII
Translation
General
Services

financial resources' (Laffan, 1997, p. 40). This greater independence evoked demands for greater political control of finance and resources at the Community level, and the 1975 budgetary treaty gave the Parliament, alongside the Council of Ministers, an enhanced formal status as the budgetary authority.

The Union's funds derive from four sources. These are the proceeds of any customs duties levied on imports from outside the Union, the proceeds of various levies on the import and export of agricultural produce, a sum of money from each member state equal to the yield of a rate of value added tax (VAT) set from 1986 at 1.4 per cent (gradually reduced to 1 per cent between 1993 and 1999) on a uniform base of goods and services, and finally a further contribution based on the size of each member state's Gross National Product (GNP). This fourth source of funding was introduced in 1988 and it is expected that by the end of the century half the Union's resources will derive from it (Laffan, 1997, p. 46). Altogether the amount of resources accruing to the European Union must not exceed a percentage of the total GNP of the member states which will rise to 1.27 per cent in 1999. As Laffan points out, the Union's dependence on resources which are closely linked to the health and rate of growth of the economies of the member states means that its income may be adversely affected by slowdowns or recession. The Union has no powers to even out its financial flows. Indeed it is one of the rules of the Union budget that it may not run a deficit or borrow to meet its spending. When the Union's income is less than had been anticipated (as between 1992 and 1994), tight management is necessary and there are real constraints on administrative spending (Laffan, 1997, p. 47).

These resources finance the activities of the Union. Less than 5 per cent of the total budget finances the administrative and staff costs (including pensions) of the institutions of the Union. This modest figure for running costs reflects the extent to which the implementation of Union policies is carried out within the member states. About 83 per cent of the budget goes to finance the Common Agricultural Policy and the Structural Funds. The EU finances the provision of such services – whether these be, for example, infrastructural projects financed by the cohesion fund or payment for set-aside agricultural land – but does not itself provide them.

The budgetary authorities of the European Union have, since 1975, been the Council and the Parliament. Their relationship was over a long period a difficult one: '[t]he sharing of budgetary power between the Council and the Parliament inevitably led to serious contention ... on issues of substance and procedure' (Laffan, 1997, p. 7). But budgetary peace, achieved since the late 1980s through a succession of high-level agreements between the Commission, the Council and the Parliament on the broad parameters of Community financing, does not necessarily mean that the Commission, which carries the bulk of the responsibility for the formulation, implementation and monitoring of EU policies (see Chapter 7), is adequately resourced to carry out its functions. Indeed, the 1999 Committee of Independent Experts, which examined the allegations of fraud and mismanagement of resources, suggested that some of the problems were at least partly caused by a lack of properly authorised administrative resources. A major plank of the proposals for reform of the Commission put forward in 2000 was that there should be much greater attention in the future to the matching of resources and responsibilities.

The budget is divided into two parts: Part A, 'administrative expenditure', and Part B, 'operating expenditure'. The Commission is developing a proposal for the introduction of activity-based budgeting, which, if agreed, would have the effect of merging Part A with Part B, possibly with effect from the budget for 2001. Part A provides the resources for the number of staff, both permanent and temporary, approved by the Council and Parliament as joint budgetary authorities. Traditionally the Council in particular has been very reluctant to increase the administrative budget for the Commission in line with the increased size of the Community and the widening scope of Commission responsibilities, and the Commission itself has been reluctant to press its case for more staff, knowing the response it would be likely to receive. No doubt the Council's intention has been to exert pressure on the Commission to redeploy resources and increase efficiency. The Parliament, on the other hand, has been more inclined to increase the Commission's proposed budget for existing programmes, or even for new programmes not yet approved by the Council, without at the same time increasing the staff resources required to implement such programmes. In relation to both parts of its budget the Commission is liable to find its proposals altered. In all the horse-trading which is involved the Commission's staff resources are seldom a high priority. This is not so great a problem for the two other major institutions: the Council and the Parliament are themselves both jointly budgetary authorities, and have arrived at a working arrangement which ensures that neither interferes with the other's running costs proposals.

The staffing of the European Union

The staff of the Union is its third major resource (see Table 1.2). It is with the nature, operation and dynamics of the staff that the bulk of this study is concerned. It is important first to consider the size and structure of the staffing provision. As a consequence of the budgetary arrangements described above the staffing of both Council and Parliament, although starting from a much more modest base, has grown at a faster rate than the staffing of the Commission (see Figure 1.6). Staffing in other bodies has also been held back. The Committee of the Regions has particularly resented being obliged to share a large part of its administrative

FIGURE 1.6 *Growth in staff numbers*

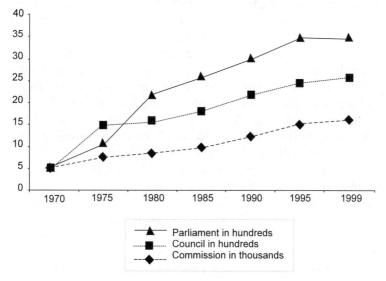

TABLE 1.2   *Authorised staff numbers in the EU institutions*

	Permanent posts	Temporary posts
European Parliament (including Ombudsman)	3491	611
Council of Ministers	2584	37
Commission:		
administration	16 511	690
research and technological development	3638	74
Office of Official Publications	525	0
Court of Justice	727	234
Court of Auditors	458	94
Economic and Social Committee	508	17
Committee of the Regions	209*	0
EU Agencies (see Table 7.2)*		1185

*   Includes both permanent and temporary staff.
Sources: Final budget of the European Community, OJL39, 12 February 1999, p. 129 and General Report on the Activities of the European Union 1999 (European Union, 2000): paras 1056 and 1062.

services with the much longer established Ecosoc. It failed in its attempt to achieve recognition in the Treaty of Amsterdam as a fully autonomous institution, but fulfilled some of its desire to enhance its political clout by running its own administration when the common organisational structure was dissolved during 1999 and replaced by a co-operation agreement setting out the arrangements for assigning staff to the joint services which the institutions continue to share.

It is surprisingly difficult to state with any certainty how many people really work for the European Union. The difficulty is particularly acute in relation to the European Commission. Middlemas (1995, p. 244) asserts that when DG XIII (Telecommunications, Information Industries and Innovation) moved premises in 1989, about 200 more officials were found than DG IX (Personnel and Administration) knew about. One interviewee told us that the existence of the Commission's consolidated telephone directory was a development of the early

TABLE 1.3   *DECODE figures for European Commission staffing*

Type of staff	Numbers
permanent and temporary staff	20 880
auxiliary staff	1033
detached national experts	760
casual staff	606
local agents	2133
in-house service providers	1836
extra-mural service providers	3765
TOTAL	31 013

Note: These figures are derived from the DECODE (Designing Tomorrow's Commission) report. The figure for permanent and temporary staff includes 1834 staff at Joint Research Centre establishments and 606 staff at the Commission's delegations in non-member countries. The figure for local agents includes 1919 staff at overseas posts.
Source: European Commission (1999), p. iii.

1990s in response to the requirements of the budgetary authorities who insisted that the Commission should know exactly who was working for it, and where.

One might suppose from the figures in Table 1.2 that the Commission employed some 21 438 people in 1999, but this would be a serious underestimate. An internal review of the Commission's organisation and operation (European Commission, 1999), based on a census of staff in April 1998, reckoned that there were in fact some 31 013 people working for the Commission at that time (see Table 1.3), and the figure is not likely to have been any lower a year later.

The Commission likes to compare its relatively modest size favourably with that of other administrations. For example, Hay notes that the Commission's policy and executive services are about the same size as the French Ministry of Culture or the British Lord Chancellor's Department (which administers the courts and legal services), and smaller than the total staff of the City of Amsterdam or Madrid (Hay, 1989); and Martin (Martin, 1995) notes that in the mid-1990s there was less than one

European civil servant (0.8) for 10 000 European citizens, while there are 322 national civil servants for the same number of citizens. But such comparisons are of doubtful relevance, since the work of the Commission is very different from that of a city or even a national administration. The Commission is directly responsible for the implementation of very few policies (in most cases that is the responsibility of the member states) and that is what generally requires large numbers of staff.

When account is taken of the staff of the other main EU institutions – 10 155 in Table 1.2 – it is apparent that the EU institutions as a whole employ over 40 000 staff. In addition there are also the European Investment Bank and the European Central Bank, whose staff are not covered by the main EU budget.

Permanent officials: grades and levels.   Under Article 1 of the Staff Regulations, an official of the Communities means 'any person who has been appointed, as provided in these Staff Regulations, to an established post on the staff of one of the institutions of the Communities by an instrument issued by the appointing authority of that institution'.

Staff are divided into categories: A, B, C, D and LA. A grade staff, who carry out the Commission's policy work and fill all senior positions, and LA staff, who fill posts in the Commission's language services, require a university degree or equivalent qualification. Exhibit 1.1 shows the grade levels within this category. Staff in category B, mainly responsible for executive tasks such as the Commission's own financial and personnel services, require two A-level passes (or the equivalent school-leaving certificate in other EU countries). Category C is for secretarial and clerical staff, who must have the equivalent of five GCSE passes. The messengers, drivers and other manual staff covered by Category D are required to show only that they have completed their compulsory education.

In principle (but see Chapter 4) staff are recruited at the lowest grade in their category (for example, for category A at A8, or at A7 if they have two or three years' professional experience). At the levels between A8 and A4, the rank to which a permanent official may normally expect to rise in the course of a full career with the Commission, there is no link between grade and function, which means that there is considerable flexibility in the level

---

Exhibit 1.1   Grade structure of category A

Category A has 8 grades:

A1:   Director general (or deputy director general)
A2:   Director (or principal adviser)
A3, A4 or A5:   Head of unit (or adviser)
A4 or A5:   Principal administrator (or head of section, deputy head of unit)
A6 or A7:   Administrator
A8:   Assistant administrator

---

at which policy work can be done below the level of Head of Unit, and no expectation that staff at, say, Grade A5 will have more junior A grade staff working for them. Staff in the most senior grades, from Directors General (A1) down to and including all Heads of Unit (often A3, but sometimes A4), are expected to manage the staff reporting to them, though some very senior staff, such as a Principal Adviser at Grade A2, may have no staff beyond immediate secretarial support.

Temporary staff.   Large numbers of temporary and other staff work in various capacities alongside the staff permanently engaged under the statutory regime. These fall into several distinct categories. The first group of such staff are the temporary staff covered by a special set of terms and conditions within the framework of the Staff Regulations. The Commission is the main employer of such temporary staff and small numbers of them are found in all parts of it, but the most significant concentrations are among scientific and technical staff in the Directorates responsible for the management of research programmes, and at the various establishments which together comprise the Community's own Joint Research Centre. In July 1994, of 3009 staff paid from research appropriations, 2103 (about 70 per cent) were on temporary contracts (Petit-Laurent, 1994, p. 41). This emphasis on temporary appointments for research staff reflects a policy dating from 1976 which is designed to encourage mobility within the Commission's research services and between these and national research centres, and to make it easier for the Commission to adjust its research programmes to changing requirements (Hay, 1989).

Another large group of temporary staff is found in the *cabinets* (private offices) of the Commissioners (see Chapter 10), where at the same date 221 staff were on temporary terms, out of a total of 303. This is a convenient arrangement because it allows Commissioners to bring in staff to work closely with them if they so wish, without the need for the lengthy recruitment and appointment procedures which apply to permanent staff. However, over the years many staff who have joined the Commission in this way have been appointed to permanent positions when they have completed their period of service in the commissioner's *cabinet*.

Detached national experts. 'Detached national experts' (DNEs) – staff on secondment from various administrations or private companies in the member states – form a distinct category of temporary staff with their own terms and conditions. The Spierenburg Report (1979) criticised the European Communities for their lack of openness towards the different national administrations, and recommended both a rolling programme of four-year temporary appointments and the utilisation of national experts seconded from their home administrations for short periods ranging from one month to one year. The institution most involved in such exchanges is the Commission where the first exchanges had in fact taken place in 1977, when five Commission staff were seconded to national administrations for a few months and 25 came to the Commission. Numbers of outward secondments have remained small, in the region of 20–30 a year since the early 1980s, but inward secondments grew rapidly from about 1985 onwards. The figure was generally thought to have stabilised at around 600–650 since 1991, but the DECODE report found 760 such staff in May 1998 (European Commission, 1999, p. 9).

The numbers are not so very large when measured against the size of the Commission as a whole, but their significance lies in their concentration, since they account for about 15 per cent of all A grade staff, 30 per cent of staff at A4/A5 and even higher proportions than that in some Directorates (Petit-Laurent, 1994,

p. 13). The Spierenburg committee thought that the presence of more than about 20 per cent temporary staff at A4/A5 would distort the European character of the Community administration (Spierenburg, 1979, p. 38). The DECODE report does not show concentrations at A4/A5, but it does show that by 1998 the heaviest concentrations of DNEs were to be found in the more technical directorates such as statistics, nuclear safety, customs and taxation. Even so, there were more than 40 DNEs in each of the directorates responsible for industrial policy, employment and social affairs, and relations with East and Central Europe (European Commission, 1999, pp. 9–10).

The terms of service of the detached national experts in the Commission were set out in a Commission decision dated 26 July 1988 (revised 20 September 1991). They are defined in Article 1 of that decision as national and international civil servants or private sector employees temporarily serving with the institution under the staff exchange scheme. Their salaries are paid by the national, regional or local administrations or companies which provide them and they must be citizens of a member state. The Commission covers their living expenses in Brussels. They may work at the Commission for a period of not more than three years and not less than three months. As they are not part of the statutory staff, they have no access to internal competitions and cannot normally be integrated into the statutory staff. However, it does not prevent them from applying and being recruited to temporary staff posts (Spence, 1997a, p. 80). Initially limited to category A, the exchanges have been extended to category B. Community civil servants on secondment to national administrations remain subject to the Staff Regulations.

The role, and above all the number, of national experts on secondment was criticised in a report of the Committee on Institutional Affairs presented to the European Parliament in 1993. The rapporteur of the Committee, Mrs Cassanmagnago-Cerretti, acknowledged the advantages of the presence of national experts in the Commission. 'Not only do they bring their skills to the Commission, they also take back to their national administrations a greater understanding of the institutional structures of the Community and the problems which it faces' (Cassanmagnago-Cerretti, 1993). This understanding is very important given the necessarily close collaboration between the Commission and national administrations, and it was the main reason why the Commission encouraged the increase in such secondments which has taken place (Hay, 1989, p. 50). However, as Mrs Cassanmagnago-Cerretti pointed out, the presence of so many national experts is not without disadvantages: some member states are over-represented, and some people fear that such a strong representation of national civil servants and their exercise of authority on behalf of the Union could weaken the independence of the European civil service (Cassanmagnago-Cerretti, 1993, pp. 6–9; Penaud, 1993, p. 67; Petit-Laurent, 1994, p. 14).

Consultancies and contracts.   A third category of temporary staff includes those engaged by the Commission under various forms of contract. In the late 1980s, under intense pressure from the Iberian enlargements and the 1992 internal market programme, the Commission found a convenient device to circumvent the squeeze on its resources in the creation of so-called 'mini-budgets'. This procedure entailed the allocation to relevant staff costs of some of the money intended to finance particular expenditure programmes under Part B of the budget, thereby circumventing the limitations on staff numbers and administrative expenditure imposed under Part A.

Mini-budgets were condemned by the Court of Auditors in 1990, and subsequently in two reports on the staff policy of the Community institutions which were made for the European Parliament by the Committee on Budgets. In 1992 the report by Mr James Elles, the Committee's Rapporteur, stated that almost one-third of the staff working for the Commission came from outside and were paid in part from the operating section of the budget. Moreover, in some DGs the number of outside staff was greater than the number of statutory staff. The report emphasised the need for greater budgetary transparency, which mini-budgets do not permit (Elles, 1992, pp. 6–11). Mr Elles's 1994 report noted that the mini-budgets had been deleted and all relevant costs were included in the Commission's administrative budget. However, the conversion of posts from mini-budgets into the normal budget was not yet complete, and in 1994 considerable staff expenditure still remained, particularly under the headings of research and structural funds (Elles, 1992, pp. 8–13).

At their peak the mini-budgets covered several thousand staff. Even in 1994, after three years of budgetary reform leading to the re-integration of about 1000 posts into the proper administrative budget, there were still more than 4000 external staff under contract to the Commission (excluding the detached national experts), equivalent to almost 25 per cent of the official staff complement. Some services, such as the European Social Fund (60 per cent), the Internal Market directorate (30 per cent) or the Human Resources Task Force (69 per cent), were heavily dependent on external resources in one form or another (Petit-Laurent, 1994, p. 13). The situation was not much better by the time of the 1998 census for the DECODE report. There were still 1836 people not counted as Commission employees, but contracted to provide services on Commission premises, and another 3765 not on Commission premises. The latter group included 863 staff in technical assistance offices (a device not unlike the mini-budget), as well as 252 staff working on EC aid programmes under the European Co-operation Agency, 947 full-time consultants and another 383 person/years of studies, and 474 person/years of interpreter and translation services. The other institutions also call upon freelance and contract staff. For example, the European Parliament makes considerable use of freelance interpreters and has devised a special retainer system whereby they can be deployed as required to cover Parliament's meetings.

Conclusion

It is apparent from this brief survey of the resources available to the institutions of the EU that we are examining an administration under intense pressure. It is by no means clear that its administrative resources have been allowed to grow at the same pace as its membership and responsibilities. The Commission in particular started out with a culture which preferred small size and unbureaucratic procedures; and even when it could bring itself to demand more staff, the Council of Ministers was reluctant to approve more than minimal increases. The largest institution, the Commission, is no longer small, and a multi-national, multi-cultural organisation with complex and challenging responsibilities is not easy to administer. Its failings have been catalogued in a long series of critical reports since at least 1979 (see Chapter 8), and the Santer Commission (1995–99) did more than most of its predecessors to address them, but the crisis of mismanagement which led to their early resignation confirmed that solutions had not yet been found, or at all events applied. President Prodi gave Commissioner Kinnock, one of only two vice-presidents, responsibility for designing a thorough programme of reform for the new Commission. He quickly launched an ambitious reform programme, but it remains to be seen whether he will be able to find the long-term solutions which have eluded his predecessors, and, if he does, whether there will be the necessary commitment at all levels of the EU institutions to resource and implement a reform programme on the scale which is required.

Chapter 2

History and Models

This chapter outlines the early development of the administrative services of the European Union, and evaluates the influence of various models of administrative organisation on its evolution. Most national administrative systems, even when they have undergone major change as a result of social and political upheaval, are deeply embedded within the society in which they operate, both reflecting and shaping many facets of that society. The administration of an international or supranational body is different in the sense that it has to be created, often at great speed, to serve a new purpose. But it is not created in a vacuum. Its authors bring to the task their own experience of administrative systems, both positive and negative, and this has a major influence both on what is adopted and on what is discarded. In the case of the institutions which were to evolve into the European Union, the initial task may have been limited to the management of a European market for coal and steel, but many of those who joined the organisation in its early years were attracted to a loftier objective in the construction of a much wider European project. Those who shared this approach, including Monnet himself, were reluctant to adopt administrative procedures which might constrain the development of that project, but it was not long before others, faced with the task of making the new institutions operate effectively, found it necessary to create appropriate administrative structures, and in doing so they turned naturally enough to the administrative models with which they were familiar. The tension between these two approaches to the administration of the European Union lives on in the reluctance of some of its administrators, mindful of the flexibility and informality of the early days, to embrace administrative reform.

The beginnings of the Community services

The creation of the European Coal and Steel Community involved decisions not merely on its shape and political and economic objectives, but also on how it was to be organised, where its offices were to be located and what staff it would need. This period has been closely studied by Yves Conrad and this section draws heavily on his work (1989, 1992). An interim committee was established to sort out these matters, and at an 'epic' conference in Paris on 23 July 1952 a number of important decisions were made (Conrad, 1989, p. 29), including the language policy to be adopted, and the location in Luxembourg of the Community's offices. The timescale was extremely brief. The High Authority was installed in office on 10 August 1952. Jean Monnet was offered the presidency, and so became responsible under the Treaty of Paris for the administration and for seeing that the High Authority's decisions were implemented. It was not until the beginning of October that Monnet called a meeting to begin to sort out how the High Authority should organise the necessary work. The solution adopted, initially *de facto* and subsequently in a regulation on the organisation of the body, placed full control of the administration in the hands of the president, rather than delegating oversight of any of the divisions or services to other members of the High Authority.

Despite Monnet's own long experience of policy-making in both public and private sectors nationally and internationally, he had spent relatively little time within standard administrative organisations. The League of Nations, of which he had been Deputy Secretary General, had minimal administrative services. He did not want a heavy or hierarchical organisation. The first vice-president of the High Authority recalled that he wanted a small, flexible organisation, of some 200 staff (quoted from an interview with M. Coppé in Conrad, 1989, p. 21), and the Belgian delegation to the talks preparing the Treaty of Paris noted that if the number of officials was kept down to the size of the administration preparing the Schuman plan, influences other than those of the French would not be able to make themselves heard and Monnet's authoritarian methods would be perpetuated. The coal and steel industries were especially concerned that the High Authority's services should not be too *dirigiste* and should include some staff who knew the sector, but their views had no influence.

The officials who made up the services of the new body conformed rather well to the profile that Downs categorises as 'zealots' (Downs, 1967; Mazey, 1992). Many came to their posts, Conrad concludes, in the hope of actually being able to achieve something useful, but acquired a measure of European idealism as they rubbed shoulders with 'convinced Europeans'. They worked long hours in pursuit of their goals, in a markedly unhierarchical and informal way. Monnet himself had trusted collaborators amongst the senior officials, especially Pierre Uri, the economic adviser who had come with him from the French Planning Commission. He would discuss his ideas with them, and then ask them – sometimes two or three of them in parallel – to draft papers for him. He was quite likely to ask a desk officer to undertake a task for him without going via the head of the division, and the officials themselves, if they needed information or advice, could and would go directly to the relevant person without passing via the hierarchy. As one of them said to Yves Conrad:

> The administrative organisation of the ECSC was very agreeable (*amusant*) for someone like me who had come from the public service ... If you were concerned with a matter involving a particular division you wrote a note to the person who was dealing with it, not to the division ... I have to say it was very effective ... much more effective than the normal procedure which does have to be respected in a big administration. (Conrad, 1989, p. 102).

While the relatively informal and non-hierarchical nature of the working relations may have been effective, it led to overlap, duplication and lack of co-ordination in certain areas. Although Monnet, reluctant to lose the flexibility of the early stages, seems to have resisted organisational definition, several officials were designated from the beginning to organise the administrative and financial arrangements needed, and within a few months 11 divisions had been set up. Their areas of activity and responsibilities were ill defined, and territorial disputes soon arose. Several divisions might be working on the same problem and, since there was little co-ordination, the High Authority might find itself faced with several differing submissions. By November 1953 it was clear that better co-ordination was required, and six standing working groups including members of the High Authority were set up, to which any proposals which the administration wished to put to the High Authority had initially to be referred. One of these was a working group for administrative questions, chaired by Monnet, with three other members of the High Authority, its secretary (Max Kohnstamm) and the Director of the Administration and Personnel division. In May 1954 this working group produced a statement of the responsibilities of the divisions, and noted that there was a good deal of overlap and duplication.

Another area in which the fluidity of the organisation produced problems was the area of financial control. The Treaty provided for a *Commissaire aux Comptes*, or auditor-general. Monnet thought that a simple financial audit was all that would be required, and the work could be contracted out to a firm of accountants. The German view was that the auditor-general should look at all the Community's income and expenditure as well as its assets and commitments, and should be entitled to express views on the merits of the expenditure. M. Urbain Vaes, a Belgian, who was the auditor of the Société Générale de Banque, was appointed to the High Authority. His first impression was one of such disorder and confusion that he thought the task was desperate; he begged friendly banks in Brussels to let him have some inspectors whom he set to doing an initial audit in the offices. Conrad observes that there were difficulties between a new body, whose administrative organisation was far from fully formed, and an auditor who was used to well-structured administrative organisations which were precise about details (Conrad, 1989, p. 67).

The adoption of staff regulations had to await Monnet's departure. The Treaty of Paris had provided for a Committee of the presidents of the four institutions (the High Authority, the Court of Justice, the Council of Ministers and the Parliamentary Assembly) to take decisions on the numbers of officials and their terms and conditions. One of its first decisions was to set up an inter-institutional committee to draw up staff regulations (a *statut du personnel*), but its main area of work was budgetary. Monnet himself accorded no priority or urgency to the establishment of the staff regulations. A draft was in fact produced quite quickly, and applied from 1 July 1953 as a 'provisional regulation' for the staff of the Court and the Assembly. The presidents of the four institutions seem to have been conscious that they were at the start of a long and possibly far-reaching process, which could lead to the establishment of a 'European civil service'. The fact that the Schuman plan was followed so speedily by detailed, if eventually unsuccessful, plans and a (never ratified) Treaty to create a European Defence Community (EDC) supported such a view. They were anxious that the staffing provisions for both ECSC and EDC should be consistent. The High Authority, however, dragged its feet, although the terms of the provisional regulation were in fact applied to staff contracts that came up for renewal. Conrad judges that Monnet was apprehensive about the emergence of administrative rigidities.

It was his successor, René Mayer, who pushed the work of drafting the *statut* forward, and it was adopted in July 1956, just over a year after he had taken office. Despite Jean Monnet's initial resistance, there is with hindsight a certain inevitability about the adoption of a statutory framework by an emerging policy-making bureaucracy drawing, to an important extent, upon former members of the civil services of the member states. 'The essence of a continental European bureaucracy was in its creation of a distinctive social class', and such bureaucracies 'are associated with formalism and hierarchy – the insistence that rules and procedures be observed' (Page, 1997, pp. 7–8). Both these features demand a clear statutory definition in order to entrench them. As Jacques Rueff, then a judge at the ECSC Court of Justice with special responsibility for managing its budgetary and administrative questions, said in 1953: 'We have, rather blindly, chosen the option of a statutory framework [a *statut*] by analogy, because we want to create a situation closer to that of national administrations than that of international organisations. We felt that supranational civil servants [*un corps de fonctionnaires supranationaux*] were, in fact, almost national civil servants, whose nationality was supranationality' (quoted in Conrad, 1992, p. 64; author's translation).

The creation of the European Economic Community in 1958 resulted in the fairly rapid creation of a much less fluid and more complex organisation than the ECSC had been in its early days. There were a number of reasons for this. First, the scope of the EEC was much wider. Nine Directorates General were established (External Relations, Economic and Financial Affairs, Internal Market, Competition, Social Affairs, Agriculture, Transport, Overseas Countries and Territories, and, last of all (Siotis, 1964, p. 244), Administration and Personnel), sub-divided into 32 directorates (Cassese and della Cananea, 1992, p. 83). A general secretariat was also created as a horizontal service, while the statistical service, the legal service and the press and information service were, until the merger of the three Communities, under the control of a group of Commissioners, one from each Community.

The greater complexity and scope of the EEC also explains the emergence of the Commissioners' *cabinets* as key actors in the system. Such private offices, which had been a feature of the French administrative system since the latter half of the nineteenth century, had been established to support the members of the High Authority in the ECSC (Ritchie, 1992, p. 99). There was an almost automatic assumption that the new Commissioners would need such support. The first President of the Commission, Walter Hallstein, 'wanted to keep them small. However, several Commissioners, including the French and Italians, argued that substantial *cabinets* were necessary because of the heavy workload' (Ritchie, 1992, p. 99). Indeed the *cabinets* were virtually the first administrative services to exist for the new Commission, during the period between January and March 1958 when the division of responsibility between Commissioners was being decided. Apart from them there were only a handful of other staff, mostly Belgian, charged essentially with housekeeping duties. For some weeks the head of President Hallstein's *cabinet* acted as secretary to the Commission (Noël, 1992, p. 146).

A second reason for the more structured creation of the EEC Commission services was the nature of the personal preferences of President Hallstein. Unlike Monnet, he had behind him substantial experience in a national bureaucracy and he brought to the EEC the hierarchical traditions of the German administration:

he wanted the administration of the EEC to be 'a great administration' whose senior officials would command equal status with the very top ranks of the national administrations (Noël, 1992, p. 150). 'The hive and all the frames were in place, and only then were the bees placed in the cells of the honeycomb' (Noël, 1992, p. 158). If the overall structures were seen as important, the subsequent management of the staff was not, and President Hallstein's interest in such matters was described, even while he was still in office, as 'limited' (Siotis, 1964, p. 224). The consequences of the approaches adopted in these early days were profound, and are explored in later chapters. Here it is worth noting that the system quite quickly attracted the comment that it combined the less desirable features of both French and German systems. The next section of this chapter considers the nature of those models.

Models of administrative organisation

The design of administrative organisations is certainly a political matter (Pierre, 1995, p. 11) but, once the crucial political decisions identified above had been taken, many other aspects of the design followed fairly automatically as the result of a relatively unthinking application of an accepted model broadly common to most of the six founding member states. The crucial decisions – as much implicit as explicit – were that the Communities, as a new type of 'supranational' body, should have a staff that was not simply an international secretariat like those that had served the Congresses and Conferences of the Concert of Europe in the nineteenth century, the League of Nations and the United Nations, or even regional bodies such as the International Commission for the Rhine. The notion that the services constituted a secretariat, or had anything in common with 'traditional' international institutions, was quite forcefully rejected (Siotis, 1964, pp. 228 and 244). Instead the view was taken that, since the European Community was destined to be an evolving institution moving towards integration, it should be endowed with an administrative service, analogous to those which had served the cause of national integration in many of the member states, comprising permanent officials, not persons on secondment or temporary contracts.

Since an explicit analogy existed between the services of the Communities and national civil services, and given that both Monnet and Hallstein were not greatly concerned with the minutiae of organisational design, it is not surprising that the emergent structure broadly conformed to the dominant model of public administration in the six founding member states. The administrative work of the Commission has been marked by the long predominance of French administrative style and practices and hence by a mentality which looks to French culture and administrative norms as the unstated model of public administration (Spence, 1994a, p. 65). However, the French influence is not unchallenged: for example, the procedure under which a reserve list is used in recruitment (see Chapter 3) reflects Belgian influence, whilst the right retained by the administration not to respect in its choice the precise order resulting from a competition comes from Italy (Ziller, 1988). German influence was also strong. Indeed, in 1964 Siotis scathingly observed that 'simply bringing together the principles and practice of public administration as they have developed in France and Germany' had resulted in 'fragmented and superficial solutions'.

The principles and practices of these two countries diverge in important respects, but they do broadly belong to the same family of administrative models. This is the model which Pierre (Pierre, 1995, p. 8) calls a public law Weberian *Rechtstaat* model. Ziller points out that it was Napoleon's administration which had perhaps come closest to Weber's ideal type, although he remarks that there is a distinction between the two concepts. Weber's model is an ideal-type, while the Napoleonic model is simply a convenient shorthand – he calls it a myth – for a collection of observed characteristics (Ziller, 1993, pp. 71–2). Pierre sees it as constituting one of the two globally dominant models, the other being the 'Anglo-Saxon' model. Cassese (Cassese, 1987, p. 12) identifies three models: the German model 'dominated by legalism, rigidity and administrative planning', the French characterised by 'the rigidity of the structures and the flexibility of the bureaucracy, and the English model by the flexibility of both'. He argues that the organisation and working rules of the

Commission are halfway between a French ministry and the German Economics Ministry, with personnel management conforming most closely to a French model, whilst the emergence of manuals of working methods and the use of *ad hoc* or permanent inter-service working groups owes much to the later influence of British models. The features of the various models are thus of key importance in understanding the way in which the administrative structures of the European Union have evolved.

The Napoleonic model

Discussing models of administration is difficult because of the risk of falling into imprecise, rather subjective and overly generalised assertions about styles, characteristics and culture that amount to little more than national stereotyping. Nevertheless, crucial features of the French model, which can for convenience be described as Napoleonic, can be identified. All-embracing, systematic and coherent, this powerful model derives from the administrative reforms introduced into France by Napoleon Bonaparte. He had at his disposal administrative structures which the Revolution had taken over from the monarchy but which had been developed and extended by the exigencies of war. He understood the crucial role of good organisation and needed its support for his military endeavours. At the same time, to ensure both stability and his own dominance, he was keen to ensure a system of checks and balances within society to prevent any one element from becoming dominant.

From this perspective the administration had a key position for two reasons. First, it could provide, through its scope, its expertise and its technical competence, a counterweight to political forces. An echo of this type of approach can be perceived within the EU administration. This is not to argue that the EU administration is in any sense antidemocratic. Liesbet Hooghe's survey of 106 top Commission officials between 1995 and 1997 found that most of them 'believe that the era of benevolent technocracy in the tradition of Jean Monnet has come to a close' (Hooghe, 1999b, p. 358). There is nevertheless a widespread sense that the role of the administration is to 'construct Europe', if necessary despite the reticences and national reflexes of the member states. Even an official whose approach could be described as 'inter-governmental' told Hooghe: 'I am an official servant of the European construction' (1999b, p. 358).

Second, the officials who comprised the Napoleonic adminis-tration were engaged for a lifetime career, linked by a loyalty to the Empire and the Emperor, subject to standard conditions and hierarchies, and developed a common *esprit de corps*. Thus they constituted a social force which could equal and balance the other two organised bodies within society, the armed services and the church. Napoleon certainly saw the material advantages which an official career could offer as an important tool for attaching members of the aristocracy and the leading families to his person and his regime. Later commentators (Rouban, 1998) have seen the administration as a mechanism for social stability. By offering relatively disadvantaged families the prospect of mer-itocratic entry to a guaranteed career and an enhanced social standing for their offspring it channelled aspirations and frustra-tions which, without some hope of an outlet, would have spilt over into social disturbance and instability. The guarantee of reg-ular advancement is hence an important feature of the career of officials. The administrative services of the European Union are so tiny that the ascription to them of a role of this kind would be ludicrous. However, traces of these approaches can be found in the *stagiaire* system, which seeks to attach young people to the ideals of the EU by bringing them into the administrative services for brief periods at the start of their careers, in the notion that officials enjoy a specific and protected status, and in their resist-ance to performance-based career progression.

The general features of the Napoleonic model, as they related to France, have been brilliantly characterised by Vincent Wright. He notes that it was a model 'attractive to tidy minds in untidy countries' (Wright, 1994, p. 116). It was, however, simply a model, never and nowhere fully realised and always subject to the 'untidy realities' of real life. The French administration of course came closest to it, and the model's widespread influence was due in part to its imposition on large areas of Western Europe during the period of Napoleonic conquest. It was also due, after the downfall of its creator, to the effectiveness of his organisation and the combination of elements adapted from previous practice with rationalised and legally coherent structures, which ensured continued survival and influence beyond the French borders. It evolved steadily throughout the nineteenth and twentieth centuries, and in France was subject to considerable restructuring in the aftermath of the Second World War. But it remains as a powerful point of reference, and its key features shaped the thinking of many who influenced the development of the EU structures. These key features can be identified in relation to the legal context and the structure of the administration.

The Napoleonic model: the legal context. The administration, in this model, operates within a codified and pyramidal legal structure. Legal systems which derive from Roman law assume a rational and hierarchical structure in which powers are delegated downwards, with their extent and limits specified by the texts which govern them. The law itself proceeds in a rational way, with specific details flowing logically from general principles. Very precise wording allowing for every contingency is not needed, since the legislator is providing a principled framework from which appropriate action can be deduced. Three other characteristics are important. The first is that the legal structures and principles that underpin policy-making are common to many continental European countries, having developed not so much within the framework of specific nation states as within a more widespread and shared academic and intellectual culture (Ziller, 1993, p. 275). The second is that within this framework there is a particular place for administrative law, which is seen at one and the same time as protecting both the administration and its subjects, through a system separate from the civil law structures which govern relationships between private individuals. French administrative law concepts have been influential in all the founder member states of the EU, and in many of the states which have acceded more recently (for example, Greece and Portugal). Third, law is codified, so that the logical connections are clear and the whole corpus of a particular type of law – civil law, for example – is brought together in a single framework. The *Code Napoléon* has had a marked influence on the development of codified legal systems in much of the EU apart from the UK,

Ireland and Scandinavia (Ziller, 1993, p. 279). These concepts have not only had an important impact on the development of EU law but also on the nature of the administrative services, since these are based upon a legal framework that defines the principles of their structure and their operation (see Chapter 3).

The Napoleonic model: structures and frameworks.   A second key characteristic of the Napoleonic model is the nature of its structures. Officials enjoy a distinct, legally defined, and normally lifelong status, conferred upon them by due legal process and only removable in the case of serious disciplinary offences. They are *fonctionnaires* (persons endowed with a specific mission) rather than employees. They cannot be sacked (other than as a major disciplinary penalty) or made redundant and, whether serving or retired, their conditions of service, pay and pension rights are governed by specific provisions of administrative law, not by the labour law which applies to employment. Advancement is largely a matter of seniority, a feature which is particularly marked, for example, in Spain, but an administrative pyramid is preserved by the fact that enhanced grade and pay does not automatically imply the occupation of a more responsible or commanding post. Internally the administrative structures tend to be very hierarchical, partly because of the concept – linked to the notion of law as emanating outwards from central principles – that authority to act in the name of the state (*puissance publique*) is specifically delegated downwards but only to a certain point. Consequently, within the administration proposals, drafts and letters normally flow upwards to the person who has the authority to act – usually the director or director general – rather than issuing from any particular level. At its most extreme this hierarchisation turns the official into a 'passive person'. As Jean-Luc Bodiguel has pointed out with regard to Spain, for instance, if performance is irrelevant to career prospects, any initiative is a one way risk; success brings no reward while failure may result in disciplinary consequences (1994, p. 56).

Such structures characteristically downplay the role of management. If performance is not a key feature in career advancement, management is deprived of one of its major tools.

Ambitious and able officials find their rewards in the quality of their response to intellectual challenges. In so far as senior officials do head up large groups of staff, their function is liable to be interpreted, as Michel Crozier demonstrated in the 1960s for the French administration (Crozier, 1964), as involving the rather impersonal exercise of their authority, essentially through command and control. Personnel issues are assigned to separate structures, such as a Ministry for the Civil Service, or a Directorate General for Personnel. Since such bodies cannot actively manage staff who are not under their control and may be very distant, they proceed by the elaboration of a regulatory framework. This relieves the operational units of any sense of responsibility for management, since all they have to do is apply the framework. This attitude, clearly evident in the French administration, can be traced also in the European Commission, where the 1997 management reform proposals (Modernisation of Administration and Personnel Policy, or MAP 2000) were opposed by many senior staff on the grounds that they were 'a *technical* hierarchy, not a hierarchy for the management of resources and the leadership of a team. In their view this is the job of the administration and not their business' (European Commission Directorate General for Personnel and Administration, draft report on the MAP 2000 programme, September 1999; emphasis in the original).

Related to these features is the importance, within such systems, of formal and external controls. If a key feature is that the legal framework should have been properly applied, then verification by external inspection is also important. Hence, in the French system, the function of inspection and external control has always enjoyed high prestige. However, the relatively rigid exoskeleton of regulation and inspection which encases the administration encourages the use of initiative, ingenuity and personal contacts to find ways around it – in France, for example, the notorious *système D* (*débrouiller* – to find a way through: Dupuy and Thoenig, 1983). Moreover, those at the summit may see regulations and procedures as part of the command and control mechanisms for subordinates, and one of the perquisites of success and authority as being relatively free from such constraints. This arrogance, at Commissioner level, had disastrous consequences in 1999.

The Germanic model

The notion of administration as a science or at least a technique that requires specific and professional skills goes back in Germany to the Prussian administration of the early eighteenth century. It implies, as in France, the attribution of a distinctive and lifelong status to officials, on the basis of procedures which involve first the establishment of eligibility through highly selective examinations and practical placements, and second recruitment into a particular post. In practice, since the examinations establish eligibility for legal as well as administrative posts, a high proportion of German officials are legally trained.

In the Germanic model, as in the French, officials operate within an administrative law framework and on the basis of terms and conditions set out in legislation, both at federal and state (*Land*) level. Two features of the German model are important because of their impact upon the administration of the European Union. The first is the *Ressortprinzip*, a constitutional principle which confers upon each minister full autonomy within a policy area and its ministry. This autonomy includes the management of personnel resources, subject only to the provisions of the civil service law. The consequence is rather pronounced compartmentalisation, exacerbated at federal level by the fact that the ministries have no role in service delivery or implementation, this being the preserve of the *Länder*.

A second important feature of the German system is the role which representatives of the staff play in the management of careers. In structures which bear some resemblance to the *Mitbestimmung* (joint decision-making) structures found in industry and commerce, staff representatives are involved both in initial recruitment and in promotion procedures. This tends to increase the rigidity of the system, and enhance the importance in promotion procedures of seniority rather than performance, since the trade unions tend to regard the minimisation of discretion as the best way to protect the interests of all those they represent. In Germany it also tends to increase compartmentalisation, since in any ministry the staff representatives are liable to favour their own colleagues rather than outsiders from another ministry when there are vacancies to be filled. The impact of the establishment of a version of this system in the institutions of the European Union is discussed in Chapter 5.

The Whitehall model

'Britain is different' has been a constant refrain of those who have sought to compare administrative models. The Irish administration draws many of its structures and approaches from a Whitehall model, although divergences have grown up over the past 80 years. Explanations can be sought in political, social and economic history, but in the context of developments within EU administration a number of features seem particularly salient.

The British and Irish civil services both have a rather more sparse and fragmentary basis in formal legislation than their continental counterparts. Both are regulated primarily by prerogative powers exercised by the government, although in the UK in the name of the Crown. This consequently makes them quite open and amenable to structural change. During the 1980s and 1990s a profound shift has occurred in both countries, away from the concept of administration as primarily the provision of advice and policy formulation and in favour of an emphasis on resource management, performance, incentives, and the devolution of responsibility. The absence of a codified legal structure has certainly facilitated these changes.

In both the United Kingdom and Ireland, the civil service's role in supporting ministers is regarded as involving a good deal of attention to the political context in which the minister is operating. In the process of policy formulation, not only technical but also political factors are taken into account. Both countries share the view that in order to fulfil this role the civil service must be visibly apolitical. There are therefore limitations on political activity by serving civil servants and a concomitant obligation to serve the government of the day with loyalty and energy. While this has not ruled out the appointment of special advisers to ministers, it has meant the absence of a political screen between the minister and officials of the sort constituted in some countries by the existence of *cabinet* structures (see Chapter 10).

The British and Irish administrations have a strong tradition of relying upon custom and practice, inculcated into officials, especially senior officials, through an induction based on an apprenticeship model – learning by doing under the supervision of superiors – rather than extensive formal pre- or post-entry training. This custom and practice may take written form, as statements of procedures or codes of practice. These, because they are not laws or legal regulations, can be relatively easily changed and adapted. They provide guidelines as to proper behaviour, and they result in internalised forms of control. Rather than relying upon inspectors to assess, after the event, whether actions have conformed in a proper and regular way to the letter of the regulations, such systems depend on the general ethos of the institution, and on managers in particular, to inculcate and inspire appropriate attitudes and responses so that, before any event, they can be confident that the right action will be taken. This approach has had some impact on the operation of the administration of the European Union and has resulted, for example, in the production of handbooks of administrative procedures for both the Commission and the Council. Since the 1998–9 crisis in the European Commission was caused in part by contempt for formal rules and by improper behaviour, one response has been to produce more explicit statements of what is expected, and a number of codes of conduct have been elaborated.

Other international administrations

Having identified some of the features of the various national models which have influenced the shape of the administrative services of the European Union, we should recall that they are by no means the only administrative bodies to draw officials from a wide range of backgrounds. The United Nations 'family of organisations' (Mango, 1988, p. 42) employs over twice as many staff as the European Union, drawn from a far wider range of national backgrounds. Unlike the European Union there is a high degree of subject specialisation and fragmentation, since staff are permanently assigned to one particular organ of the United Nations and reflect the specialist orientation of their organisation (for example, the Food and Agriculture Organisation or the World Health Organisation). The main tasks of the staff of these organisations fall into three categories: about two-thirds of all the staff, including over half the professional and senior staff, undertake what may be described as support and 'housekeeping' duties. At the lower levels they are usually locally recruited and not required to serve outside their countries of origin. The wide geographic dispersal of the headquarters of the various organisations explains the rather high proportion of staff of this kind. Support services are also provided by the linguists, who are responsible for the translation into the six official UN languages of the large amounts of paperwork which the organisations engender. The second category of tasks is secretariat duties. However, the similarity with national or even EU officials is limited, since the United Nations does not have extensive pro-active general policy-making functions. The question of whether the secretariat should be wholly confined to a reactive support role or should have a more activist approach has never been fully resolved. The third category of tasks is those related to the administration and provision of technical assistance and economic development programmes.

Perhaps more closely analogous to the services of the EU are those of other international organisations based in Europe. Since 1958 six of them (NATO, Western European Union, the Council of Europe, the Organisation for Economic Co-operation and Development (OECD), the European Centre for Medium Term Weather Forecasting, and the European Space Agency) have formed a consortium to harmonise their pay, the classification of their posts in ranks and grades, and, since 1976, to operate a single pension scheme. The Parliamentary Assembly of the Council of Europe, through its Sub-Committee for a European Civil Service, has since at least the early 1980s – recommendations 944 (1982) and 1000 (1984) – been urging upon its member states the desirability of creating a European Civil Service with 'a progressive approximation of the employment conditions' of the staffs of the European Communities and the Council of Europe. However, the member states have shown no enthusiasm for the institutional development of a 'European civil service' of this type. Given the complexities and difficulties of finding a way through the wide range of varying concepts and related practices outlined above within the single framework of the EU this is perhaps unsurprising, especially since the membership of the other organisations involved is much wider and not in all cases confined to Europe.

Conclusion

This account of the origins and early development of the administrative services of the European Union explains how the main models of administrative organisation within the member states have influenced the development of the services. Features drawn from French, German and British models have all been built into the foundations of the EU administration, because those who brought their professional and cultural experience with them seem to have found their working environment more analogous to a national government than to an international secretariat, and to have drawn accordingly on the models with which they were familiar. The remaining chapters explore the strengths and weaknesses of the structures which have been erected on these foundations.

Chapter 3

A Law-based System of Administration

Of central importance within the law-based system of administration that the EU institutions adopted are the Staff Regulations and the Financial Regulation. This chapter outlines the provisions of these regulations, which determine the character of the institutions' human resources and financial management policies, lay down the rights and obligations of all staff, and accord to staff and union representatives a privileged position alongside management in their administration. We examine the cumbersome formality of the disciplinary provisions, which have not in practice been successful in preventing the development of corrupt and fraudulent practices, and the reasons for the relatively stunted development of a more positive culture of loyalty and accountability.

The Staff Regulations

Following the precedent set by the High Authority of the ECSC in 1956 (see Chapter 2), the EEC and Euratom adopted staff regulations in 1961, and on 29 February 1968, following the merger of the three Communities, the Council adopted Regulation 259/68 setting out a single *statut* which now applies to officials of the Commission, the Council of Ministers, the Parliament, the Court of Justice, the Court of Auditors, the Economic and Social Committee, the Committee of the Regions and the EU agencies. The only EU institutions not covered by the *statut* are the European Investment Bank and the European Central Bank. Frequently amended over the years, the consolidated text contains nine Titles and eleven Annexes (Exhibit 3.1), providing a

Exhibit 3.1   The Staff Regulations

TITLE I   GENERAL PROVISIONS
This title defines who are officials of the European Union (Article 1), and the formal structures within which they function, including for each institution an appointing authority and a Staff Committee, for management and staff respectively, and one or more Joint Committees in which both are represented, as well as Disciplinary Boards, Reports Committees, an Invalidity Committee (Article 9) and a Staff Regulations Committee (Article 10).

Annex I sets out the structure of categories and grades.

Annex II lays down the composition and procedures of the committees.

TITLE II   RIGHTS AND OBLIGATIONS OF OFFICIALS
Officials must act 'solely with the interests of the European Union in mind', neither seeking nor taking instructions from anyone other than their hierarchical superiors (Articles 11 and 21). This title also sets out broad principles governing conflicts of interest, integrity and discretion, election to public office, the protection of official information, and the residence requirement (Articles 12–20).

In addition the rules cover privileges and immunities, the right of association and access to the official's own personal file (Articles 22–26). The detail on privileges and immunities is set out in a separate Protocol.

TITLE III   CAREER OF OFFICIALS
This title provides a framework of regulations governing each event in an official's career, from recruitment and appointment (Articles 27–34) to termination of service on retirement or other grounds (Articles 47–54).

Annex III lays down the basis on which competitions are held for recruitment.

Annex IV lays down the basis on which allowances are granted to staff retired early under Articles 41 or 50 of the Staff Regulations.

TITLE IV   WORKING CONDITIONS OF OFFICIALS
This title deals with hours of work and entitlements to leave and public holidays.

→

⟶

Annex IVa deals with half-time work.

Annex V deals with the calculation of entitlements to annual leave, special leave on compassionate grounds, and travelling time.

Annex VI deals with the calculation of compensatory leave or remuneration to be paid to officials in categories C and D who have worked overtime.

TITLE V   EMOLUMENTS AND SOCIAL SECURITY BENEFITS OF OFFICIALS

This title deals with remuneration and expenses (Articles 62–71), social security benefits: for example, for illness or invalidity (72–76), pensions (77–84) and recovery of overpayments (85). Rates of pay for each grade are set out in the main body of the Regulation, but:

Annex VII contains details of four allowances, and seven types of expenses which can be claimed.

Annex VIII contains details of the pension scheme.

Annex XI lays down detailed rules for the annual pay round (la méthode).

TITLE VI   DISCIPLINARY MEASURES

Annex IX contains the rules for disciplinary proceedings.

TITLE VII   APPEALS

This title provides for appeals against decisions taken by the appointing authority to be dealt with in the first instance internally, and ultimately by the European Court of Justice.

TITLE VIII   SPECIAL PROVISIONS APPLICABLE TO CERTAIN CATEGORIES OF OFFICIALS

The special provisions for scientific and technical staff in the field of nuclear science are laid down in Title VIII; those applicable under Title VIIIa to officials serving in third countries are specified in *Annex X*.

TITLE IX   TRANSITIONAL AND FINAL PROVISIONS

Formal provisions required to bring the Staff Regulations into effect.

basis in law for all the formal events of an official career, from appointment to resignation or retirement, and for the relationship between the EU institutions and their employees both individually and collectively. There is a parallel regulation setting out the conditions for other employees – temporary staff, auxiliary staff, local staff and special advisers – and a raft of other more detailed regulations.

Although the Staff Regulations and associated texts encompass a mixture of general principles and specific procedures, the latter mostly set out in the Annexes, they are not as lengthy or as detailed as, for example, the non-statutory codes of terms and conditions produced for British civil servants. In this they resemble civil service legislation in a number of the member states. Their importance should not, however, be underestimated for two reasons. First, they are often criticised for the constraints which a rather rigid, law-based framework imposes on the scope for management to introduce change. Since the texts are a Regulation adopted by the Council of Ministers, amendment entails laborious procedures involving consultation first with staff representatives and then with the inter-institutional staff regulations committee before a proposal can be put to the Council of Ministers, which itself may take many months to reach agreement. Changes recommended by Commissioner Kinnock in January 2000 were not expected to reach the Council before December 2001, and such targets are usually optimistic.

Second, the legal nature of the framework has given rise to a large volume of litigation. Article 236 of the Treaty Establishing the European Community (the Treaty of Rome) provides that 'The Court of Justice shall have jurisdiction in any dispute between the Community and its servants within the limits and under the conditions laid down in the Staff Regulations or the Conditions of Employment.' In the early years of the EEC, litigation by officials against the institutions as their employers formed an important proportion of the work of the Court of Justice. The outcome was the development of a jurisprudence which supplies a certain amount of detail to fill in the general framework of the regulations. With the growing role of litigation in the development of the EU, cases involving officials were delegated to the Court of First Instance (CFI) set up under powers granted by the

---

Exhibit 3.2   The law and the reassignment of officials

Several cases before the Court of Justice during the 1990s illustrate the extent to which Community officials are prepared to utilise legal proceedings to challenge decisions about their deployment within the Community service. In joined cases 116/88 and 149/88 (judgment in March 1990), the Court made it clear that any decision to move an official from one post to another taken against the will of the official concerned must be undertaken with great care, and must state the grounds on which it is taken, since it constitutes a measure adversely affecting the official within the meaning of Article 25 of the staff regulations. However, the Court has been careful to avoid substituting its own judgment for that of management – it did not uphold the grievances in the case in point – and in joined cases T-59/91 and T-79/91 the Court of First Instance refused the arguments of a grade A4 official against reassignment, as the result of an internal reorganisation of his Directorate General, to duties which he alleged were of lower status than his previous tasks.

Single European Act. Indeed it was the growing backlog of such cases which prompted its foundation (Church and Phinnemore, 1994, p. 282) and in 1992 they constituted 79 out of the 115 actions brought before the Court (Nugent, 1994, p. 232). The number of actions brought under the staff regulations has continued to grow (155 in 1997) but by then they constituted only a quarter of the CFI's workload. This legal oversight protects staff from arbitrary decisions or the abuse of management procedures governing such matters as recruitment, promotion, deployment and pay, but it tends to reinforce the rigidity which the regulations impose; for example, it has become surprisingly difficult for management to take staff away from work of lower priority when they are more urgently needed elsewhere (see Exhibit 3.2).

Pay and conditions

The system for determining the pay and material conditions of EU officials is a rather rigid one, related (Page and Wouters, 1994, p. 202) to notions that the official should be independent,

with a guaranteed status which should not depend upon the outcome of a trial of strength between employer and employee
(although these nevertheless do occur, as in 1991: Guérivière,
1993, pp. 33–7; Page and Wouters, 1994, pp. 208 and 211). This
status is conferred and protected through the exercise of legislative power. The officials of all the EU institutions have the same
salary scales, laid down in the Staff Regulations, which have to
be amended every time pay is increased.

Achieving a consensus for such changes in the Council of
Ministers is difficult and time consuming, so in 1976 the Council
adopted a Regulation setting out a complex formula, known as
'the method', for conducting the annual review and adjustment of
remuneration. In accordance with Article 65 of the Staff
Regulations, the review is based on an index prepared by the
European Community Statistical Office in agreement with the
national statistical offices of the member states. The index is prepared in September in the light of the position in the member
states on 1 July; the implementing Regulation usually receives
Council approval in December; and the increase is then paid,
backdated to July. The formula involves looking both at the cost
of living in Brussels and at changes in the purchasing power of
official salaries in national administrations. The intention is that
officials of the Union should enjoy a comparable standard of living regardless of where they work. The method has been criticised on the grounds that 'a rise for paper-pushers in Athens or
Lisbon ... automatically raises the salary of a French or German
Community official. In consequence the Community staff got a
rise of 7.7 per cent between 1 July 1990 and 30 June 1991, in
contrast to 2.5 per cent for French officials in the same period'
(Guérivière, 1993, p. 34).

Over the years there have been various pay disputes. In 1981,
when the Council tried to avoid implementing the increase recommended by the Commission on the basis of the formula, the
Council was successfully challenged by the Commission before
the Court of Justice on the grounds that they had acted illegally
under their own regulation (ECJ Case 59/81). When the method
itself was last reviewed in 1991, the negotiations gave rise to
widespread strike action. Annex XI of the Staff Regulations,
which sets out the current method, expires on 30 June 2001, and

difficult negotiations can be expected, particularly if they become linked with other proposals for changing the Staff Regulations in order to facilitate the Prodi Commission's reform programme. In 1998 a rumour that the Council might make a similar connection between pay negotiations and reform proposals (the ill-fated Caston Report) brought almost the whole of the Commission staff out on strike for one day (the day before a holiday weekend), and largely succeeded in heading off those reforms.

A number of elements enter into the calculation of the rate of pay any official will actually receive. The basic salary is set on the scales laid down in the regulation. In addition, all officials working outside the state of which they are nationals receive an expatriation allowance of 16 per cent of basic salary. If they have a family, they are further entitled to a family allowance of 5 per cent of basic salary, or a minimum flat rate (whichever is greater), and an allowance for each dependent child. Category C officials employed in jobs which require keyboard skills receive a fixed rate supplement.

EU officials do not pay national income tax or social security contributions on their salaries. They do pay any other tax or duty, for example on income from other sources (Page and Wouters, 1994, p. 207), and there are two 'community taxes': one is a progressive income tax which rises to 45 per cent on salary earned in the top band, and the other is a flat rate 'levy', described when it was introduced in 1981 for 10 years as a 'crisis levy' and converted in 1991 for a further 10 years into a 'temporary levy' at 5.8 per cent. Deductions are also made for the pension scheme, and for sickness and accident insurance. The pension scheme provides for payment of 70 per cent of final basic salary after 35 years service, and pensions are increased annually in line with pay. The sickness insurance scheme covers the reimbursement of between 80 and 100 per cent of medical costs. Page and Wouters estimate, on the basis of Commission budget figures, that the cumulative effect of deductions set against allowances means that on average officials take home about 85 per cent of their notional basic salaries, although clearly this will vary markedly as between the highest and lowest paid, and depending upon the official's family circumstances (Page and Wouters, 1994, p. 207).

Service in the European Community is often portrayed as offering attractive material conditions (Brigouleix, 1986, p. 37). In so far as this is so, it is the probably inevitable result of a 'levelling up' process. 'The salaries paid must be attractive even to those of the most affluent country. There can be no question of discrimination between officials from different member states' (House of Lords, 1988, p. 17 para. 62). An implicit comparison with the private sector is also a factor (Brigouleix, 1986, p. 38; Guérivière, 1993, p. 34). 'I was in a major oil company, and I am a *polytechnicien*', one official told Bernard Brigouleix. 'Don't you think, given those career prospects, I would have done as well there by now?' (Brigouleix, 1986, p. 38). As the then Director General of Personnel told the House of Lords Select Committee:

> Our salaries are normally better than those which people are paid in their member state, yes that is true, to differing degrees, according to where you are. If you are a Portuguese a Community salary ... would be more above your present salary than if you are British, and that would be more again than if you are a Dane or a German who are more or less at the top of the scale and where the margin is something that we begin to worry about. (House of Lords, 1988, p. 17, q. 43).

Precise comparisons are difficult. Spence concludes that 'the differences with national public service salaries and conditions have been reduced over the years, particularly at senior levels' and that a proper comparison ought to be with national diplomats posted to Brussels, not with national officials employed at home (Spence, 1997a, p. 76). His figures for 1994 show EU officials in each category in the middle or bottom of a league table covering France, Germany, Denmark and the United Nations. Jean de la Guérivière estimated that in 1991 French A grade officials in the middle ranks would be taking home about double the amount which their counterparts in Paris could officially expect (Guérivière, 1993, p. 34). But as a highly qualified young Frenchwoman working as an official in DG IV wrote angrily to *Le Monde* in 1991 when industrial action in the Commission was drawing attention to salary rates, 'All our salaries are public and published. On the other hand, who knows what bonuses are received by senior officials in the national administrations, a taboo subject in France if ever there was one?' (Guérivière, 1993, p. 36).

Most of the additional benefits to which EU officials are entitled are related to the need to live away from their 'home' country. So in addition to expatriation allowances and the possibility of education costs being met (European schools are free to EU officials), officials receive generous installation allowances on first appointment (Staff Regulations Annexe VII, Article 5), resettlement allowances on retirement (Article 6) and return travel costs for themselves and their family to their place of origin, once a year if it is between 50 and 725 kilometres by rail from the place of work, and twice a year if the distance is more than 725 kilometres (Article 8). Purchases required to set up house on first appointment (including a car) are tax free, as are 100 litres of petrol a month for senior officials, but the Brussels supermarket for officials is no longer subsidised, and '[d]espite public perceptions to the contrary, the Belgian and Luxembourgeois governments' offer of special European employee number plates for cars brings with it no privileges or immunities' (Page and Wouters, 1994, p. 209).

Normal working hours and leave arrangements are also set out in the Staff Regulations. The normal working week should not exceed 42 hours (Article 55). However, an agreement with the unions in the 1980s provided for flexible working hours with a normal week of 37½ hours (Coudurier, 1994). As in most organisations this provision does not withstand a long working hours culture in some parts of the institutions (see Chapter 5, page 113) even if elsewhere clock-watching and a fairly easy life may seem to be more usual (see Exhibit 3.3).

Provision for leave allows between 24 and 30 working days annually, which must include at least one period of two consecutive weeks (Article 57 and Annex V, Article 2). In addition, staff are entitled to the national public holidays of the countries in which they are stationed, and (if these are not holidays in that country) to 10 statutory days, including one on 9 May to celebrate the anniversary of the Schuman declaration. They are also entitled to extra days for long return rail journeys to their place of origin, although in practice such journeys are almost invariably made by air.

Exhibit 3.3   Working hours

In her somewhat acerbic comments on life in the Commission for six months in 1994 as a detached national expert Michèle Coudurier recorded her surprise at being asked, when discovered in her office at 6.30 p.m., whether she normally worked late. In her previous post, leaving the office before 8 p.m. seemed like an early departure. Empirical observation from an office close to the lifts led her to conclude that the normal time of arrival was 9 a.m., and lunch was taken from 1 till 3 p.m. There was a wave of departures as 5 p.m. struck, and then a steady stream between five and six, another peak at six, and after six most people had left. On Fridays departures moved forwards by an hour. Further observation led her to conclude, however, that the Commission's zeal for harmonisation had not extended to its own working hours. Some DGs (for example, that for the budget) had a reputation for hard work, while the higher one rose in the hierarchy, the more one exceeded the $37\frac{1}{2}$ hour norm. 'It is very common to see Directors General, Directors and Heads of Unit – and their deputies – in their offices until late – and keeping some of their staff late too.' But she observed an almost total absence of any checks upon hours worked (or not worked) by any staff (Coudurier, 1994, letters V and X).

The Financial Regulation

The Financial Regulation establishes a framework of financial management and control which applies to all the EU institutions financed through the budget. Coverage is in fact identical with that of the Staff Regulations (see above). The structure of the Financial Regulation is set out in Exhibit 3.4. By making comprehensive rules governing the raising and spending of all EU money, the intention is to ensure that the EU's resources are deployed in accordance with the purposes intended, and in no other way. The first line of defence is the budget itself (Title I); no money can be raised or spent if it is not justified by a specific entry in the budget. The second is the division of responsibility between the financial controller, the authorising officer and the accounting officer (Title III), based on the French model of financial management, which is intended to ensure that no one person (or even a chain of persons within a single line of management) is responsible for all parts of a financial transaction. The authorising officer, typically a senior line manager, is responsible for three formal acts: the commitment of expenditure before money is spent, the validation of expenditure when invoices are presented, and the authorisation of payment for items of expenditure which have been validated. However, the first stage – commitment – requires prior approval (called the visa) from the financial controller, and the final stage – payment – is the responsibility of the accounting officer. The unintended consequence of these arrangements has been to allow the authorising officer to rely too heavily on the responsibility of the financial controller who gives the visa and the accounting officer who makes the payments. In the Commission, recognition in the early 1990s that line managers attached insufficient importance to these financial rules, which they tended to regard as obstacles to be got around, led to adoption of the programme of sound and efficient financial management launched by Commissioners Liikanen and Gradin in 1995 (see Chapter 8). However, in 1999 the Committee of Independent Experts felt there was still some way to go before the authorising officer was made to feel fully responsible for the sound financial management of an expenditure programme. The Committee of Independent Experts also considered that 'the independence of the Financial Controller vis-à-vis the auditee was compromised by the mere fact that both visa and audit functions fell under the responsibility of the financial controller, one branch of whose staff was therefore responsible for auditing the other' (European Parliament, 1999b, para. 4.11.12). The Prodi Commission is proposing to introduce, by 2002, a new structure, in which the visa would be abolished altogether, and an enhanced internal audit function would be independent of any remaining responsibility of the financial controller.

A third range of safeguards is provided by the scrutiny of expenditure *ex post facto* by internal auditors, external auditors (the Court of Auditors) and ultimately the European Parliament. Title VI lays down the procedures which require each institution to provide an annual report on which the Court of Auditors in its turn must report to the Parliament and the Council of Ministers in

Exhibit 3.4   The Financial Regulation

TITLE I
The general principles under this title establish the centrality of the budget in the management and control of EU resources. No revenue may be raised or expenditure authorised if it is not in the budget. To this central principle has been added since 1990 an emphasis on sound financial management, including economy and cost-effectiveness, and requirements for the prior evaluation and subsequent review of expenditure programmes (Articles 2–3).

TITLE II
This title lays down the rules for drawing up the budget (Articles 12–18), and rules for its structure and presentation (Articles 19–20).

TITLE III
This title (Articles 21–55) sets out the respective roles of the authorising officer, the financial controller and the accounting officer in the implementation of the budget, including rules for the commitment, validation, authorisation and payment of expenditure.

TITLE IV
This title covers the conclusion of contracts (Articles 56–64) and rules for the keeping of inventories (Articles 65–68) and accounts (Articles 69–72). The EU applies to its own contracts the same procedures and obligations as it imposes on contracts for public works, services and supplies in the member states (Article 56); above a certain value the Advisory Committee on Procurement and Contracts must be consulted (Article 63).

TITLE V
This title relating to the responsibilities of authorising officers, financial controllers, accounting officers and administrators of

→

→

advance funds (Articles 73–77) provides the basis for disciplinary action and compensation if the terms of the Financial Regulation are not complied with.

TITLE VI
Presenting and auditing accounts (Articles 78–90). This title lays down the annual reporting and auditing cycle, including the respective roles of the Court of Auditors, the Council of Ministers and the Parliament.

TITLES VII–XII
These titles set out special provisions applicable to:

ı   research and technological development appropriations (VII – Articles 91–7).
ı   the European Agricultural Guidance and Guarantee Fund, guarantee section (VIII – Articles 98–104).
ı   external aid (IX – Articles 105–20).
ı   the management of appropriations relating to staff serving in offices and sub-offices in the Community and in delegations outside the Community and to their administration (X – Articles 121–3)
ı   financial participation by third parties and outside bodies in Community activities (XI – Articles 124–32).
ı   the Office for Official Publications of the European Communities (XII – Article 133).

PART II
Provisions applicable to borrowing and lending operations by the European Communities (Articles 134–7).

PART III
Transitional and final provisions (Articles 138–43).

a prescribed form which includes 'a statement of assurance as to the reliability of the accounts and the legality and regularity of the underlying transactions' (Article 88a). It is on the basis of this statement that the Parliament, acting on a recommendation from the Council, closes the books for the financial year in question by giving a discharge to the Commission (Article 89). It was the refusal of the Parliament to give this discharge for the 1997 budget in November 1998 which precipitated the crisis leading to the appointment of the Committee of Independent Experts and ultimately to the resignation of the Santer Commission in March 1999.

Staff representation

The ideology of social partnership, which seeks to minimise adversarial relationships over working conditions, is strongly present in the EU's elaborate arrangements for staff representation, reflecting post-war developments in the original member states. In France the long battle to achieve for civil servants the right to belong to a union ended with the 1946 civil service law, which also reflected the Gaullist desire to associate employees with the personnel management of their institutions. In Germany the desire to avoid damaging social conflict saw the introduction of *Mitbestimmung* (workers' representation) into large enterprises. In this context it is unsurprising that a Staff Committee was provided for as early as the 1956 ECSC Staff Regulation (House of Lords, 1988, p. 90, q. 382). Article 9 of the current Staff Regulations provides additionally, in each institution, for staff to be represented on one or more Joint Committees, a disciplinary Board and a Reports Committee. Finally, under Article 10, representatives of all the institutions and of their staff committees come together to form a Staff Regulations Committee which must be consulted on any proposal for a change in the Staff Regulations.

The function of the Staff Committee, which is the principal forum for the discussion of human resources policies in each institution, is to 'contribute to the smooth running of the service by providing a channel for the expression of opinion by the staff' (Article 9 of the Staff Regulations). In addition the Committee has a role in 'the management and supervision of social welfare bodies set up by the organisation'. Hence, in the Commission, the

Exhibit 3.5   Joint Committees at work

If there is, for example, a need for a general competition for the recruitment of translators of Dutch language, it is the important task of the Joint Committee to advise the Commission on the level at which it is wise to launch such a competition. If it were proposed to run the competition at A5 level, rather than, say, A8, the Joint Committee might have to put into the balance the need to recruit experienced officials against the aspirations of the officials already working at the Commission who have promotions expectations. This is where the Joint Committee intervenes ... The Joint Committee has advice to give on whether it is appropriate to make a full competition with written and oral examinations, or whether it is more appropriate in these circumstances to have a limited examination, let us say only at the oral stage or even to have only an examination on the diplomas produced by the candidate.

Source: Evidence of Mr Joern Pipkorn, Commission Legal Service, 27 January 1988 (House of Lords, 1988), p. 92, q. 38 and 388.

Staff Committees send representatives to the Social Services Board, to the Sickness Insurance Board and the Joint Welfare Committee. At local level there are joint committees for health and safety at work, and, for example, in Brussels for the management of the canteen and the crèche (House of Lords, 1988, p. 114, q. 497). More importantly, the Staff Committees send representatives to the Joint Committee and to other committees such as the Promotions Committee, the Reports Committee, the Disciplinary Boards, the Staff Training Committee and the juries (selection boards) for recruitment competitions (House of Lords, 1988, p. 90, q. 382). In the early 1990s there were in the Commission some 17 permanent committees, and a number of other *ad hoc* committees, amounting to about 25 in total.

The Joint Committees – one for each EC institution – consist of a chairman appointed by the institution, and an equal number of members appointed by the institution and the Staff Committee. These Committees give advice on matters such as the holding of recruitment competitions, and the terms in which vacancies are advertised (see Exhibit 3.5).

The views of the Joint Committee are powerful, though not binding. 'Of course if [the institution] does not follow the advice it might run into difficulties. It is difficult to systematically disregard the advice of the Joint Committee but it happens occasionally' (House of Lords, 1988, p. 92, q. 389). If the Committee fails to deliver the advice required the institution can legally proceed without it after an appropriate interval (Staff Regulations Article 10a) (House of Lords, 1988, p. 91, q. 383).

The Reports Committee lays down the general policy and framework for staff reporting (see Chapter 5). Perhaps more important, though not provided for in the Regulations, are the Promotions Committees of the Commission, one for each category, which consider all promotions up to and including promotion to grade A3. The Committees are structured like the Joint Committee. That for A grade staff is chaired by the Secretary General of the Commission. A similar Committee exists for staff training in the Commission, organised in two tiers: local sections which give advice on specific issues, such as the refusal of a request to be released for training, and a central committee which is concerned with general issues and the Commission's overall training policy (House of Lords, 1988, p. 95, q. 399).

The role of the unions

Although the arrangements for staff representation derive from an ideology which requires staff to have a voice in matters of personnel management, in practice it is the unions who put up candidates for election to the Staff Committee, and oversee the selection of members for the various other Committees. In 1988 the three major Union federations signed a joint declaration agreeing that representation on such committees would be divided up in proportion to their electoral results. Having established structures for staff representation, the EC institutions initially paid very little attention to the bodies which aggregated and organised staff opinion. Unions and staff associations were not even recognised until 1972, when the right to belong to such bodies was added to the Staff Regulations (Article 24a). In 1974 the Court gave the unions and associations the right to be heard in cases where they had a general interest (House of Lords, 1988, p. 93,

q. 390), and in the same year the Commission concluded a framework agreement granting them recognition and representative status. A further agreement – the *Social Contract for Progress* – was signed in June 1989. For the staff of the Council of Ministers a 'protocol for negotiations' was signed in 1988 with one of the unions. The Economic and Social Committee signed an agreement with unions representing its staff in 1977, and a further agreement in 1989, while the first framework agreement for bargaining between the European Parliament and its staff was concluded in July 1990 (Penaud, 1993, p. 39). These agreements allow for union business to be conducted in working time, and provide for a regular series of meetings between the unions and management at the level of the Director General of Personnel (these meetings are called 'technical' consultations). In the Commission, if agreement cannot be reached at that level, the unions have the right to be heard by the Commissioner in what are known as 'political consultations'.

In 1974 the Council of Ministers rejected an attempt to get a right to strike written into the Staff Regulations, but in 1975 the Court of Justice implied that it considered absence for a strike not unlawful (House of Lords, 1988, p. 93, q. 391). For the Commission, the 1974 agreement recognised three principles: first, that all members of the staff had the right to strike except those required by the Commission to work; second, the list of those who would be required to work would be the subject of an agreement between the management and the unions; and finally, those who wished to work should not be prevented from doing so. On remuneration and pensions, a consultation and conciliation procedure exists between the Council of Ministers and the unions representing the staff of all the institutions through a committee with one representative of each member state and an equal number of union members, chaired by the Secretary General of the Council (House of Lords, 1988, p. 94, q. 391). Although key issues such as pay and reform have continued to precipitate strikes from time to time, the reduction in strike activity since the early 1970s may in part be a consequence of this more structured mechanism for bargaining.

Union representation within the EC institutions is, as in many of the member states, fragmented along political lines. In the

1970s and most of the 1980s there were three recognised union organisations and recognition was also accorded to three national-level Italian union confederations which incorporate unions representing the staff at the Ispra research centre in Italy. In the Commission the three leading organisations in 1999, with 20 of the 27 seats in the Central Staff Committee, were the *Union Syndicale* (9 seats), *Renouveau et Démocratie* (6 seats) and *Fédération de la Fonction Publique Européenne* (FFPE) (5 seats). *Union Syndicale* and *Renouveau et Démocratie* share a socialist ideology. The latter, which had some personal connections to radical parties such as the Italian former Communists and the Scottish National Party, broke away from the *Union Syndicale* in the early 1990s. They objected, perhaps understandably given the numerous scandals that emerged in the later 1990s, to the domination of the *Union Syndicale* by people closely linked to the Belgian Socialist Party and related networks of freemasons. In the first half of the 1990s the FFPE, with a less politically aligned and militantly 'trade union' stance, ran the bureau of the Central Staff Committee with two other organisations, the *Syndicat des Fonctionnaires Internationaux et Européens*, with a Christian Democrat (Catholic) orientation (2 seats in 1999), and the latter's 1988 offshoot, the *Syndicat des Fonctionnaires Européens* (3 seats in 1999). The 1989 Social Contract was also signed by the Association of Independent Officials for the Defence of the European Civil Service, whose place has since been taken by two other groups with an independent stance, of which only one currently has any seats on the Central Staff Committee.

A costly structure

These elaborate arrangements for staff and union representation prompt questions about their costs and benefits. Under a 1988 agreement, the Commission, for example, undertook to provide resources both for the unions and separately for staff committee representatives, who in fact are also union representatives. As a result, the Commission was funding about 50 full-time union officials, almost the equivalent, we were told by an official, of a separate DG for staff representation. 'Whereas ten or twenty years ago a political consultation might involve six or eight people now [1995] it is forty or sixty.' Yet European officials are not very strongly unionised. Membership figures are not published, but in 1988 a union officer said that the unions 'have approximately, I would have thought ... one third of the staff as members and two thirds are, frankly, fed up with the unions' (House of Lords, 1988, p. 118, q. 528), and in late 1999 membership was still said by the Commission to constitute no more than 35 per cent of their staff, and possibly as few as 18 per cent (*The Independent*, 20 October 1999). Despite the plethora of unions, their programmes do not vary greatly; all of them have as a priority 'preserving the *acquis* of the *statut*'. The style of bargaining, especially when it derives from French and Italian traditions, may at times be confrontational, but the leading organisations generally prefer to arrive at a consensus and avoid votes. This cosy alliance, which in the past has led to accusations from rival organisations that the dominant unions (*Union Syndicale* and the *Fédération de la Fonction Publique Européenne*) are too much in the management's pocket, may not survive if the Prodi Commission maintains a radical reform programme.

This complex structure provides parallel channels for the achievement of objectives. If a union is defeated in the Central Staff Committee it may then, in its separate capacity as a union, ask for a technical consultation meeting with the management in an attempt to regain the lost ground. Costly as these arrangements are, they might be worthwhile if they acted as an effective channel of communication between staff and management, reducing militancy and facilitating constructive change. The sense of protection and independence, which the existence of the *statut* enhances, has as one of its corollaries a relatively weak sense of any obligation to co-operate in management initiatives, which are seen as being illegitimately imposed by force. Such institutionalised alienation might be offset by strong staff and union representation, but in the 1990s the administration seems to have concluded that the arrangements allow too much scope for relatively unrepresentative unions to obstruct communication and frustrate necessary change. Following his appointment as Vice-President for reform, Commissioner Kinnock therefore moved quickly to instigate a fundamental review of the Commission's arrangements for union consultation, with a view to reducing the cost and the complexity, and giving a stronger role to the central staff committee which represents all staff. He also appealed directly to staff by ensuring that major consultation documents were made available to them electronically.

Compliance and discipline

The Staff Regulations establish a legal framework for the exercise of administrative responsibilities within all the institutions of the EU, but much depends on the provisions for enforcement and how rigorously they are applied. The obligations of EU officials, as set out in Title II of the Staff Regulations, are very broad and general. They forbid officials to seek or accept instructions from any outside body, including national governments. No honours, favours, gifts or payments of any kind may be accepted from any outside source without the permission of the appointing authority (Article 11). There is a major emphasis (Articles 12–16) on the prevention of conflicts of interest. The regulations forbid the keeping or acquisition of interests in bodies which are subject to authority of the EU institutions, or which do business with it, and they require permission to be sought for outside activities. They specify that officials leaving certain posts must notify their previous institution of posts and activities that they take up in the three years following their departure, and the institution concerned has the right to forbid such activities. An obligation of discretion is laid on officials, who are prohibited from conveying unpublished documents or information to unauthorised persons, or publishing matter relating to the work of the institutions without permission, which, however, may only be refused where such publication is deemed prejudicial to the interests of the Communities. Other articles in this Title lay a duty of obedience to hierarchical superiors upon officials, with minimal rights of appeal against instructions deemed to be irregular. Officials must inform their immediate superior if they judge that they have received such instructions, but must then carry them out, provided that they are confirmed in writing, unless they involve breaches of the criminal law or safety standards.

The scope for disciplinary proceedings under Title VI is also wide. They may arise from any failure to comply with obligations under the Staff Regulations themselves or, under Articles 73–75 of the Financial Regulation, in any circumstances where the authorising officer, financial controller or accounting officer has failed to comply with the Regulation and the rules for its implementation. In the most serious cases, including major allegations of fraud, the investigating magistrates (in some countries it would be the police) may be called in to conduct a criminal investigation, in which case any disciplinary proceedings are suspended until the judicial procedures have run their course. A less public procedure which the Commission often employs to bring irregularities and cases of fraud to light, particularly if senior officials are involved, is to set up an administrative inquiry, usually entrusted to a serving director general, or sometimes to a group of three such officials, who may be able to gather a solid body of evidence with a view to instituting disciplinary proceedings if appropriate. The CIE was critical of this approach, which, in its opinion, was often started too late, took too long, and too often resulted in the senior officials concerned being allowed to take early retirement under the generous provisions of Article 50 of the Staff Regulations when they should have been subject to disciplinary proceedings (European Parliament, 1999a, paras 4.20–22).

Article 22 of the Staff Regulations (Financial Regulation, Article 76) provides for compensation related to the scale of damage suffered by the EU as a result of the official's misconduct, though no monetary sanction under Article 22 has ever been applied (European Paliament, 1999b, para. 5.10.15). Articles 86–89 set out the full range of disciplinary measures – from written warning to loss of post and pension – and the procedures for determining them. However, the use of these procedures is difficult and time-consuming, as it probably needs to be if the rights of the accused party are to be adequately safeguarded, and the difficulty is compounded in the case of alleged financial irregularity by the technical complexity of the issues which may arise. For this reason the Committee of Independent Experts recommended new procedures for financial affairs, whose purpose would be to identify the persons concerned and fix their individual responsibility (European Parliament, 1999b, paras 4.9.24–28). This would then provide a secure factual basis for the application of the disciplinary procedures under the Staff Regulations.

Even where the facts can be reliably established, the conduct of disciplinary procedures, whether for financial or other forms of misconduct, may present difficulties as a result of the very broad and general framework of rights and obligations set out in the Staff Regulations. The regulations, the more detailed rules attached to them, and the operational procedures manual of the Commission do not provide detailed guidance as to the standards of conduct expected of officials (for example, in the acceptance of hospitality). The reform proposals put forward by the Commission in January 2000 envisage the establishment by December 2000 of an inter-institutional committee on standards of behaviour in public life, whose purpose would be 'to support officials in maintaining high standards of ethical behaviour' and to monitor the implementation of codes of conduct in each institution. Codes of conduct for Commissioners and for their relations with departments were adopted in 1999, and a further code establishing guidelines for good administrative behaviour in relations with the public has been under consideration since 1997, though the relevance of this must be fairly limited in a bureaucracy which provides relatively few services direct to the public. It may be some years before the development of codes of conduct for EU officials is anything like comprehensive.

Meanwhile there is still much uncertainty, and the past judicial decisions of the European Court of Justice, to which officials who have been subject to disciplinary procedures may appeal, provide the only guidance as to whether specific behaviour is unacceptable (Dellis, 1994, p. 2). However, disciplinary measures, though becoming more frequent than they used to be, are still relatively rare (European Parliament, 1999a, para. 9.4.21). Dellis argues that, while officials recruited through a careful and competitive selection process may be little inclined to contravene regulations, the slow and cumbersome nature of the disciplinary process makes the Community authorities notably disinclined to embark upon such procedures (Dellis, 1994, p. 8). In 1993, for example, only 18 cases were brought to the point where a sanction was imposed, but they included two cases of assault on a colleague, eight cases of forgery or use of forged documents, four cases of fraudulent behaviour relating to recruitment competitions, and one each of corruption and sexual harassment. There is also a tendency to leniency in the imposing of sanctions. We were told that disciplinary boards could be harsh in cases of embezzlement for personal gain, or where a serving official had been found guilty by an external court of sexual offences, but one of the people we interviewed used the expression 'There but for the grace of God go I' to characterise the more sympathetic position adopted by disciplinary boards in many other cases, particularly where hard-pressed managers, or staff for whose actions they carried managerial responsibility, might have found ways around some of the more tiresomely bureaucratic procedures governing such matters as appointments or the awarding of contracts. The CIE also criticised the leniency of penalties imposed by disciplinary boards (European Parliament, 1999a, para. 9.4.23).

The public impression of widespread financial malpractice is probably exaggerated. It has been fostered by the determination of the European Parliament to focus attention on these matters, for reasons which included the opportunity to enhance their own powers, and seized on enthusiastically by the press. The Committee of Independent Experts was able to substantiate only a small number of the allegations of mismanagement, fraud and nepotism, focused primarily on the responsibilities of the Commissioners themselves, though these were sufficiently damaging to cause the Commission to resign in March 1999. But it would be equally wrong to conclude from the apparent paucity of disciplinary proceedings against officials that misconduct is rare and that there is no need to question the efficacy of the legal framework within which they operate. The CIE laid bare a culture within the Commission, particularly in respect of financial irregularities and mismanagement, which tolerated the bending of rules, was slow to uncover wrongdoing, and was also reluctant to take decisive disciplinary action when it did.

It is important to make a clear distinction at this point – one respected by the CIE but often fudged by hostile commentators (for example, *The Guardian*, 12 November 1994) – between 'fraudulent behaviour in the member states against the financial resources and allocative functions of the EC' committed by 'individuals, groups, organizations or the member states themselves' (Mendrinou, 1994, p. 82) and fraudulent or dishonest behaviour by EU officials. The former has long been recognised as a major problem. In 1998 approximately five-sixths of the Community budget was allocated to agricultural, regional, social and economic cohesion programmes under which payments are made – and then claimed against the Community budget – by national authorities within each member state acting within the framework of the regulations governing those programmes. The Court of Auditors and the European Parliament both began to be seriously exercised in the early 1980s by the scale of fraud arising under these programmes, with the European Parliament producing three reports on Community fraud between 1984 and 1989 and the Commission setting up new programmes, notably the establishment in 1988 of the Unit for the co-ordination of fraud prevention (UCLAF) under the authority of the President of the Commission, to estimate the extent of such fraud and monitor the progress of the member states in repressing it. Since then the regulations governing the major shared management programmes have been tightened up, and the powers of UCLAF (for example, to initiate inquiries on its own account), as well as the resources available to it, have been progressively strengthened (see Chapter 7), with UCLAF being replaced in 1999 by the Fraud Prevention Office (OLAF). However, the concerns of the Court of Auditors have not been allayed, and in 1999 the CIE still found ample scope to criticise the Commission as well as the member states for their failure to clamp down on irregularities and abuses which may have defrauded the Community budget of very large sums of money. For four years the Court of Auditors has not been able to give a positive statement of assurance on expenditure under the budget, estimating the rate of financial irregularities in payments under the Agricultural Fund at between 3 and 4 per cent, and as much as 10 per cent under the Structural Funds (European Parliament, 1999b, paras 3.12.2 and 3.17.9). These estimates are based on sampling techniques, and irregularity is not the same thing as fraud, but they are a worrying indicator of where fraud may lie hidden.

Compared to this problem, the extent of fraud actually involving EU officials seems, as far as it can be estimated, rather small, though not insignificant. For example, a case in 1995 (T-12/94) resulted in the demotion of a Commission official through whose hands a substantial sum of money (450 000 Belgian francs) had passed. The Personnel Directorate General suspected that the money had been retained by the official concerned, but had not undertaken extensive forensic and investigatory inquiries, or called in the police, and was held by the Court of First Instance, which upheld a demotion but annulled the dismissal of the culprit, not fully to have proved the facts. The rarity of corruption prosecutions has not prevented the emergence of lurid allegations linking the staff of the Commission much more extensively to the frauds carried out in member states. These allegations were afforded a degree of verisimilitude by the spectacular suicide in 1993 of the Commission official from the Agriculture Directorate General responsible for policy on the support of tobacco farming, who fell to his death from an upper window of the Directorate General's office building in Brussels.

There have been other well-publicised cases where fraudulent activity in the member states has been linked to Community officials. In 1996 two former officials of the Commission – the Head of the Tourism Unit and another man who had held a temporary contract within the unit, both of whom had been suspended in 1994 and then dismissed in 1995 – were arrested by the Belgian police on suspicion of corruption. These allegations involved the receipt of kickbacks from companies to whom funds for the promotion of tourism were assigned (*The Guardian*, 6 January 1996). This was only the third time that officials had appeared before Belgian courts, and the Commission has in general been reluctant to lift the diplomatic immunity its officials enjoy; despite a request from the Belgian authorities it refused to do so some months later for the Director General responsible for tourism as well as the Director and another subsequent head of the Tourism Unit, until after he had taken early retirement in the interests of the service (European Parliament, 1999a, paras 2.3.18–20). Meanwhile the new Director General had set up a task force involving Financial Control and UCLAF as well as his own directorate, which in July 1998 published a report of past management of tourism policy that identified 236 cases of undue payment and 718 cases of excess payments since 1990 concerning in total more than seven million European Currency Units (ECU). Some of those involved were facing legal proceedings in the member states, others required further investigation (European Parliament, 1999a, paras 2.3. 19–22).

It is the extent of such irregularities and their link with proven cases of fraud which no doubt caused the CIE, whilst recognising that 'an irregularity is not a criminal offence in a judicial sense', to go on to describe such widespread irregularities, by no means confined to tourism, as 'the soil in which fraud can grow'. Their judgment was severe: 'tolerance of the slack administrative practices, poor regulations, over-complicated payment mechanisms, excessive exceptions and derogations, lack of transparency etc. which tend to lead to abundant irregularities and errors, amounts to tolerance of a relatively high level of fraud' (European Parliament, 1999b, paras 5.1.4–5).

Loyalty and accountability

Financial probity is not the only aspect of the moral code and values of officials to have come under scrutiny in one or more of the member states. Much of the discussion which has led to the formulation of a code of ethics for British officials has centred around the nature and extent of an official's duties of loyalty and accountability. The question is a complex and subtle one, and is experienced in widely varying ways within the different member states.

Notions of accountability and loyalty are in most West European countries linked to traditions about the political neutrality of the civil service. In all European countries this is seen as involving a downward-looking concept of 'fairness': officials must not allow their personal convictions to influence their behaviour towards any member of the public calling upon the services of the administration. This concept has relatively little application within the Union, which is only in very few areas a direct provider of services or implementor of legislation. In a number of countries it is also linked to an upward-looking notion of support for any democratically elected government, regardless of its political colour. Many countries take a somewhat sceptical view of the human and psychological possibility of such support. Within the highly legal framework of the German system, for example, the obligation of loyalty and political neutrality is expressed in the requirement for an official to uphold the constitution (the Basic Law), whilst loyalty to the government of the day amongst the most senior officials is ensured by the practice of making appointments to the most senior posts which take into account the political views of the officials concerned. In France the *cabinets* and the designation of the most senior posts in the civil service as 'discretionary' posts (to and from which officials can be moved as governments change) fulfil a similar function. It is hardly surprising that the tensions which such a system provokes in France are found also in the European Commission (see Chapter 10 below, and Page, 1997, p. 132). Only in the countries with systems based on the 'Whitehall model' (the UK and the Republic of Ireland) is the notion of an upward-looking neutrality taken to its fullest extent, with the requirement that the civil servant is accountable to, and must serve with equal energy and loyalty, the government of the day, however constituted.

Within the European Union the focus for loyalty is less clearly defined. There is neither a regime as such – for 'ever-closer union' is usually perceived as a process – nor a government of the day with a specific manifesto towards which loyalty may be exacted. The *statut* is clear: there is a formal duty of hierarchical obedience enunciated in Article 21. But this in itself is never likely to be sufficient to shape a general internalisation of moral attitudes or a specific ethos of accountability and loyalty. And beyond that the *statut*'s requirements are mostly negative, prescribing what an official must not do (for example, seek instructions from elsewhere). The internalisation of such restraints may help to define the parameters of acceptable behaviour, but it does not shape a positive ethos of accountability. The consequence is the very distinctive relationship between the political and administrative levels within the European Union, which are described in Chapter 10. The absence of an ethos of accountability may be linked to the general democratic deficit of the European Union, but serves also to underline the extent to which the Union is still far from comparable with any nation state.

Conclusions

Despite the disturbing evidence of mismanagement and even irregularity assembled by the Committee of Independent Experts in 1999, there seems to be no reason to suppose that the institutions are a hotbed of criminality, corruption or disloyalty. Equally, however, the fact that the EU possesses a law-based system of administration has not in itself been enough to ensure probity. What may be missing, in the EU as in the public services of some of the member states, 'is the transformation of mere discipline into a genuine ethical stance' (Dellis, undated). The existence of disciplinary regulations does not in itself imply the existence of an internalised, agreed, if uncodified and even unspoken but widely shared standard of conduct, and certainly not a uniform one. In some national systems such a standard may find expression in texts and codes of conduct setting out a general framework for good behaviour, and may be inculcated into new entrants by the examples, practices and sometimes the explicit training offered by longstanding officials. These in turn may be influenced by patterns of behaviour more widely expected and practised within the surrounding society, although it is frequently recognised that the requirements of public democratic accountability may demand different standards in public officials from those that might be accepted in private business.

In this respect the EU faces particular difficulties, given the differences in social structure and context between the countries from which officials come. These reach the level of farce when, as in a disciplinary case that went to appeal (case C-403/85), an official pleaded his 'latin temperament' as justification, or at least mitigation, of an assault upon his superior. At a more profound level the sense of moral obligation towards, say, a family member or a patron that arises in a country with strongly clientilistic social patterns may differ from that found in more individualistic countries. In response to a reporter's question about the appointments she had made, Commissioner Cresson is said to have replied: 'Should we only work with people we have never seen before?' (*The Economist*, 6 March 1999). No doubt Jacques Blanc, the first President of the Committee of the Regions, would have defended his appointments policy on a similar basis (see Chapter 5). Similarly, standards of punctiliousness in relation to financial procedures may vary, even in the absence of any intention of dishonesty or fraud.

The drive by Commissioners Liikanen and Gradin to tighten up the financial control procedures within the Commission (Sound and Efficient Management, or SEM 2000), which began in 1995, derived in part from a desire to impose a more uniform standard of conduct in this respect which would override such national differences. The Prodi Commission in its early months adopted codes of conduct for the Commissioners themselves and for their *cabinets*, together with proposals for a code of conduct for officials, despite the fact that such texts had hitherto been virtually non-existent for the institutions of the European Union, as indeed for the large majority of the countries from which EU officials are drawn. It remains to be seen whether the appointment of a new Commission in 1999, with its commitment to root and branch reform, the probable creation of an inter-institutional committee on standards in public life and adoption of a code of conduct for each institution, will succeed in repairing the deficiencies of a law-based system of administration which is regarded as having failed to impose acceptable standards of behaviour. It can take a long time to change the rules and even longer to inculcate a new culture.

Chapter 4

Getting In

The principles which govern recruitment to the institutions of the European Union give priority to recruitment on merit, whilst also emphasising the importance of geographical balance among the nationals of the member states. Article 27 of the Staff Regulations stipulates that 'recruitment shall be directed to securing for the institution the services of officials of the highest standard of ability, efficiency and integrity'. The same article provides for geographical balance by stating that officials shall be 'recruited on the broadest possible geographical basis from among nationals of Member States of the Communities', whilst adding that 'no posts shall be reserved for nationals of any specific Member State'.

These principles find expression in three distinct routes of entry to a permanent appointment as an official of one of the EU institutions: the classic route via competitive entry competitions, the 'parachute' which allows some staff to be recruited to senior positions without having to undergo a competition, and the 'submarine' approach which may take several steps over several years to convert an initially temporary contractual relationship into a permanent appointment. This chapter reviews how staff are recruited by each of these routes, and considers in the light of the evidence how successful the recruitment procedures of the EU have been in meeting the objectives laid down in the Staff Regulations, and in striking an appropriate balance between them, arguing that measured against these objectives, recent performance has been disappointing.

The development of the recruitment process

Since at least the 1968 consolidation of the Staff Regulations, recruitment has operated on the basis that the officials of the

Community institutions should join an independent and structured service which provides a full career for those who work within it. That was not how things were at the beginning. The first officials of the ECSC were recruited on an informal basis and on short-term contracts or secondments. 'The only rule was that all candidates had to be approved by a member of the High Authority of their own nationality' (Conrad, 1992, p. 67). In practice, from 1953 the directors of the High Authority's divisions were asked to nominate candidates and, since no formal recruitment procedures existed until March 1955, the result was a subjective, indeed clientilistic, system of recruitment. While on the one hand the ECSC had rejected Monnet's initial vision of a very small and loosely organised body of officials, it had also rejected any suggestion that the service should resemble other international secretariats and be composed of temporary secondees who would make their careers within the services of their countries of origin. Jean Monnet overrode the hesitancy of some of his colleagues in the High Authority to persuade them that a post in the ECSC's service should be incompatible with continued membership of a national civil service or the holding of a public office (Conrad, 1989, p. 65).

The early practice of the Commission was similar, many appointments being made by co-option, mostly from national administrations. Most of the officials appointed under these arrangements had some required specialised knowledge or were known to be committed to European integration, or both. Going back to figures produced in 1970, when most of the staff had still been recruited under these procedures, 46 per cent of category A officials had come from the public services of national governments, 25 per cent from national professional organisations and trade unions, 24 per cent from the private sector, and only 5 per cent had entered service with the Commission as their first employment (Coombes, 1975, p. 92).

The informal and clientilistic features of the early recruitment system were mitigated, but not entirely banished, by the development during the 1960s of clear and formal staff regulations administered by the Personnel and Administration DG (DG IX), which gradually put the recruitment process on to a fairer and more regular basis. If the service was to offer the substantial guarantees of a career service and the statutory framework of Staff

Regulations to those who worked within it, then it was important that there should be a well-defined process by which the service was entered and those guarantees acquired. Although the disadvantages of a poorly defined recruitment system were recognised more than 30 years ago, some aspects of the old, informal approach survive in the process of recruitment and appointment to senior positions (see below), which is still heavily influenced by the Commissioners and their senior *cabinet* staff, and in the less formal procedures characteristic of the submarine approach.

The recruitment procedure

Each of the EU institutions is responsible for appointing its own staff, though they can and sometimes do co-operate with one another in the running of particular competitions (for example, for Italian-language typists). When a post falls vacant in any of the EU institutions, the first step is to consider (Article 29 of the Staff Regulations) whether it can be filled by transfer or promotion of existing staff, either within the DG where the vacancy has arisen, from another part of the same institution, or from another Community institution. At intermediate levels it is usually possible to fill most posts by these means, though some with particular requirements may have to be filled by external recruitment (for example, where the EU has acquired new responsibilities). One important source of experienced staff at intermediate levels is the supply of detached national experts, mainly staff on secondment from national administrations. Another way to plug a gap quickly is to appoint a consultant on a temporary contract. When all these expedients have been exhausted, most of the remaining vacancies which cannot be filled internally tend to be in the basic grades (A7/6, A8, B5/4, C5/4, D3/2).

The next step is to check the availability of resources. The number of permanent and temporary officials each institution can recruit is limited by the number of additional posts approved by the budgetary authority in that year's budget and any posts approved in the previous year which have not been filled or otherwise become vacant through retirements, transfers and resignations. However, since the recruitment process may take up to a year to complete and the budget may not be approved until shortly before the financial year begins, the forward planning of competitions is difficult. In the past the difficulty has been compounded by exchange rate fluctuations. In 1987/88, and again very suddenly in 1993/94, a rapid decline in the value of the ECU in relation to the Belgian Franc caused the Commission to freeze all recruitment, disrupting the competitions and delaying the appointment of successful candidates. This difficulty should not recur under a single currency regime.

The recruitment procedure followed involves the following parties:

- the appointing authority;
- the staff committee;
- the joint committee;
- the recruitment unit; and
- the selection board.

The appointing authority is the administrative body regulating relations between the institution and its employees or future employees (in effect, the employer). Normally each institution would have one appointing authority, but the Commission has two, one in the Personnel and Administration DG for administrative appointments, and another in the Research DG for appointments under the research budget. The appointing authority has jurisdiction over all decisions about the competition. It decides whether to open a competition in the first place, which procedure to use, and what to say in the public notice and the application form. It appoints the selection board, receives its decisions and transmits them to the candidates.

Staff interests are represented in the Staff Committee which appoints members to the selection board, in the Joint Committee which has to be consulted before a competition notice is issued, and within the selection board itself. The Staff Committee has the right to designate one member of the selection board (Staff Regulations, Annex III, Article 3), but in practice, following a position adopted by Commissioner Ortoli in 1976, it designates half the members of the selection board whenever appointments are being made to more than a single post.

The Joint Committee (the common Joint Committee where the competition is for posts in more than one institution) consists of a chairman appointed each year by the appointing authority, and an equal number of members from the appointing authority and the Staff Committee. The Joint Committee must be consulted before the appointing authority adopts a competition notice. Although many proposals are adopted without amendment, that is not always the case and many of the significant features of the institution's recruitment procedures can be traced to initiatives of the staff representatives (Zito, 1992).

The recruitment unit is part of the Personnel and Administration DG and is responsible for the practical and administrative organisation of the competitions, including the provision of secretariat services to the selection boards. The selection board appointed for each competition, one for each language where appropriate, is independent. It does not represent the administration or the Staff Committee or the unions. It is normally composed of officials with other jobs, or recently retired officials. It is rare to use outsiders (Zito, 1992, p. 72). This imposes an additional burden on busy staff, but has the advantage of involving the operational departments throughout the recruitment procedure. The members of each selection board must be competent to make an objective assessment of the performance of the candidates (Dubouis, 1984, p. 244). The boards are responsible for taking all decisions as to who is admitted to tests, what marks are awarded, and who should appear on the final list of those successful.

Recruitment by open competition: general competitions at career entry level

Although all the institutions follow much the same procedure, and the major competitions themselves follow much the same pattern (see below), each institution sets its own tests to satisfy its own requirements, unless it chooses to collaborate, so that there is a good deal of variety within a broadly similar pattern. The Staff Regulations merely require recruitment (except to grades A1 and A2) to be based on qualifications or tests, or a combination of the two.

Whilst some competitions may be open to a very wide range of candidates, others may be more restricted. For example, at the time of enlargement, there are always competitions limited to nationals of the new member states. In some cases the competition may be restricted to those with particular languages (for example, in December 1996, English or German for the Council of Ministers and the Committee of the Regions); or a competition may be structured in such a way as to reserve some appointments for candidates with degrees in particular subjects such as law, economics or statistics, or for people with particular types of experience such as external relations or aid management (for example, in March 1998, for the Commission). In addition to such special qualifications, candidates for A7 competitions are generally required to have had two or three years of relevant graduate-level work experience, and candidates for A8 competitions (professional experience not required) must have obtained their degree within the past three years. Finally, there is usually an age limit, though it was set at 35 for the 1996 Council competition, and 45 for the 1998 competitions for the Commission and the European Parliament, and there are suggestions that it should be removed altogether.

Competitions are advertised in the Press at the same time as the formal competition notice appears in the Official Journal (and on the Europa website), together with the application form. The competition notice is a legally binding document whose terms must be respected by the appointing authority, by the selection board and by the candidates. The recruitment unit has the task of checking that the applications comply with the formal and general requirements, such as nationality, provision of references and fulfilment of any military service obligations. In principle, the greater the number of applicants, the greater the chance of securing recruits of high quality, but the sheer volume of applications – over 55 000 for the Commission's 1993 A7/A8 competitions; 30 000 in 1998 – must make it difficult to give each application adequate attention. It has been alleged that in the early stages at least the emphasis is on elimination rather than selection. Candidates have to be very careful not to make mistakes, however small, in completing the application form and supplying the required supporting documentation.

The next stage is for the selection board to examine whether candidates comply with the specific requirements for the post, of which the most significant are age, qualifications and professional experience. However, where there are very large numbers of applications, the selection board may initially reject only those who do not meet the nationality and age requirements, leaving the other requirements to be checked only when numbers have been reduced to more manageable proportions by the pre-selection stage.

Where numbers are very large, the pre-selection stage is arguably the most important in the whole competition. It may have to reduce a field of 30 000–50 000 candidates to no more than 2000–3000. The test takes the form of two or more multiple-choice papers; one will be designed to test knowledge of any specialist expertise which may have been required, whilst the others will aim to test more general administrative skills, knowledge of the EU institutions and policies, and finally the candidate's chosen second language. The marking scheme allows the various elements to be differentially weighted, but all candidates must reach the pass mark in all papers, usually 50 per cent. All the tests, except the language test, are the same for all candidates, and the competition takes place on the same day in as many as 38 different centres across the EU. So when cheating was reported at the tests in September 1998 in Rome and in Brussels – some candidates left the room and used mobile phones to check their answers – the whole competition had to be annulled and re-run six months later at vast expense.

Candidates who survive the pre-selection stage and whose applications are found to meet all the other general and specific requirements are invited to sit a further written examination. These further written tests also vary from one competition to another. Where there has been no pre-selection stage (for example, the 1998 competition for the European Parliament and the Court of Justice), the written test will be more extensive and include some multiple-choice papers and a language test similar to those otherwise used in the pre-selection stage. Otherwise the written tests usually consist of a general essay (about 2 hours), an essay on a specialised topic (for A7) and a dossier exercise (three to four hours) which may, for example, require the candidate to draft a speech and a summary on the basis of an official EC document.

About half of those who sit the written examinations are invited to attend a final interview in Brussels where they appear before the selection board for 45 minutes, to answer questions which further test their knowledge, their ability to make a clear oral presentation in response to questions, and finally their ability to speak and understand a second language.

About half the candidates who attend the final interview are declared suitable for appointment and informed that their names have been placed on the reserve list, from which candidates may be drawn for actual appointment as and when specific vacancies arise. This procedure is envisaged in the Staff Regulations which provide in Article 30 that 'the Selection Board shall draw up a list of suitable candidates. The appointing authority shall decide which of these candidates to appoint to the vacant posts.' The reserve list normally contains about twice as many candidates as the number of posts to be filled. This is probably just as well, since the procedure is so drawn-out that some candidates will have found other jobs by the time they are finally declared successful. The reserve list concept is further justified by the fact that the competitions are generally organised before knowing the budget and therefore the number of posts to be filled. However, even if new vacancies arise and there are successful candidates available but unplaced, they cannot be appointed to any post for which the competitions were not organised (Mordt v. CJCE, 27 June 1991, Rec.p.II 407 in case T-156/89, cited by Dubouis, 1994, p. 246). The use of the reserve list also permits the adjustment of the results of a competition, which might otherwise result in a high number of successful candidates from one nationality, undermining the principle of geographical balance (Bodiguel, 1994, p. 162).

The recruitment procedure described up to this point is organised for each institution by its central Personnel DG. The choice of candidates for a particular post is, however, decentralised. Once the reserve list appears, it is circulated to DGs, who use it to see whether there are suitable candidates for vacant posts which cannot be filled by internal transfers. They ask for one or more candidates to be called in for interview. A candidate may be called to several interviews before being offered a job, or he or she may not be called for interview at all before the final expiry date of the reserve list which lasts one or two years (Zito, 1992, pp. 77–80). Much depends on the initiative of the candidates themselves in ensuring, with the help of such contacts as they may have in the Commission or in their national representation, that their names are actively considered for the posts for which they are best suited. It may be argued that, given the relatively impersonal nature of the recruitment up to this point, the use of the reserve list provides for a degree of flexibility in ensuring that a candidate's personality and aptitude for a particular post are taken into account.

The Staff Regulations provide for appeal against decisions of the appointing authority to the Court of Justice and its Court of First Instance. The appointing authority has wide powers of assessment (from the French administrative concept of *pouvoir d'appréciation*) recognised both by the Staff Regulations and the Court (Judgment of Tribunal of First Instance, 25 February 1992 in Schloh v. Council, T-11/91, Rec.p.II-203, cited in Dubouis, 1994, pp. 248). This discretionary power of assessment reduces the chances of success on appeal to the Court of First Instance on such grounds as discrimination, abuse of power or unequal treatment (*rupture d'égalité*: judgment in case C-107/90P, Hochbaum v. Commission, 17 January 1992, Rec.I-157, cited in Dubouis, 1994, p. 248).

Pre-entry training

As a result of the intense competition which these competitions attract, many candidates undertake a substantial course of training to prepare for them. Quite apart from professional training in law or economics, successful candidates will have acquired a good theoretical knowledge of the European Communities and how they work. They may have studied European Law or European Studies at university in their own country or at the Collège d'Europe in Bruges, or have attended preparation courses such as those run in France by Paris I, Strasbourg III and Montpellier I. National administrations also train their own staff and others for the competitions. The UK Cabinet Office has recruited 20 to 30 young graduates each year since 1991 into a European Fast Stream programme, which prepares them for the competitions by up to four years' experience of relevant work in government departments, together with appropriate training. In France the Ministry of the Economy has developed a traineeship scheme for young civil servants from various administrations wishing to enter the European Union competitions (Penaud, 1993, p. 26). The Commission itself offers about 1000 six-month traineeships (*stages*) every year to EU citizens, and another 2–300 to citizens of other countries. This traineeship scheme does not form part of the recruitment procedure for permanent officials. A *stage* is nevertheless normally a valuable experience which can help prepare a candidate for the competition although, in 1997 a *stagiaire* in DG V was dismissed for publicly criticising the Commission for overstaffing, idleness and lack of worthwhile tasks (The European, 1 August 1997). Indeed, before 1993, the *stage* was seen as a way to avoid formal competitions. Since that time, however, a lapse of one year has been introduced before temporary contracts can be offered to former trainees (Spence, 1997a, pp. 92). Even so, the *stage* is one way to mark oneself out from others on the reserve lists to which successful candidates are assigned (Abélès, Bellier and McDonald, 1993, p. 35).

A more specialised training programme, intended to lead to employment if successfully completed, is offered by the Joint Interpreting and Conference Service (JICS). Candidates under the age of 30, with a university degree in any discipline, well informed on current economic and political affairs, and with a good knowledge of at least three Community languages, can be trained in six months to provide simultaneous interpretation at Community meetings provided that they undertake to remain in Brussels as JICS interpreters for at least two years after completing the course.

Senior appointments

Many of the public service systems within the member states of the Union, including France, Germany, Italy and Spain, distinguish both legally and in practice between what may be described as career grade posts, and the most senior posts. In these systems progression up the career grades for those who start at the appropriate junior level has tended to be a largely automatic process, heavily dependent upon seniority. At the most senior levels, however, appointment to a particular post is a matter for the discretion of the political head of the department, who is likely to take factors such as the political allegiance of the appointee into account. In some systems it is possible for such posts to be filled by external appointment rather than by promotion from amongst those already in the service in the grades below. The reason for such arrangements is the conviction that political heads of department must be entitled to choose as their closest collaborators in the most senior posts people in whose personal and political loyalty they can have complete confidence. In practice such posts are often filled by candidates from within the public services, who are likely to have the necessary professional expertise. But the choice is discretionary.

These practices find their echo in the arrangements which apply under Article 29 of the Staff Regulations, which accepts that 'a procedure other than the competition procedure may be adopted by the appointment authority for the recruitment of Grade A1 or A2 officials'. In practice the competition procedure is never used at these senior levels (Guérivière, 1993, p. 41), but that does not mean that the selection process is not highly competitive. All such appointments require the approval of the College of Commissioners, and in the past they have been the subject of much secret wheeling and dealing among the Commissioners and their *chefs de cabinet*, but in 1999 the Prodi Commission adopted a new code of practice which at least places some limits on their freedom of manoeuvre in this respect. Vacancy notices are to be published with a detailed job profile, candidates will be assessed by the Consultative Committee on Appointments (a group of Directors General) on a transparent basis against criteria related to the job profile, and those placed on the short-list must all be interviewed by the Commissioner concerned (and in the case of candidates for A1 posts by the Commissioner responsible for personnel as well) before the Commissioner makes a recommendation to the full College. Where it is decided to resort to an external appointment, the same procedures will be followed, but the post will first be publicly advertised, as was done for five A1 posts in 1999.

Although the procedures are now more transparent and more professional than they were, they still allow the Commission a flexibility in senior appointments similar to that which exists in France, Germany, Italy and Spain, and the importance of these appointments is such that *chefs de cabinet* are likely to continue to invest up to 20 per cent of their time in this activity. As in many of the national systems, this permissive authority in senior appointments is balanced by the appointing authority's equally unfettered right of decision to retire such staff 'in the interests of the service' under the terms of Article 50 (Dondelinger, 1985). This enables senior staff to be moved or removed when this is required by the arrival of new tasks or new Commissioners, or when space has to be made for senior staff from new member states. Of even greater importance is the possibility of maintaining an appropriate balance of nationalities among the most senior staff within the institutions. Indeed this balance has assumed a sufficient importance in the eyes of the member states for the attribution of 'political responsibilities', the criterion for discretionary appointments, to have extended beyond posts at A1 and A2 to encompass an increasing number of posts at A3 level (Guérivière, 1993, p. 41).

Such appointments are known as *parachutage*. Below the top two grades, some form of competition has to be arranged, but this may well take the form of a special competition, open only to existing temporary staff. For example, a special competition for a particular post at A3 or A4 level may be held when room needs to be found, at the end of a Commissioner's mandate, for a *cabinet* member brought in some years earlier on temporary appointment terms. The most detailed study of *parachutage* has been made by Edward Page (Page, 1997). Using biographical data on 2300 officials in all the institutions mostly at grade A4 and above (Page, 1997, p. 20), his work shows that around half of all senior officials were parachuted in to the institutions, and in the A1 and A2 grades of the European Commission 70 per cent of the posts are filled by officials who did not start in the basic career grades (A7-A8). Even below the top two levels, where *parachutage* is provided for in the Staff Regulations, he estimates that 45 per cent of A3s, and even one in three of all A4s, did not begin their careers at A7 or A8 level (Table 4.1). This does not mean that the officials concerned had necessarily been parachuted into the job they currently held. Page defines a parachutist

Table 4.1   *Parachutists and career officials in the Commission Directorates General and Central services in percentages (early 1990s)*

Grade	% Career	% Parachuted	Number
A1	18.2	81.8	33
A2	34.3	65.7	105
A3	55.1	44.9	354
A4	66.7	33.3	54

Source: Page (1997) p. 51.

as a person whose first job in the Commission was at a senior level (that is, not at the normal career starting point), but he points out that once in, such people tend to stay in the service of the EU for a long time, and tend then to arrive at the most senior posts (Page, 1997, pp. 49–51).

Parachutage and the impact of the cabinet system

The much contested practice of *parachutage* is sometimes linked to the alleged planting of national flags on certain posts. In the 'highly contentious struggle between different member states' over the filling of important new positions or the replacement of retiring senior officials (Page, 1997, p. 50) the outcome may be the promotion of an appropriate long-serving career member of the institution's staff. It may equally be the promotion of an official parachuted into the DG earlier on at the next level down with precisely that progression in mind, though this is not a risk-free strategy. Or it may be the introduction of a senior person with no previous direct experience of work in the institution, as will inevitably be the case for those appointed from new member states soon after their entry. If member states are to achieve appropriate representation of their officials at all levels, they will not, and do not wish to, wait 20 years or more while career grade entrants work their way up. So with the repeated waves of enlargement it is scarcely surprising that Page finds that before the 1995 enlargement the six original member states had the six lowest proportions of late entry officials in all the institutions.

The processes are not simple, however, or straightforward, and a simplistic linking of geographical balance, 'national flags' and *parachutage* would be misleading.

Parachutage is also a means by which members of Commissioners' private offices, their *cabinets*, may move into permanent posts. Here again the linkage with national balance is not straightforward. The 20 Commissioners are supported by about 300 staff, of whom about one-third are category A staff, chosen by the Commissioner personally. Commissioners constitute their private offices largely from their own compatriots. There has long been a requirement for at least one 'foreigner', and President Prodi has insisted that each *cabinet* must include staff of at least three nationalities, but this still allows the majority of the *cabinet* to be of the same nationality as the Commissioner. They come from many different backgrounds, including the permanent staff of the Commission, the national administration of the Commissioner's member state, or from the private sector. Although some Commissioners may pick their team principally from amongst existing officials of the institutions, as Neil Kinnock did in 1995, Edith Cresson, consistent with the practice followed by most French ministers, brought almost the whole of her team from Paris. As the term of office of a particular College of Commissioners comes to an end, both Commissioners and their *cabinet* staff will be on the lookout for permanent appointments to posts which will reward loyalty and strenuous service, and exploit a very wide overview of the operations of the Commission. A *chef de cabinet*, equivalent to an A2 official, may be appointed director or director general; an assistant principal private secretary may be appointed director (A2) or head of unit (A3) (Bodiguel, 1994, p. 160), though this can be more difficult because appointment to A3 requires a specific competition. Page found that within the EU as a whole, of 1174 top officials (grades A1–A3) for whom he had data, 12 per cent had served in a *cabinet*. Two-thirds of these were parachutists and one-third of them career officials. However, in the highest ranks – A1 and A2 – the proportion with experience in a *cabinet* rose to 32 per cent.

It is not disputed that many temporary staff in *cabinets* find permanent posts in the Commission when the Commissioner who appointed them moves on. But there will be individuals of many different nationalities seeking posts, and not all *cabinet* members necessarily seek subsequent posts in the services of the institutions. Some may have been on secondment from elsewhere and return whence they came. The impact of the parachuting of former *cabinet* members is more important for perceptions of career progress (see Chapter 5 below) than it is for national balance. *Parachutage* creates some resentment because it is perceived as making it harder for career officials to reach the highest levels (Bellier, 1994a, p. 256; Page, 1997, p. 81). Former members of a *cabinet* who are absorbed into the permanent service of the Commission block the progress of others and distort the pattern of promotion (House of Lords, 1988, p. 17). Even in the case of those recruited to the *cabinet* from the permanent staff of the Commission, their return sometimes gives rise to difficulties: for instance, a reorganisation may have to be arranged to create senior posts irrespective of the need to improve services (House of Lords, 1988, p. 16).

The extent to which *parachutage* occurred at the end of the last Delors Commission in 1994 gave rise to criticism (Guérivière, 1993, p. 42) as a particularly blatant departure from the ideals of a European Union public service detached from national or political considerations. The Santer Commission adopted a Code of Conduct designed to mitigate such criticism of *parachutage* appointments associated with the dispersal of their cabinets. Nevertheless it remains the case that in a system heavily influenced by informal networks, staff who have the necessary pull (or *piston*), especially with the *cabinet* of their own national Commissioner, can progress rapidly. The converse is also true: informal networks can form harsh judgements against which there is no appeal, and in a highly competitive environment senior staff who are thought to have made errors of judgement, or who fail to keep their support networks in good repair, are liable to find themselves rather suddenly faced with a requirement to 'take Article 50'. The circumstances of such events are frequently shrouded in a degree of mystery, barely concealing suggestions of cabal and back-stabbing, but the risks and the rewards at this level are recognised as considerable, and the departure terms are generous. As a result, while individual cases may give rise to speculation and even concern about what has occurred, and the worst features may now be mitigated by the adoption of codes of good conduct both for promotions of *cabinet* staff and for the use of Article 50, there is no very strong pressure to change the arrangements which apply to senior appointments.

The submarine approach

The Commission has long been adept at finding ways around its own rules. The Spierenburg Report describes the procedures devised for external recruitment of staff at A3 and lower levels in the following terms:

> As there are no special rules like those for Grades A1 and A2, these recruitments (at A3) are made by devious procedures, the appointee being brought in on a temporary contract and subsequently established as a full official by means of an internal competition at which because of his special experience he is sure of being successful. A similar procedure also operates for appointment of outsiders at A5/A4, which has a generally disruptive effect on career prospects. These purely formal competitions – the so-called 'rigged competitions' – are understandably unpopular with staff; and they do not even provide a guarantee that the Commission will select the best possible candidate. (Spierenburg, 1979, para. 104).

A slightly more elaborate way of securing, ultimately, a permanent post at the Commission is by means of the unofficial *sous-marin* route which David Spence describes in the following terms:

> If a seconded national official is sought by a Directorate General yet cannot take the normal competition route, e.g. on grounds of age, he or she may be employed on a contract as a consultant, thereafter obtain the status of auxiliary agent, graduate to a full temporary agent contract and thus be eligible for the internal competition for establishment, for which the age requirements are waived. (Spence, 1997a, p. 80).

This suggests that co-option, much practised in the early days and criticised by Spierenburg, survives in this more sophisticated variant. A particularly blatant example appears to have been the early staffing of the Committee of the Regions (*The Guardian*, 1 December 1995). It is alleged that the Committee's first president, Jacques Blanc, a former French Prefect, staffed the committee very largely from people already known to him, if only to get it up and running quickly without having to wait 12–18 months to obtain staff through a normal recruitment competition. Even when eight posts were advertised internally in the summer of 1995, they all went to people already working for the committee on temporary contracts, in much the way described by Spence.

Limited internal competitions certainly provide an important route into the EU institutions for temporary staff. Members of the large group of temporary research staff frequently apply for permanent status under internal competitions, and some are successful, but it is the 200 or so staff in the Commissioners' *cabinets* and the group of about 300 temporary staff scattered around the other parts of the Commission who are probably most relevant as candidates for the limited competitions leading to appointment as permanent officials.

One of the advantages of the *sousmarin* route into Commission employment is that the recruitment procedures for temporary staff are less formidable than those for permanent appointment, and the subsequent competitions for conversion from temporary to permanent status, being limited to staff already employed as temporary staff, are also less intensely competitive, if only because not so many candidates can compete. When a DG has one or more vacancies for temporary staff, it draws up a job profile. The profiles are sent to the Personnel and Administration DG, which advertises the posts and their strictly limited duration in the press, setting out the job profile and the academic and/or professional experience required. Several candidates corresponding to each profile are then identified, and transmitted to a selection board composed of one representative of the Personnel and Administration DG, one staff representative chosen by the central Staff Committee and one representative of the DG in which there is a vacant job. The choice of the candidates is then made from this list by the Personnel DG, with the agreement of the DG concerned. The main difference in this process from that used to select permanent officials is the absence of any written test. The unions would like to see written tests instituted for the recruitment of temporary staff, but the Personnel DG has resisted this, arguing that the CVs sent by candidates are a sufficient basis on which to make an assessment, subject to confirmation at an interview similar to the oral test faced by candidates for permanent posts, and conducted under the same procedural conditions of legality, equality and confidentiality.

Under a policy dating from 1988, temporary staff (except research) should not normally be employed for longer than five years, but in that time they should have the opportunity to compete twice in internal competitions for permanent posts (Bodiguel, 1994, p. 164). Spence reports that following a large influx of temporary staff in 1989 to deal with the consequences of the Single European Act and the 'Delors I' Package, the Commission advertised an internal competition in February 1994 to allow about 100 temporary staff to obtain permanent status (Spence, 1997a, p. 78). A further competition was advertised in September 1994, mainly to deal with temporary staff leaving *cabinets* at the end of the Delors Presidency and seeking appointment at levels below A2.

It is impossible to say how many staff gain access to permanent posts at the Commission by way of temporary appointments followed by limited internal competitions, but the evidence from 1994 (when there were no open competitions at A7/A8 other than for nationals of the new member states) is that entry by the back door is by no means unusual. The Commission has recognised the dissatisfaction which this can cause, and by a decision of 13 November 1996 attempted to tighten up the system, but it is likely to remain a significant avenue of recruitment for as long as temporary staff have to be appointed on contract to get the work done, leading to periodic demands that the posts so created must subsequently be integrated into the establishment plan approved by the budgetary authorities. This has been the pattern throughout the 1990s, and a further integration of temporary posts is included in Commissioner Kinnock's reform programme.

Issues in recruitment policy

Despite the development of formal procedures, recruitment to the Community's services has never been unquestioned or uncontested, and not only at the more senior levels. Some of the issues which arise relate to the fairness of the competitions as a means of selecting officials 'of the highest standard of ability, efficiency and integrity' (the merit principle) in a Community of fifteen member states with very different cultures reflected in their educational systems and professional training. Others are related to the need to recruit staff 'on the broadest possible geographical basis from among nationals of Member States of the Communities', whilst still others arise from the impact on regular recruitment at career entry grades of the alternative procedures, which have allowed some staff to be recruited at all levels on a less competitive basis.

Recruitment on merit

Even during the brief period 1988–93 when entry competitions were being held on a regular basis, there was a good deal of dissatisfaction with the ways in which they operated. If the way in which the recruitment process is framed and operates has the effect of discouraging applications from certain groups of candidates, then the principle of recruitment on merit is not fully respected. A particular bone of contention has been the difficulty of finding means of achieving a fair competition for people whose national educational and administrative cultures may vary widely. In the UK, for example, recruitment to managerial and administrative positions, both in public service and in the private sector, has tended to depend importantly upon an appreciation of the general qualities, transferable skills and personality of the candidate, rather than upon a more formal assessment of knowledge. This approach both reflects and is reflected in the nature of the education system. By contrast, in France, detailed specific and relevant knowledge, committed to memory, is regarded as a crucial factor, and the educational and recruitment context reflects this.

Some of these problems have been recognised for many years, and taken into account as recruitment procedures have evolved. For example, the Spierenburg report recommended that the perceived imbalance in recruitment should be addressed first by publicising competitions more effectively in the different member states, particularly through more regular contacts with universities and public authorities; second, by a greater decentralisation of the places in which the tests were conducted; and third, by the appointment of external assessors so that the diverse national cultures would be better represented. During the 1980s the numbers of candidates for the main competitions grew, and the geographical distribution widened, but concerns remained about the outcome. It was partly in an attempt to deal fairly with the growing numbers of candidates that general knowledge qualifying tests were introduced. But these have been described as 'somewhat akin to the board game *Trivial Pursuits*' and suffer, as David Spence points out, from the difficulty that 'school systems vary nationally and *Trivial Pursuits* involves varying cultural criteria' (Spence, 1997a, p. 73). More frequent A8 competitions were introduced in response to pressure from some member states (especially the UK) who felt that good generalist arts graduates were being disadvantaged by the bias in the A7 competitions in favour of degrees in law or economics.

There have also been persistent concerns that EU recruitment may discriminate against women. In 1988, for example, although one-third of the candidates admitted to the written test for A7 were women, only two were appointed alongside 41 men (Penaud, 1989, p. 14). One of the main aims of the new guidelines for recruitment adopted by the Commission in 1991 was to attract more women, especially into category A. This was one reason why it was decided to hold A8 competitions every year (a policy which has since been disrupted as a result of enlargement), and A7/6 competitions less frequently. Because the candidates for A8 competitions are not required to have had working experience, which is required at A7/6, these competitions are more attractive to young women, who are more easily recruited before their mobility is inhibited by commitments to a partner or family. Around 52 per cent of candidates for the 1993 A8 competition were female, compared to 37 per cent at grade A7. As a result of the new policy, women comprised 31 per cent of the A8 grade on 1 January 1994, by comparison with 13.5 per cent for category A as a whole. Research carried out by the Commission also showed that the general knowledge test discriminated heavily against women. A psychometric test had to be abandoned on the same grounds in 1992. The general knowledge test was therefore replaced in 1994 by a test of knowledge of the European Union and its policies. Over the five years 1995–9, the success rate for women from Sweden and Finland entering the Commission at Grades A7/6 and A8 was markedly higher (51 per cent for Finland, 46 per cent for

Sweden), and the corresponding figure for Austria was an encouraging 36 per cent. The increase from five to ten in the level of representation of women at A1/2 which followed the 1995 enlargement may also have helped to encourage the recruitment of women. By 1999, 30 per cent of all recruits at grades A8 and A7/6 were women (50 out of 165), which suggests that gender bias at career entry grades is being reduced; but the proportion of women in category A in 1999 was still only 19.4 per cent, and the eight women recruited at the higher A4/A5 level comprised only 13.6 per cent of the intake (European Union, 2000, para. 1068).

A further problem is the fragmentation of competitions, which may make it difficult for potential candidates to be aware of what openings there are throughout the institutions of the Union and what their procedures are. The Spierenburg Report criticised the holding of separate competitions and proposed joint competitions for all the institutions. Since that time, an increasing number of inter-institutional competitions has been organised for B and C grades (Bodiguel, 1994, p. 162) and, as we have seen, the Council of Ministers shared its 1996 A grade competition with the Committee of the Regions, and the Parliament shared one of its A grade competitions with the Court of Justice in 1998. Discussions have taken place on the creation of an inter-institutional office which could organise competitions on behalf of all the institutions (Zito, 1992, p. 81). As the largest institution of the European Union, the Commission is still inclined to discourage such developments, because it feels it has least to gain and most to lose by subordinating its requirements to a collective programme. Nevertheless, it cannot altogether resist the pressure to co-operate, and between 1994 and 1998 it was involved in 49 inter-institutional competitions (European Union, 2000, p. 432).

Geographical balance

A second major source of recruitment problems is the link between recruitment and the successive enlargements of the Community. With every new accession openings in the services of the Community have had to be found for nationals of the new member states. As a consequence the staff has been recruited in a series of national waves, following the growth of the European Union, leading to an uneven age profile, with undesirable consequences for promotion prospects and career development. These upheavals have had the effect of temporarily blocking almost all normal recruitment from sources other than the new member states. For instance, over the three-year period 1986–88, the Commission recruited 1320 Spanish and Portuguese officials who were selected as a result of 106 competitions. This compared with a normal recruitment level at that time of about 550 staff per year. To facilitate this influx provision was made for some staff to take early retirement – about 446 officials chose to do so – while an extra 939 posts were created, reflecting the fact that enlargement entails additional duties for the Commission (Hay, 1989, pp. 25 and 39).

The 1995 accession of Austria, Finland and Sweden created similar problems. Between 1995 and 1999 the Commission recruited more than 1100 officials and nearly 300 linguists from the new member states, whilst requesting only 550 new posts and taking no steps to encourage early retirements. As a result there were no open competitions for the nationals of other member states at the normal graduate career entry grades (A7/A6 and A8) for several years. Open competitions were launched in December 1996 for the Council, and in March 1998 for the Parliament and the Commission, but there is no promise of a return to regular annual competitions and the prospect of a wave of further enlargements encompassing six and eventually as many as a dozen or more new members over the first decade of the new millennium causes any return to a predictable and regular recruitment programme to recede further and further into the distance. The EU institutions like to see themselves as offering a career service to graduates of the highest quality from all the member states, but the unpredictable irregularity of open competitions acts as a serious deterrent to potential candidates. Finding a fair, balanced and flexible means to resolve this issue will be a major challenge for the institutions and the member states.

Despite the irregular pattern of recruitment, the institutions have succeeded in maintaining a reasonably fair geographical balance in category A (see also Chapter 6), where most countries are within one or two percentage points of what might be their theoretical representation, based on their share of seats in the European Parliament (Bodiguel, 1994, p. 159), albeit with two significant exceptions, namely Belgium, which has 12 per cent against a theoretical representation of 5 per cent, and the UK, which also has 12 per cent but against a theoretical share of 15 per cent. At the level of directors general the Commission maintains a particularly careful balance between nationalities, and this balance is also maintained, but with increasing flexibility, at the levels of director and head of unit, at which level the flexibility is now substantial. At the B, C and D levels, merit is the only factor which influences selection. The over-representation of Belgium and Luxembourg reflects the high level of interest from host-country nationals who are five to fourteen times more likely to apply for competitions than the nationals of other member states. This high level of attraction exists for all grades, but it is highest in the B grades (37–42 per cent of applicants), where the Commission recruits disproportionately from within relatively small groups of potential applicants, largely if not exclusively located in and around Brussels, and likely to be already associated with the Community system in one way or another.

Alternative recruitment

During the 1990s the alternative recruitment tracks, which were meant to be exceptional, have become increasingly significant. Enlargement is not the only reason for an uneven recruitment profile. Another main cause has been the spasmodic growth of functions, usually following the adoption of new Treaty provisions at inter-governmental conferences. For example, the Single European Act of 1985 led to a major programme of work to realise the single market by 1992, and considerable numbers of additional staff were needed to carry it out. The progressive development of the Common Foreign and Security Policy (CFSP) and the work on Justice and Home Affairs under the Treaty of European Union has also generated additional work requiring increased staffing provision at all levels in those parts of the Commission and the Council which are charged with putting them into practice. Successive budgetary agreements have progressively shifted the burden of Community expenditure away from agriculture and into a wide range of other programmes, including regional assistance, educational exchange programmes, aid programmes for Eastern and Central Europe, and also humanitarian aid. Such programmes require staff to manage them, but the Commission, under pressure from the Council to keep down the level of administrative expenditure, has been reluctant to ask for additional resources. Neither has it had much success in transferring staff from areas of relative decline in Community activity to areas of growth (see Exhibit 3.2 and Chapter 5). Instead the Commission has plugged the gap by the deployment of detached national experts and by relying on temporary, auxiliary and agency staff, many of them not scoring at all against Part A of the budget (administrative expenditure) because they have been hired through the diversion into administration of funds provided under Part B of the budget (operational expenditure) for the programmes themselves. This device, known as a mini-budget, was gradually regularised under the Santer administration, but in 1999 the Committee of Independent Experts still found that some of the Technical Assistance Offices, which typically were appointed under contract to manage the programmes, were carrying out work which should more properly have been undertaken by officials. The growth of mini-budgets and their subsequent regularisation through the conversion of temporary posts into permanent ones has provided extensive opportunities for staff initially recruited on a temporary basis to make themselves indispensable, and ultimately to secure appointment to a permanent post in the manner described above.

Conclusions

Measured against the declared objectives of recruitment on merit and on the broadest possible geographical basis, the recent performance of the EU institutions has been disappointing. The difficulties are formidable, but the fact is that since 1993 the primacy of the merit principle has been substantially sacrificed, first in favour of the nationals of the new member states, and then in favour of those who had got their foot inside the back door as a result of irregularities in staff management (the so-called mini-budgets). One of the tests of the Prodi Commission's commitment to management reform will be their success or otherwise in restoring a fair, open and regular recruitment programme.

Chapter 5

Getting On

Career progression

Twenty-five years ago relatively informal career management procedures were still adequate for a small administration. As the Spierenburg Report says: 'In the small Commission administration of the early days, when officials were well known to each other, it was not difficult to lay one's hands on the right person to fill a particular post' (Spierenburg, 1979, p. 79). By the end of the 1970s, as Spierenburg recognised, that position was no longer tenable, and more formal procedures were required in the interests of equity, good management and staff morale. These were put in place during the 1980s, and increasing efforts were made to apply an equal opportunities policy as between men and women; but old habits die hard, and there is bound to be an element of subjective judgement and personal chemistry, particularly in senior staff appointments. This is necessarily complicated by the need to maintain an appropriate geographical balance, most notably in the Commission, where it is fiercely contested by the national networks, centred on the different national Commissioners and their *cabinets*, which strive to realise that objective in the most advantageous way for their own national interests. As a result, internal appointments in all the institutions, especially at the more senior levels, remain a battle-field on which the interests of the Community and its own permanent staff are in continuous tension with those of the member states. Some individuals have flourished in this environment, many others have been de-motivated, and arguably the institutions themselves have been the biggest losers if as a result they have not made the best use of their staff.

Internal appointments and promotions

Although external recruitment occurs at all levels, the staff of all the institutions of the European Union are recruited to a career service in which, normally, appointments are made to the starting grade for each category, vacancies in the higher grades are filled by promotion from below, and most staff can expect promotion to a senior grade within their category if their career extends over a period of 20 years or so.

The statutory foundations of the career service are laid down in Articles 43–46 of the Staff Regulations. Under Article 44 all staff are entitled to advance by one incremental step within their grade every two years. There are eight such steps in most grades (except A1, A2 and A8, which have six steps, and D4, which has only four), and each such step is worth 4.5 per cent of the basic salary for that grade. Progress to the next grade is governed by Article 45, which provides for promotion to be determined by a combination of seniority and merit. The key sentence reads as follows: 'Promotion shall be exclusively by selection from among officials who have completed a minimum period in their grade, after consideration of the comparative merits of the officials eligible for promotion and of the reports on them.' Article 43 provides for such reports to be made on all staff at least once every two years, with the exception of grades A1 and A2.

Opportunities for promotion

Article 4 of the Staff Regulations provides that 'no appointment or promotion shall be made for any purpose other than that of filling a vacant post'. The number of promotions which can be made in any one year therefore depends on the overall number of posts in the budget and the number of vacancies which arise. These will fluctuate from year to year but an average pattern can be discerned (see Exhibit 5.1).

Staff who reach A4 after 20 years or so can become dissatisfied if they can see no further prospect of promotion in the course of a career which normally extends to age 65, and there has been persistent pressure (expressed, for example, in both the Spierenburg and Petit-Laurent reports) for the normal career progression to A4 to be slower, or for more internal promotions

Exhibit 5.1   Career expectations

On average the best staff recruited to category B or C may expect to reach grade B1 or C1 respectively over a period of 15 to 18 years; there are competitions restricted to serving officials for further promotion into the next category. In category A the average period for promotion from A7 to A4 is 15 to 20 years. Whilst A4 is the ceiling for a normal career in category A, there are opportunities for the best staff to be further promoted, though the pyramid narrows sharply towards the top (1 post at A3 for every 2 at A4; 1 post at A2 for every 3 at A3) and considerations of geographical balance become increasingly important from A3 upwards. At the top of category A, about one in four of the staff who reach A4 can expect promotion to A3, and about 90 per cent of A3 appointments are internal. Over the decade 1982–92 there were only 25 temporary staff appointments at grade A3, whilst over the same period 280 A4 staff were promoted (Bodiguel, 1994, p. 169).

to A3, or both. There is also pressure for more promotion opportunities from one category to the next, though it is already the case that about 20 per cent of the intake into categories B and C comes from the categories below (Hay, 1989, p. 34). Moreover, too many internal promotions between categories would risk exacerbating, in the sensitive upper reaches of the administration, the geographical imbalance which already exists in favour of the host nations, but is even more pronounced in the lower categories.

Promotion procedures

Within the lower categories promotions are agreed within a promotions committee, on which the staff have equal representation. The committee checks the reasons for any accelerated promotions which may be recommended, examines the files of staff with a given level of seniority who have not been recommended, and checks that the promotions are consistent with budgetary considerations.

Different procedures apply to category A, where promotions are decided by a committee chaired by the Secretary General. All the Directors General are members, and each submits a list for their own service drawn up following consultation with their deputies and with staff representatives. The latter have no input to the separate arrangements which have been made for consultation among DGs about appointments to Head of Unit posts (Bodiguel, 1994, p. 169), which may be at any level from A5 upwards. Such appointments are a critically important first step on the ladder leading to senior management positions, and the exclusion of staff representatives is much resented, particularly following the increase in Head of Unit posts at levels below A3 which used not to carry management responsibilities. The exclusion has so far been stoutly defended by management, on the grounds that those appointed to such posts will be exercising management responsibilities, but the effect is also to make it easier for management to give more weight to considerations of merit, and less weight to seniority and the dubious evidence of formal systems of staff reporting, in making such appointments.

Staff reports

Whilst age, seniority in the grade and length of service play an important part in determining eligibility, a more subjective assessment of merit is a key factor in the selection of candidates for early promotion. The starting point for this assessment is the staff report which is made every two years by the official's immediate superior, usually the Head of Unit, and countersigned by a senior manager. After the necessary personal information (name, department, grade and seniority), there is a half-page space for description of duties carried out over the reporting period, a note on languages used followed by a self-assessment of language skills, and an account of publications and new knowledge gained during the reporting period. This is followed by an assessment of 14 aspects of performance under the three headings listed in Article 43 of the Staff Regulations, namely ability, efficiency and conduct in the service (see Exhibit 5.2).

Exhibit 5.2   Framework for staff reports

I Ability
  I.   Knowledge required for post occupied
  II.   Proficiency
        A.   comprehension
        B.   judgement
        C.   articulateness – written word
        D.   articulateness – spoken word
        E.   organisational ability

II Efficiency
  I.   Quality
  II.   Speed
  III. Consistency
  IV.   Versatility

III Conduct in the Service
        A.   Sense of Responsibility
        B.   Initiative
        C.   Ability to work as a member of a team
        D.   Ability to get on with people

Each of these 14 qualities is marked against a five-point scale (excellent, very good, good, adequate, unsatisfactory) and there is a small space on each line for comments (optional). There is then a page headed General Assessment, which invites the reporting officer to mention the official's most outstanding qualities, the areas in which there is scope or need for improvement (with suggestions as to how this might be achieved), the official's ability to adapt to different duties and, where relevant, an indication of progress or lack of progress. The present report reflects reforms (notably five points on the scale instead of three, and the safeguard of countersignature by a more senior reporting officer) which were recommended in para. 81 of the Spierenburg Report.

The official sees the assessment in full and has the opportunity to add his or her own comments. Open reporting is widely supported on the grounds that openness is an effective defence against any personal prejudice or animosity on the part of the reporting officer, but it is also criticised on the grounds that it leads to bland and ultimately meaningless reporting. The blandness of the reporting is liable to give rise to parallel systems of confidential reporting which are all the more damaging because they are subject to no formal rules whatsoever and their very existence has to be denied.

There is some evidence that the Commission's reporting systems are or have been subject to both these perils. It is widely understood that reporting officers hardly ever use anything but the top two marks (excellent and very good), which seriously undermines the value of a five-point marking scale, and the general assessment is usually completed in perfunctory and uncritical terms. Such meaningless reporting may be due to top officials being 'too busy or too lazy' to carry out their assessment and reporting responsibilities properly, as a senior official of the Commission alleged (quoted in *Financial Times*, 30 September 1996), adding, 'Because of this everybody in the Commission is rated as a genius.' But apparent laziness, or the according of a low priority to actions which require a face-to-face management role for senior staff in relation to their colleagues, may also be a reflection of an administrative culture which has generally eschewed the notion of management of resources, whether human or material, and preferred to deal with people through regulation, not leadership.

The existence of a parallel set of confidential personnel files covering all staff within the translation service over a period of ten years from 1981 was confirmed by a judgment in the Court of First Instance (cases T39/93 and T553/93) on 11 October 1995. Such blatant quasi-formal arrangements may be exceptional, but the weakness of the formal reporting system is bound to increase reliance on more informal information networks when choices have to be made for promotion purposes among large numbers of staff, whose claims are all supported by favourable written reports. This weakness is widely acknowledged, and there have been suggestions for reform, but there is no great enthusiasm among managers for the painful process of more rigorous appraisal, and those who have considered instituting reforms within their own Directorate General have been dissuaded by the fact that any unilateral action would tend to unfairly penalise their staff in competing for posts elsewhere within the Commission.

A reform of the staff reporting procedure was attempted in 1997–98, but abandoned in the face of union opposition, leaving the matter to be pursued by the Prodi Commission in the context of its management reform policies. The present reporting system makes no attempt to identify specific goals as a basis for assessing performance, and this will have to change if the reporting system is to play its part in a more positive approach to staff management.

Informal networks

The importance of informal networks has been recognised for many years. Michelmann noted in 1978 the existence of nationality-based networks run by the *cabinets* with an informal system of 'credits' for officials negotiable at promotion time (Michelmann, 1978, p. 482). A year later, the Spierenburg Report identified a number of concerns about promotion and career development, which suffered from:

- uncertainty from year to year about the number of posts authorised by the budgetary authority;
- the irregular shape of the career pyramid caused by successive waves of recruitment;
- direct recruitment from outside into the intermediate and higher grades; and
- the Commission's own promotion procedures, which resulted in more rapid promotion in expanding Directorates General than in those whose numbers were stable (Spierenburg, 1979, p. 94).

The Report went on to propose reforms intended to ensure the transition from 'a period of unplanned development to a steadier one with better career opportunities', and although not all the specific recommendations have been implemented, the origins of many of the more formal arrangements described above have their roots in the Spierenburg Report.

However, the continuing importance of informal networks, and the extent to which such arrangements can have a demoralising effect on staff, was still very much apparent in the survey of Commission staff carried out by the French consultancy CEGOS during 1988. In response to a question in the survey, staff said the best way to ensure promotion is to have the right connections, followed by seniority, luck, the right nationality, service in a *cabinet*, the will to succeed, ability, qualifications, knowing when to keep quiet and – last of all – producing results and hard work. Just over half said of their promotion prospects: 'It doesn't matter what I do, promotion won't come any faster' (Spence, 1997a, p. 75).

Mobility is an important factor in promotion and career progression. However, in none of the institutions is there an organisation responsible for planning career development, and in the Commission, despite repeated screening exercises since the late 1980s, management has found it difficult to impose mobility by obliging staff in areas where the workload has diminished to move to areas where more staff are urgently needed. The staff themselves are often reluctant to move, and their senior managers may be reluctant to relinquish their posts. In the European Parliament Julian Priestley, the (British) Secretary General since 1997, has introduced rules requiring all staff at A3 level to move after a maximum of seven years in post, and staff below A3 must move after five years. In the Commission the introduction by President Prodi of a similar requirement for Directors General to move on after a maximum of seven years resulted in the transfer to new duties of some very longstanding incumbents, including Guy Legras, who had been head of the Agriculture DG for more than 15 years. But such enforced mobility is still rare within the EU institutions. Normally the initiative lies with staff themselves, and if they choose to remain in the same post for a very long time, it is extremely difficult for management to move them against their will, particularly if they have satisfactory reports, as nearly all staff do. Within the Commission between 1990 and 1997 an average of only 800 staff (about 4 per cent) moved from one DG to another each year, and in 1997 only 54 staff moved between the Commission and other EU institutions (Williamson, 1998, p. 48).

Leaving career management in the hands of the individual member of staff may suit the most confident and ambitious, but it may also open the door to patronage and favours. 'Mobility works by personal obligations ... "I know you, I like you, so whenever I get a vacant post I will tell you before the post is published because I think it will be nice for you"' (House of Lords, 1988, p. 112, q. 482 and 486). Those who are more cautious or less well connected tend to regard mobility as more of a threat, detrimental to their career prospects and tantamount to a disciplinary measure (see Exhibit 3.2). It may also be seen as putting at least a temporary brake on promotion possibilities.

> With the way the promotion system works, people tend to believe that there is a quota for each Directorate General and that the Director General is concerned with the morale of his staff and therefore prefers to recommend for promotion someone on his staff rather than someone who has just left it. (House of Lords, 1988, p. 115, q. 506).

The suspicion surrounding mobility illustrates the high levels of stress associated with career progression, and the continuing tension between the preference of many staff for a rigid but predictable system and the preference of management for greater flexibility.

Training

There are, broadly, three models for the training of administrative civil servants in Europe. The British model is an apprenticeship model, where a large proportion of the skills and knowledge required for the effective fulfilment of duties is acquired on the job and under the guidance of senior officers, supplemented nowadays by an increasing range of short-term or part-time training modules. The French model involves the intensive training of future civil servants, who have already had relevant higher education or experience, at the entry to their career, a process which also prolongs the selection period in the sense that it results in the deployment of new officials into varying career patterns on the basis of their performance. The German pattern requires a quite high degree of specialised training before recruitment, and relatively little in-service provision. In the early days training in the European Community resembled the German approach, but more recently the Commission's growing programme of in-service training has inclined towards the British model.

Recognition of the contribution which in-service training can make to effective performance was slow to develop. Training was not part of the administrative culture of a pioneering organisation, and there were no post-entry training programmes in the 1960s, since the Commission felt able to rely on the education received by officials before their entry into its services (Coombes, 1975, p. 91). However, training divisions were established in the ECSC in 1965 and in the Commission in 1968. A first programme of in-service training was organised in 1970, and in 1972 the Staff Regulations were amended to provide for the facilitation of 'such further training and instruction for officials as is compatible with the proper functioning of the service and is in accordance with its own interests. Such training and instruction shall be taken into account for purposes of promotion in their careers'(Article 24). The wording of this provision suggests that management was by no means convinced that in-service training was likely to benefit the organisation, though it might be useful to staff seeking promotion. However, a training programme developed gradually through the 1970s and 1980s, with an emphasis on the language skills required in a multi-cultural environment, and on the growing demand for information technology.

Training finally received a higher profile in 1989 under President Delors' 'Social Contract for Progress', which led in 1991 to the adoption of what was known as 'The New Training Policy'. Moreover, an ambitious target was set, but never met: a total of six months' continuing training for each official in every period of ten years. Training programmes multiplied in the early 1990s, with a tripling of the Commission's budget between 1991 and 1995, but fell back a little between 1995 and 1998 (see Table 5.1). However, training received a further boost from the MAP 2000 programme (see Chapter 8), and in Commissioner

Table 5.1 *The training budget (in millions of ECU)*

	1995	1998	% change
Language training	4.1	3.7	–9.8
General training	3.7	2.9	–21.6
Computer training	1.9	1.9	–
TOTAL	9.7	8.5	–12.4

Source: Williamson (1998) p. 42.

Kinnock's reform programme, which envisaged that the training budget would have to be at least doubled.

Language training, which is organised on an inter-institutional basis, has always been the most important feature of the EU's training programmes, essential as it is in a multi-cultural environment. Quite apart from the demand generated by the staff themselves, Petit-Laurent noted that it would be important to train some staff in languages such as Portuguese or Greek, if the Commission's relations with the national administrations in these countries were not to be left largely in the hands of staff who happen to have those nationalities and hence those languages (Petit-Laurent, 1994, p. 103). Computer training has also become increasingly important as the Commission, like most other large administrations, has introduced more and more computerised systems, data-bases and word-processing facilities, and it is noticeable that this element remained stable (Table 5.1) when languages and other training fell back between 1995 and 1998.

The third category – general training – includes courses designed to prepare staff for internal examinations for promotion to a higher category, training in practical matters such as procurement or financial management procedures, and post-entry induction training. The Commission has for some years run post-entry training courses for all new staff on such topics as the rights and obligations of an official, the social and administrative environment (where to find the crèche, the library, the medical service, and so on), an introduction to the major Community policies and to the history of the European institutions, and these courses continue to be offered, with some elements spread through the probationary period. But it is only since 1995 that there has been a special course for newly recruited staff at grade A8/A7. The concept had been agreed in principle by the Commission on at least three occasions since 1981 (Petit-Laurent, 1994, p. 62), but it had always been resisted on practical grounds. Once an appointment had been made DGs were impatient for their new staff to start work and were reluctant to release them for training. Neither did new staff want yet more training on the structure of the European institutions, which they had had to study for the competitions; but when a selection of staff in their first year were asked what they would have found useful, their answers generated a list of about 20 topics, ranging from how to deal with the media to how to chair a meeting with interpreters, as well as questions of legal and financial procedure, and how to draft documents varying from legal texts to records of meetings and press releases. The course attempted to cover this ground, mixing lectures with role-play exercises and a visit to a member state to get a different perspective on the Commission. A 'new officials' programme', which will no doubt build on this experience, is to be further developed as part of Commissioner Kinnock's reform programme.

Attention to training for management is of more recent origin. The Christophersen programme of management seminars in the late 1980s may have launched a greater awareness of the need for management, but there was also some disillusion with the approach of the Danish company, Time Management, which won the contract at that time, and sought to impose on the Commission a system which required the supply of a great deal of proprietary stationery. This experience may for a while have damaged the case for management training; it was not until 2000 that the Commission could claim, for the first time, to have a comprehensive range of middle and senior management training programmes. The most significant of these is likely to be the new senior management training programme, which is to be mandatory for all new Heads of Unit. The aim, according to the Kinnock reform paper, is to create a culture of management and accountability rather than simply one of administration.

Exchanges and secondments also have a training role. Flows are very imbalanced, as rather few EU officials move out to national administrations to counterbalance the large numbers of detached national experts coming to Brussels. The exchange programme does in effect provide training for national officials in the ways of the Community, and there are also shorter-term exchange programmes, such as CAROLUS, under which members of national administrations spend short periods observing how others implement the same Community policies as they do (Petit-Laurent, 1994, p. 63). Development of a more balanced programme might facilitate the moves for which some commentators have called (Metcalfe, 1992) to position the Commission within a network of interlocking domestic and supranational institutions engaged in the development and implementation of policy.

Equal opportunities

The promotion of equal opportunities and equal treatment for working women throughout the member states has (some would say surprisingly) been one of the major fields of activity and achievement by the European Union. In the 1970s the convergence of a number of pressures, including litigation, an emphasis on social policy deriving from the context of the late 1960s, concern about the social consequences of economic and monetary union, and the actions of a number of committed individuals (Hoskyns, 1996, pp. 78–86) led to the adoption of major directives on equal pay (Directive 75/117/EEC) and equal treatment at work (Directive 76/207/EEC). While the 1980s provided a rather less propitious climate for progress on women's issues, the strength of the relevant policy networks, the context of international interest, exemplified in the United Nations Decade for Women, and the important support of the European Parliament, especially its Committee for Women's Rights, all ensured that some momentum was maintained (Hoskyns, 1996, p. 142). In 1982 the first Community Action programme on Equal Opportunities (1982–85) was approved by resolution of the EC Council of Ministers, to be followed by three more (1985–90, 1991–95 and 1996–2000).

At this time it became apparent that the Commission itself had a poor record in the field of equal opportunities, and steps began to be taken, albeit slowly and hesitantly. In 1978 a working party representing the administration and the trade unions and staff associations was set up to study the situation and make recommendations. This, combined with reference in the first and second Community action programmes to the promotion of equal opportunities within the EC institutions, led to the establishment in 1984 of a standing Joint Committee on Equal Opportunities for men and women. A very revealing report was commissioned in 1985 by the Committee and completed in 1986 (Chalude, Chater and Laufer, 1986, cited by Hoskyns, 1996, p. 164, n. 42). 'The in-depth interviews revealed both stereotypical attitudes on the part of men and procedural blocks to women's advancement' (Hoskyns, 1996, p. 151). There have since been three positive action programmes within the Commission – 1988–90, 1992–96 and 1997–2000 – supported since 1991 by an equal opportunities unit within the Personnel and Administration DG, whose tasks include the gathering and dissemination of information, raising awareness, monitoring and evaluating the progress of the action programme, and proposing further steps.

In 1994 women occupied 45 per cent of posts in the Commission, the same proportion as a decade earlier. But these figures owe much to the heavy concentration of women among secretarial staff in category C (over 80 per cent). At the top, there have been five women Commissioners out of 20 since 1995, but there were none at all until 1989, when Christiane Scrivener (France) and Vasso Papandreou (Greece) were appointed, and only Scrivener remained from 1993 to 1994. Although the representation of women in category A posts had grown from 9.3 per cent in 1984 to 13.5 per cent in 1994, they still occupied only 5.4 per cent of posts in the top three grades. This situation was perceived as shocking by the Commissioners and senior staff from Sweden and Finland, with their longer tradition of strong female representation at decision-making levels, when they entered the Union in 1995. The Commission's second positive action programme (1992–96) had already set targets of 14 per cent women in category A and 10 per cent in management posts but, as they were reached, partly as a result of the recruitment of a relatively high proportion of women at all levels from Sweden and Finland (see Chapter 4), Finnish Personnel Commissioner Erkki Liikanen

Table 5.2   *Women in category A of the European Commission staff, 1984–99*

Grade	1984 Number	1984 Per cent	1994 Number	1994 Per cent	1999 Number	1999 Per cent
A1	2	4.4	1	1.9	2	4.1
A2	0	0.0	4	2.5	20	12.0
A3	3	1.0	29	7.0	57	11.0
A4	41	5.7	90	9.2	154	12.8
A5	56	11.9	118	14.4	175	17.1
A6	72	14.8	96	16.3	225	24.2
A7	47	19.8	139	19.4	266	28.9
A8	0	0.0	44	31.9	23	35.9
Total A	221	9.3	521	13.5	922	18.9

Sources: *Women at the European Commission 1984–1994* (1994) and, for 1999 figures, Equal Opportunities Unit of the European Commission.

regularly raised them, and by the end of his tenure in 1999, the proportion of women in category A had risen to nearly 19 per cent (see Table 5.2). Although the *Kalanke* case of 1995 (C-450/93), in which the European Court of Justice ruled against preferential treatment for women, was seen as threatening the Commission's equal opportunities policy (*The Guardian*, 18 September 1995), targets as opposed to quotas were probably still legal, and the programme seems to have been unaffected. Any risk of legal challenge was subsequently blocked by the adoption of an amendment to the Staff Regulations (Reg. 781/98) which specifically recognises the right to adopt appropriate provisions 'to redress such de facto inequalities as hamper opportunities for women'.

An analysis of the promotion record of men and women up to A4 level between 1988 and 1993 suggested that in general women's chances of promotion were much the same as for men, though there did appear to be some disadvantage at the more senior levels, notably at promotion from A5 to A4 where 13.16 per cent of eligible women were promoted, compared to 15.51 per cent of eligible men (*Women at the European Commission 1984–1994*, 1994, p. 32). This imbalance existed even within the LA grades (that is, the graduate level staff of the translation and interpretation services). Despite the fact that the head of the interpretation service for many years was one of the only three women ever to have been a Director General – the formidable Mme Renée van Hoof – and that in 1994 the LA grades included more women than men (753 women and 749 men), the percentage of eligible women promoted to all grades above LA7 between 1988 and 1993 was from two to five percentage points lower than the proportion of eligible men promoted.

The representation of women at all levels of management remains a difficult area. In 1995 Commissioner Liikanen set a target of parity between men and women for middle management appointments from the new member states, and 25 per cent for middle management appointments of nationals from the old member states, but these targets have not been reached. Over the period 1995–9 only 14 of the 64 officials recruited from the new member states to middle management posts were women, and six out of eighteen at A2 director level (European Union, 2000, para. 1076). However, the progress made under Commissioner Liikanen should not be entirely discounted: the overall proportion of women in category A rose from 13.5 per cent in 1994 to 18.9 per cent in 1999; the percentage of women directors rose from 2.5 per cent to 12 per cent over the same period; and 20 per cent of new appointments to middle management posts in 1999 (14 appointments) were women (European Union, 2000, para. 1068).

The equal opportunities unit was in 1995 involved in some kind of action in 22 out of the 30 DGs and services in the Commission. Two DGs – both headed by staff from the north – were running pilot programmes, including such features as seminars, training, and a target of 30 per cent of A grade recruits to be women. A spillover effect is beginning to be seen, reflected in the implementation of Commissioner Liikanen's personnel management modernisation programme (MAP 2000: see Chapter 8), but the impetus continues to come mainly from the north, and there must be some risk that the devolution to DGs of responsibility for the application of personnel policies – a key feature of the Liikanen and Kinnock reform programmes – may take the pressure off those who are not so committed to equal opportunities.

The European Parliament has also had an active equal opportunities policy for its staff. The staff of the Council of Ministers, which is both small and relatively insulated from some of the pressures to which the Commission are exposed, has made very little progress in the area of equal opportunities. They did not set up a staff committee until 1995, and at that time had no specific programme for the promotion of equal opportunities.

The difficulties which women face in large organisations in many Western European countries in achieving career progression comparable to that of men are well documented. The pyramid of women within the EU institutions, with high numbers in secretarial and clerical grades, and sharply diminishing numbers above, is not dissimilar to that in the public services of the member states. Women – including, as our interviewees told us, some in the EU administration – may feel that they can succeed only as 'honorary men'. The factors which affect women's progress in the services of the EU institutions are not confined to those which can readily be addressed by the setting of targets. As one interviewee reminded us, in the context of the EU's services the intellectual recognition that an effective organisation needs to foster a range of management styles and approaches, including those which are more congenial to many women, has not yet been accompanied by the necessary change in structures, practices and mentalities. Although the strides which have been made in the development of equal opportunities frameworks within the member states have in many cases been due to the impact of European Community law, the record of the EU in relation to its own administrative service has not been a distinguished one. Some of the difficulties, however, are exacerbated by the particular context of the EU's services.

The prevalence of sexual stereotyping, which limits the capacity of those concerned with appointments or promotions to envisage a particular role being successfully fulfilled by a woman, was clearly identified within the European Commission through the in-depth interviews carried out for the 1985 study

(Chalude, Chater and Laufer, 1986). It persists, conditioning not only promotions but also working practices and expectations. The fact that it is assumed that senior staff will be male, so that a senior woman answering her own telephone will routinely be taken for her own secretary (interview, 1995) is banal, but telling. 'Persistent traditional view[s] of women's career profiles' (*Women at the European Commission 1984–1994*, 1994, p. 12) have a particular resonance in an organisation that is, throughout its professional levels, staffed very largely by expatriates. A lifestyle which involves separation from national roots and background, especially the more extended family, is likely to result in a paucity of the informal support networks upon which working women often rely, and the practice found amongst some senior officials of maintaining a working base in Brussels and commuting to a family home some distance away at weekends may be particularly unattractive to women. Set against this is the relatively high pay of senior Commission officials, which means that particularly in two-earner households good quality domestic help, if it can be found, may be affordable.

Other features of the working culture of the European Commission also present difficulties for the career progression of women. It is frequently admitted that the working culture of the Commission is a male-dominated one, and that women feel that only by conforming to these patterns will they be able to gain recognition and advancement. The long working hours undertaken by many within the Commission are a clear expression of such patterns. Although the Commission has child care facilities for children – a crèche and a *garderie* for school-age children – these close at 6 p.m. Yet leaving the office at six is not seen as appropriate behaviour for those who are ambitious for a good career. The example was set from the top. Pascal Lamy, Delors' *chef de cabinet*, and since 1999 one of the two French Commissioners, 'expected everyone else to work as hard as he did – which was an average of 12 or 13 hours a day, six days a week. He would call a *cabinet* member at home at the weekend and … ask why he or she was not in the office' (Grant, 1994, p. 98). The Equal Opportunities Unit is attempting to combat this mentality, and a 1995 pilot programme in one DG resulted in an instruction from the Director General that internal meetings should not continue after 5.45 p.m. That long hours may be a matter of working culture rather than necessity is suggested by the behaviour of one *cabinet* – that of a northern European commissioner in the early 1990s – which was reported as relentlessly going home at 6 p.m. every day.

Another feature of career progression in the European Commission which poses particular problems in the context of equal opportunities is the extent to which career moves can be the result of informal contact, of networks, acquaintanceship and recommendation. It remains the case, as the respondents to the CEGOS study in the mid-1980s perceived, that having the right connections is crucial to a successful career. Some types of connection (for example, those between officials of a certain nationality and the *cabinets* of the Commissioner of that nationality) are likely to be gender neutral. But many of the other types of connection, such as those resulting from professional background, political allegiance or career profile, are more strongly male-biased. With very few women in senior posts they are less likely to have access to the networks, mentors or sponsors which assist men to build a career, if only because, in the words of one newspaper:

> research shows that to get on you need mentors and sponsors – one to help you and one to put your name forward – and they tend to be men … if a man puts a woman forward, people say he must be sleeping with her, so sponsoring a woman is seen as a bigger risk for a man. (quoted in *The Guardian*, 18 October 1996).

The European Commission's Equal Opportunities Unit recognised that 'Women … have less room for manoeuvre and fewer contacts, which are essential for a high level career' (*Women at the European Commission 1984–1994*, 1994, p. 12). The impact of the Nordic countries following the 1995 enlargement, and the setting of modest, but rising, targets for career progression for women has gradually improved their position, but it is probably still the case that the male orientation of Community personnel policies over many years means that the Community institutions are not making the best use of their female staff resources.

Conclusions

Within the EU institutions generally, and particularly the Commission, the arrangements for career development have been haphazard and weak, heavily dependent on the initiative of individual staff members, and open to the pressures of personal and national patronage, in ways which are unlikely to have succeeded in making the most of a talented multi-national resource. Under Commissioner Erkki Liikanen and Director General Steffen Smidt, a reform-minded group within the Personnel and Administration DG recognised that personnel management in the Commission had failed to keep pace with the reform and modernisation programmes which had swept through the public administrations of almost all the OECD countries since the mid-1980s. In their MAP 2000 programme they set out to identify and implement a package of reforms suited to the special circumstances of the EU institutions. Some advances were made, particularly in the field of equal opportunities for women, but much still remained to be done, as the Committee of Independent Experts underlined, when the Prodi Commission was appointed in 1999 with a special mandate for reform. The reforms proposed by Commissioner Kinnock, including annual staff reports with a new emphasis on performance measured against targets set in advance, and closer attention to mobility and training, are intended to give more weight to merit and less to seniority or patronage in the management of officials' careers. However, such aspirations have been heard before, and the outcome has rarely lived up to the high hopes with which reform programmes are launched. Chapter 8 outlines the history of reform since Spierenburg, but in order to illuminate further the strength of the resistance which such initiatives have provoked in the past (not just from the unions but from many senior managers as well), Chapter 6 first focuses on some of the aspects of EU administration which make it different from national administrations – some would say unique – and the administrative culture within which change would have to take root. Chapters 7 and 8 then examine the tasks which the EU administration has to address and the way it has organised itself to undertake them.

A Unique Administration

There are aspects of the EU administration which are unique. Its staff serve an organisation which is *sui generis*. It demands their loyalty and they are appointed by the EU institutions to which they belong, yet their career chances may be significantly affected by national considerations. The location of their work, and its multilingual context, shape distinctive work and life experiences.

Provenance and its impact

Within a multi-national organisation which still lacks a strong tradition or inherited ethos the question of who the employees are is of particular interest. However open-minded, flexible and adaptable an official may be, there is always a presumption that background matters because he or she will bring into work at least some of the values, presuppositions and habits that have been acquired earlier in life. If a new European civil service is being formed, the characteristics of those who comprise it may matter. Since the 1960s such questions have been asked by scholars who were concerned to argue that bureaucracies in themselves wield considerable power which they were liable to exercise in the interests of the class from which they come or the dominant ideology which they share (Bottomore, 1964; Milliband, 1969; Hill, 1997, Bodiguel and Quermonne, 1983). A number of studies have pursued these questions in relation to senior civil servants in some of the major European countries. 'This literature invariably finds that top civil servants come ... disproportionately from the traditionally advantaged groups within a society; males from middle class families ... The European Union is no exception to this' (Page, 1997, p. 69). There is little evidence that similarity of background necessarily produces similarity of, for example, personal or professional or political outlook or goals, 'the main drawback to this kind of argument being that social origin does not necessarily determine current identification, interest or commitment'. It may none the less ease day to day interaction and create a common style.

Distribution by nationality

In one respect the backgrounds of officials of the European Union are markedly different from those of any national civil service: they hold 15 different nationalities. As we saw in relation to recruitment, the Staff Regulations explicitly forbid any discrimination on the basis of nationality except for the most senior levels but include a general commitment to a balanced 'geographical' representation. 'Nationality', with its link to 'nationalism' which 'in this milieu is something you should "go beyond", something you can "overcome" ' is accepted as an important factor and widely discussed informally, but is unacceptable in formal discourse, so 'Europe's administration is officially a world not of different nations and nationalities but of "geographical balance"' (McDonald, 1995, p. 52). Hence there are no formal agreements about what the balance should be or how it should be secured (Spence, 1997a, p. 82). Nevertheless, the need to ensure balance has influenced recruitment and appointments from the beginning and resulted in the special measures taken at each enlargement to ensure recruitment from the new member states.

National balance

Both David Spence and Edward Page have attempted to analyse the figures for national representation. Page (1997, p. 44), on the basis of 1993 figures, concludes that in proportion to member states' populations the largest countries – Britain, France, Germany, Spain and even, though to a lesser degree, Italy – are all underrepresented in the employment of the Commission, while Belgium, Denmark, Greece, Luxembourg and Ireland are overrepresented. Portugal and the Netherlands are closest to an appropriate balance. Spence, taking figures for 1974–94, agrees that the smaller countries 'are over represented as a matter of course', though noting that the balance fluctuates over time (Spence, 1997a, pp. 82–6).

The mismatch between the proportion of officials of each nationality and the proportion within the EU of the population of each country, as calculated by Page (1997, p. 45) is lowest in the A category grades, and markedly higher in the B, C and D category grades. This is in itself unsurprising. Tasks undertaken by the B, C and D grades are essentially support tasks. The conditions are unlikely to act as major inducements to undertake the type of disruption which long-term settlement in another country involves. It is hence understandable that nationals of the country where the main bulk of employment occurs should be disproportionately employed at these levels, especially since the salary levels do provide an incentive when there is no concomitant disruption (Guérivière, 1993, p. 34). In 1994 Belgians accounted for over a third of total employment in each of these categories in the Commission. For similar reasons there is a high proportion of Luxembourgeois in the lower categories of the European Court of Justice. Only Italy, with a further third of the small (and declining) number of staff in the most basic category (category D – manual and service staff) was similarly overrepresented in all the institutions. This is explained by the existence of a substantial Italian community in Belgium prior to the creation of the European Community, by the general willingness of Italians, especially from the south of Italy, to migrate in search of employment (House of Lords, 1988, p. 112, q. 469) and by the support mechanisms provided by the existence of a sizeable group of compatriot colleagues. Similar patterns are to be found in the services of the Council of Ministers (Page, 1997, p. 47). In the European Parliament, 1987 figures (House of Lords, 1988, p. 136) showed relatively high proportions of French nationals in category B and C and of Luxembourgeois in categories B, C and D, accounted for by the location of some of the activities of the European Parliament in Strasbourg and Luxembourg.

Senior posts and national balance

It is at the level of senior posts, in category A generally, but especially at levels A3 to A1, that the issue of national balance gives rise to most concern. The College of Commissioners has from the first exercised close control over senior appointments, a practice which dates back to the High Authority of the European Coal and Steel Community (see Chapter 2). There have never been formal quotas, but there was and still is an informal understanding among the member states dividing Commission posts in the top three grades on the basis of contributions to the Community budget (Coombes, 1970, p. 141). This initial 'gentleman's agreement' (Coombes, 1970, p. 141) was modified with the first enlargement of 1973. The four large states (France, Germany, Italy and the UK) would each have 18.4 per cent, Belgium, the Netherlands and Luxembourg would share a further 18.4 per cent and Ireland and Denmark would each take 4 per cent (Coombes, 1970, p. 153).

It is no longer possible for the full Commission to intervene quite so directly in all senior appointments, but the practice of maintaining a national balance persists. *Cabinets* keep information about staff of their own nationality. They ensure the claims of their candidates are fully considered, particularly where a vacant post is considered to be of national interest (Michelmann, 1978, p. 178; Spence, 1997a, p. 85). *Chefs de cabinet*, who know many of the staff concerned, are particularly closely involved in the complex manoeuvres and deals which may be associated with appointments at the top two levels. In the Santer era they reckoned to spend about 20 per cent of their time on such matters. Their machinations have been described by a *cabinet* member as 'like a game of chess, played by *chefs de cabinet*, who know the people and the vacant posts and keep it all pretty much in their heads'. The system has been more bluntly described as 'horse-trading' and denounced for leaving posts above A4 level unfilled for months (*Financial Times*, 30 September 1996).

The arrangements for posts at A1 and A2 may appear similar to those for the appointment and removal of 'political officials' in the senior ranks of the French and German civil services. However, decisions about appointments at this level are driven more by considerations of geographical balance than political allegiance. Indeed, at grades A1 and A2 'parachutists' with *cabinet* experience 'are outnumbered two to one by career officials with no obvious political connection either as parachutists or as *cabinet* members' (Page, 1997, p. 82).

The causes and consequences of national balance

There is no doubt that member states perceive the value of having their own nationals well placed at all levels of category A, and not just in the highest ranks where the national quotas are most overtly respected. Page concluded from his study, based on 1993 statistics, that, although geographical balance is most clearly respected at grades A1–A3, it is still much more evident throughout the A grades than in categories B, C and D, and is respected well below the level to which the national quota system clearly applies (Page, 1997, p. 46).

There are a number of reasons why this is so. First, member states attach a good deal of importance to it. Having officials of one's own nationality in key places provides a network of easy contacts, starting from the fact that it is possible to conduct a conversation (face to face or by telephone) in one's own language. According to Spence, France realised early that 'astute placement of key French officials ... can include the promotion as well as defence of national interests' (Spence, 1997a, p. 85). Germany came to a similar view rather later and the UK first showed signs of reacting with some concern to the situation in 1989 with the House of Lords Select Committee Report on *The Staffing of the Community Institutions* and the subsequent creation of the European Fast Stream (see Chapter 3). New entrants frequently seek to identify the posts they wish to fill, as the UK did before 1973. Austria and Sweden were both identifying and planning for the posts they wished to fill well before their accession in 1995.

Balance – and indeed imbalance – in the distribution of nationalities within the senior grades of the institutions might, as Page argues, be a consequence of a well-balanced distribution of nationalities amongst those who are candidates for appointments. On the basis of figures for competitions between 1989 and 1991 Page concluded that the imbalance amongst applicants and amongst those who were successfully declared eligible for recruitment and placed on the reserve list was markedly higher than the imbalance amongst officials in post, and suggested that this indicated that attention was paid to national balance at the point of actual selection of eligible candidates for a specific post. The UK, for example, which between 1986 and 1991 was the most seriously underrepresented member state both in terms of candidates and those proceeding successfully to the reserve list (although its candidates were somewhat more successful at this stage), has since the end of the 1990s instituted a programme of advice and support, operated through the UK Permanent Representation in Brussels, which has been quite successful in helping to secure appointments for those who have reached the reserve list.

A further, tacit factor which affects national balance amongst those working for the institutions is the explicit policy of attempting to ensure that at the senior management levels (A4 and above) the hierarchical chain comprises people of different nationalities (Page, 1997, p. 59). Even at lower levels there is a concern to avoid obvious national clusters. Page concluded that his detailed study of senior officials throughout the major institutions provided no evidence for the 'colonisation' of any parts of the institutions by officials of any particular nationality.

While there is little evidence of 'colonisation' of the entire hierarchical chain there have been frequent allegations that certain posts in the Commission, especially at A1 or A2 level, are regarded as the rightful patrimony of a particular nationality with a 'national flag' attached to them: German in Competition Policy, French in Agriculture, Italian in Financial and Economic Affairs (Page, 1997, p. 54). Technically this would be contrary to the explicit terms of Article 27 of the Staff Regulations. The rulings of the Court of Justice condemn the reservation of a specific post to one particular nationality, but they permit considerations of nationality and geographical balance when the qualifications of different candidates are similar.

Page's detailed study shows that national continuity may 'be more prevalent' among Directors General and their Deputies, and he noted for the period 1989–93 that 'the French appear to dominate among those who pass the post on to a compatriot' (Page, undated, p. 6). Since that study there have been important changes, in part because of the damage which too widespread a perception of national capture does to the legitimacy of EU policies and organisation. Director General posts were reshuffled when the Prodi Commission arrived, and Neil Kinnock publicly announced an end 'to the convention of attaching national flags to senior positions' (*The Independent*, 30 September 1999), and confirmed this by the appointment of a Spaniard to Agriculture. However, Financial and Economic Affairs remained Italian and after a brief British incumbency under Santer, the headship of the Competition DG reverted to a German.

Enlargement and the consequent reorganisation of the Commission complicate considerations of national balance and of national continuity, and involve early retirements, reorganisations and reshuffles. At the time of the 1995 enlargement, at least one Director General from each of the new member states was appointed within the first six months.

Professional background and expertise

Some of the civil services of the member states are characterised by a marked homogeneity of academic background or expertise within the senior ranks of the service. Thus, despite some broadening, officials with academic qualifications in law continue to dominate the senior ranks of the civil service in Germany and Denmark, and those trained in law or the social sciences also predominate in Spain and France. By contrast the Dutch civil service involves specific recruitment to each post on the basis of the technical skills needed for that particular post, while in Britain and Ireland a 'generalist' approach to career grade recruitment means that – as also for much graduate recruitment to private sector employment – the academic area of the degree programme of graduate entrants is irrelevant (Bodiguel, 1994).

Page's study found, as would be expected given that the possession of a university degree is a normal prerequisite for appointment to EU category A posts, that all but 1 per cent of his sample of 1131 listed a university degree. He also found that although the academic background of officials was diverse, those with qualifications in law and the social sciences dominated. There are also significant numbers of natural scientists, while the much smaller numbers of arts and humanities graduates come disproportionately from the UK, Ireland and Luxembourg. His detailed observations confirmed the 'common-sense assumptions' (1997, p. 78) both that officials of the EU tended to reflect the traditional patterns of academic background for officials in the countries from which they came, and that those with backgrounds in certain disciplines may be particularly concentrated in certain areas. Thus natural scientists are most strongly concentrated in the Joint Research Centres, in the Commission's technical agencies, and in the Directorates General concerned with science and research and telecommunications. The much smaller numbers of arts and humanities graduates tended to be found 'servicing the Commission, the Parliament and the Council' (Page, 1997, p. 78). Social scientists are most evenly distributed.

Moreover, two factors ensure that even career-grade entrants normally have working experience outside the services of the institutions before appointment. These are the extent of recruitment at grade A7 for which several years' prior professional experience is required, and the length of time between the opening of a competition and actual appointment, during which a candidate must earn a living. Page found that two-thirds of his sample of officials in grades A8 to 4 had entered the EU service after the age of 30, and might thus be presumed 'to have at least begun a career outside it' (Page, 1997, p. 75).

Page's conclusions, with which anecdotal and interview evidence are fully compatible, do not support any argument that officials within the policy-making and administrative services of the EU are markedly professionally specialised. While the disciplines of their educational formation may appear somewhat more focused than might be found amongst officials in the countries with the most 'generalist' traditions, it is hard to assert that a degree in, say, sociology, is intrinsically more relevant to all areas of EC policy-making than, say, a degree in history or modern languages. Moreover, the motivations which make a career in the EU services an attractive one may be precisely those which may have earlier incited a young person, especially in countries where the choice of degree subject is seen to have a strongly determinant influence upon career openings, to choose a degree programme in law or social sciences. Finally, the degree of mobility between the Directorates General within the Commission – if not between the institutions – militates against the presumption that EU officials are intrinsically and strongly specialised in specific areas.

Despite the rejection by Monnet, and then by Hallstein, of the notion of an administration composed of seconded officials, it seems unsurprising that 45 per cent of those in Page's sample who had previous careers before joining the EU services had been civil servants. National officials are likely to have acquired a taste for and confidence in the processes of policy-making. The national civil service may – explicitly in the case of the British European Fast Stream and in many countries through generous provision for secondment – provide a comforting fall-back position through the long-drawn-out and uncertain procedures of recruitment. In addition the national civil services are an obvious source of late entrants since candidates from that source will be known to governments and their Permanent Representatives who may be able to support them in the negotiations for filling strategic posts. Over half of the senior officials in Page's survey in the Council Secretariat, the Court of Auditors, and the Court of Justice and the Court of First Instance had such backgrounds (1997, p. 75). The Joint Research Centres mainly recruit senior officials (71 per cent) from within educational institutions (presumably particularly higher educational institutions where research is undertaken). Indeed, education and the private sector are the other two major providers of pre-recruitment experience, followed by the professions (such as law and accountancy). Journalism, politics, interest groups and the public sector industries each provided prior experience for no more than 5 per cent of officials. Late entry 'parachuted' officials (those recruited to management positions at grades A5 and above) come predominantly from national civil services, but are also more likely than career-grade entry officials to have employment experience in education and the public sector. 'As one might expect the proportions who had served as professional policy advisers was somewhat higher (9.0 per cent) among parachutists than career officials (1.1 per cent)' (Page, 1997, p. 85).

The educational and the professional backgrounds of EU officials provide no evidence to support the image of a very closed and homogeneous world. There are many factors which make for diversity and fragmentation within the services. Liesbet Hooghe's analysis of the attitudes of senior Commission officials found that prior experience in their national bureaucracies caused them 'to internalise norms and practices from previous settings [but to] reevaluate them before applying them to a new institutional context' (Hooghe, 1999a, p. 412). To set against the fragmentation which results from differing nationality – and language, see below – are points of contact: the possession, for example, by many officials of combinations in various proportions of administrative background and a familiarity with the discourse of the social sciences, including law. The administration of the EU undoubtedly is cosmopolitan and diverse, but, as Page points out, '[i]n many respects EU civil servants as a group are little different from senior civil servants in member states' (Page, 1997, p. 86).

Linguistic diversity

One notable area where the officials of the EU are different from the civil service of any of the member states is the range and diversity of their mother tongues. One of the criteria for recruitment to the service of any of the EU institutions is competence in more than one of the languages of the Community. There is a good deal of evidence from anecdote, and from anthropological observation, of the impact of multilingualism upon the working methods and atmosphere of the EU services. There are three important aspects to the consequences of multilingualism. The first is the extent of the formal requirement for translation and interpretation services. Second, some languages have tended to dominate, so that the desirability of recognising this and reducing the range of languages in use continues to be discussed. At the same time some have discerned the emergence of a kind of internal dialect, shaped by the interaction of the vocabulary and structures of several languages. Third, language use can reinforce certain networks, and underpin informal circuits of information and action.

Translation and interpretation

When Jean Monnet founded the European Coal and Steel Community he was conscious of the difficulties of forging together an institution which would involve close co-operation amongst a staff who functioned in four different languages. He did not want any language to dominate (Monnet, 1976, p. 450) and noted that this meant that the staff numbers would be 'over-burdened' with interpreters and translators. Indeed, he required the services of a personal interpreter, Ursula Wenmackers, whom he describes as *'attachée à nos pas'* (constantly at our heels) to communicate with Franz Etzel, the German Vice-President of the High Authority with whom his only common language was English, which Etzel did not speak well (Monnet, 1976, p. 45; Duchêne, 1994, p. 240). However, despite his anxiety to ensure that no language dominated he also, Roger Morgan reports (Morgan, 1992, p. 7), refused in the first few months to sign translations of the decisions of the High Authority in languages which he did not understand – and he had no German. It was for this reason that the unit of specialised legal translators *(juristes-linguistes)* was created.

All the final, formal official documents emanate from them. All such documents are produced in all the eleven official languages of the Union (Danish, Dutch, English, Finnish, French, German, Greek, Italian, Portuguese, Spanish, Swedish – and Irish for the Treaties). At meetings of the Council of Ministers and its work-ing groups, everyone has the right to speak and to receive inter-pretation in their own language, although in practice there are a number of limitations (Westlake, 1995, p. 15). Where simultane-ous translation cannot be provided between a pair of languages, interpretation may simply not be available, in which case the rep-resentatives of the countries usually, if 'under sufferance' (Westlake, 1995, p. 15), will follow the discussion through another language. The interpretation between some pairs of lan-guages in any case frequently passes through a 'core language': thus Greek may be interpreted into English and thence into Danish. These constraints have led to some informal understand-ings: for example, the Transport Working Group operates rou-tinely on the basis of six languages. A second practical limitation is the difficulty of providing enough translators' booths for all the language pairs. With the 1995 enlargement it proved impossible to accommodate sufficient, even in the brand new building of the Council Secretariat, so that interpretation into both Swedish and Finnish could not be provided at the same time.

Within the European Parliament there is similar provision for interpretation, and similar practical constraints also apply.

Plenary sessions of the Parliament, meetings of the Parliamentary Committees, and travelling delegations of the Parliament are all serviced by interpreters. So are the Economic and Social Committee of the EU and the Committee of the Regions. These, however, are all institutions of the Union which bring together representatives, delegates and members who are not employees of the Union nor involved in a more or less permanent way in its operations. The more 'internal' institutions often operate, for reasons both of practicality and effectiveness, without interpretation or with interpretation in a limited range of languages. For example, in the years after the creation of the EEC the Committee of Permanent Representatives (COREPER) used French, without interpretation, and nowadays French and English are used, still without interpretation (Westlake, 1995, p. 16). Interpretation is provided within the Commission for meetings when representatives of member states or of specialised interest groups are present and for the meetings of the College of Commissioners although 'French and English tend to dominate in practice' (Spence, 1997a, p. 94). Interpretation is provided for the hearings of the Court of Justice, but the deliberations of the judges take place without it.

The translation and interpretation services of the Institutions are organised separately and somewhat differently. As the then Director of the Joint Interpretation and Conference Service said in 1987, 'The only people who do not meet professionally are the translators and interpreters. The interpreter does not need the translator and the translator does not need the interpreter ... the mentality and work are different' (House of Lords, 1988, p. 151, q. 674–5). The Joint Interpretation and Conference Service provides interpreters for the Commission, the Council of Ministers, the Economic and Social Committee, the Committee of the Regions and the European Investment Bank. In 1998 it provided 147 068 interpreter days at 111 648 meetings. The JICS had 522 interpreter posts in 1998 but, given the fluctuating nature of demand for services, and the fact that the demanding nature of the work means that some interpreters prefer a more flexible commitment, the JICS relies quite heavily on freelance interpreters, who in 1996 covered 37 per cent of the interpreter days. Two of the Union's institutions maintain their own interpretation services: the European Parliament with 258 staff in its interpreting directorate, and the European Court of Justice with 40 interpreters. They recruit separately, and indeed relationships have not always been amicable. Good interpreters are in short supply, and accusations of poaching periodically surface.

The translation services are both larger and more fragmented. The Commission maintains its own translation service, and there is a separate translation centre for the agencies (see Chapter 7). The Secretariat of the Council of Ministers, the Economic and Social Committee, the Court of Justice and the Parliament also have individual translation services. The demands on these services are heavy. Initial working drafts of documents are usually in English or (perhaps less frequently nowadays) French (Westlake, 1995, p. 16; McDonald, 1997, p. 56), or even, paragraph by paragraph, in a bit of both. However, formal documents such as proposals, reports, decisions and draft legislation must be available in all languages before formal publication or discussion. Final versions of legally binding documents must be uniformly legally valid and precise in every language. The consequence is that nearly 21 per cent of the graduate-level officials working in the Commission are translators or interpreters. They in their turn are supported by clerical and secretarial staff. In 1994 David Spence made a rough estimate that, if the staff time spent on language-related work by staff not directly employed in the language services were also calculated into the total staff resources devoted to language work in the Commission, these resources would amount to the equivalent of some 2700 staff (Spence, 1997a, p. 94). The advent since then of two new languages means that this figure should probably be calculated at closer to 3000. Even this does not include the freelance interpreter days utilised.

Working languages

Clearly there are a very large number of meetings each day for which interpretation is not available. Indeed, 'in the internal work of the Commission there is hardly ever recourse to translation or interpretation in all languages' (Spence, 1997a, p. 93). Noting in his memoirs that he wanted an administration where the four languages would be used indiscriminately and with none dominating, Jean Monnet notes in the next breath that French was the habitual working language in the High Authority of the Coal and Steel Commission. In 1995 Martin Westlake could report that French was still 'the *de facto lingua franca* of the General Secretariat' of the Council of Ministers. Maryon McDonald observed that the officials to whom she talked in 1993 commented that 'the language of the Commission is French' (McDonald, 1997) and that at that time there was still 'a strong moral and political compulsion to speak French' which seemed 'more ideologically sound' (McDonald, 1998, p. 71).

One consequence of the domination of French until the 1990s is that concepts which developed within the French-speaking environment of the early years remain difficult to translate into English. These terms include *l'acquis* – the treaties and the body of law which set out the EU constitution and its policies – and *la construction européenne* – the process of integration, (*The Times*, 15 April 1998). The same applied to procedural matters. McDonald quotes everyday speech: 'Don't forget the *fiche financière*' and 'DG IX is trying to *supprimer la filière papier*' (McDonald, 1998, p. 72).

However, English now seems to be challenging French strongly as a working language. Indeed by 1998 it could be alleged that it was now the dominant working language in the Union's institutions, especially the European Monetary Institute, as in other, non-EU European institutions such as Europol, the police cooperation agency based in The Hague. This process is likely to continue with further enlargements. It was notable that at the Brussels launch of the enlargement negotiations in 1998 the representatives of eight of the eleven applicant states (including Romania, where a Romance language is spoken) made their formal speeches in English (*The Times*, 15 April 1998).

McDonald noted marked differences between 1993 and 1998, and our interviewing experience tended to confirm this. But the working English or French of the EU is not quite the language of Paris and London. There are 'oddities of language followed even by the native speakers' which are the result of 'multicultural tolerance' especially at the working level (Bellier, 1994b, p. 95). Grammar, vocabulary and syntax intermingle and interfere. The

---

Exhibit 6.1   A multilingual world as observed by a Frenchman

Just after encountering a group of Italians in the corridor [of the administrative offices of the European Parliament] I found two men talking to each other in German. One of them rushed over to a young woman and they greeted each other in English. As I entered the office of an Italian official who was going to introduce me to some of his colleagues he was talking to his secretary in his native language. Both of them greeted me warmly in faultless French. When the telephone rang the man I was speaking to immediately responded in English. Then he returned to French with me, until the next phone conservation, this time in German. As soon as he had put down the receiver he took up where he had left off with me again, but then stopped short. He had seen my rather puzzled expression, and realised that he was still using German.

Source: Translated from Abélès (1992), p. 250.

---

results are generally acceptable for spoken communication, although written texts cause more difficulties, since idiosyncrasies have to be ironed out when communication with the outside world is required. Nevertheless 'a German speaking French to a Dutchman about a text in English does not cause surprise' (McDonald, 1997, p. 56) and multilingualism is common (see Exhibit 6.1), though probably few can reach the level of the official in the Council Secretariat who spoke nine of the eleven languages and was learning the other two (Westlake, 1995, p. 16). And linguistic diversity has its costs. There may be a loss of nuance, and particularly of humour and of the small ways in which communication is eased (Abélès and Bellier, 1996, p. 435).

Location and lifestyle

A high proportion of the employees of the services of the European Union are making a career outside the country of their birth and education. The experience may be a rewarding one. Indeed several of the officials of the Parliament interviewed by Marc Abélès admitted that it was the chance to earn at a level a good deal higher than was on offer in their home countries (Abélès, 1992, p. 267) that induced them to take the somewhat risky step of joining the Parliament's staff in the very early days of the Treaty of Rome.

The experience is, however, frequently an ambiguous one (Abélès, Bellier and McDonald, 1993, p. 26ff). Unlike the expatriate employees of multi-national corporations or diplomats, those who make their career in the institutions of the European Union do not expect their sojourn in a foreign country to be a temporary one, and very often retain no career base in their country of origin. Equally, however, they do not expect or aim for total assimilation of their family into their country of residence, as may be perceived when they speak of the education and future of their children or their retirement.

Another symptom of the 'expatriate' nature of the life of at least some officials is the extent to which they may maintain their involvement in the political life of their home country. There are no limitations upon the rights of officials of the Community to engage in political campaigning on a personal basis. They will be granted leave for a campaign and, if they are successful, for as long as their electoral term lasts. A number of officials of both Commission and Parliament have stood as candidates in national and European elections in their home countries

The ambiguity about assimilation into the host society extends beyond political and educational concerns. European Union officials enjoy some privileges analogous to those of foreign diplomats in a host country, including a distinctive vehicle registration plate, and diplomatic immunity against criminal proceedings, as well as an allowance of leave time for travel 'home' if that is sufficiently far away. The ambiguity is particularly evident to Belgian officials working in the institutions in Brussels (McDonald, 1998, p. 36).

For the high proportion of European Union officials who are based in Brussels, where they work may affect how they live, as the anthropological study by Abélès, Bellier and McDonald, on which this section draws heavily, discovered. The linguistic division and 'pillarisation' of Belgian society result in marked social divisions, within which people of other nationalities who could not be classified into any of the accepted categories find it difficult to situate themselves. Moreover, the Brussels homes of EU staff tend to be concentrated within certain parts of the city and adjacent communes. In consequence, although the staff of the European union take full advantage of the cultural life which Brussels offers – opera, theatre, cinema – and of its sporting facilities, assimilation into, or even social contact with, the Belgian population is difficult and the expatriates and the Bruxellois 'constitute two parallel social universes' (Abélès, Bellier and McDonald, 1993, p. 26).

Community officials, then, have in common the negative experience of living outside their country of origin (except for the Belgians) and in a context where 'Eurocrats' are much criticised (Abélès, 1996, p. 117; McDonald, 1998, p. 36). In Brussels their privileges are resented and they are accused of having benefited from favourable conditions for purchase of property and progressively taken over part of the local housing stock (Abélès, 1992, p. 262). The fact that the Belgian government encouraged such purchases as a way of ensuring that Brussels remained the uncontested headquarters of the Community has scarcely mitigated the criticism. In Luxembourg one official remarked to Marc Abélès, 'When we arrive in Luxembourg we have to be willing to pay large amounts for housing. Here everything is dear and the population does not like us' (1992, p. 261)

The 'parallel universe' of the EU staff is not, however, a homogeneous one. As the numbers of EU staff and of expatriates in Brussels has grown markedly, the social networks based on nationality have tended to strengthen. In the early 'heroic' days staff numbers were small and relationships close. In Luxembourg in the late 1950s the Parliamentary Assembly had a staff of less than 100. 'Everyone knew everybody' and the atmosphere is remembered as warm, almost familial (Abélès, 1992, p. 269). 'Curiously, we see a renaissance of national attachments as numbers grow. [EU staff] contact and talk to each other, but we don't really want to get to know each other as we did in the heroic age when building Europe was the business of a few enthusiasts', a longstanding member of the EU staff told Jean de la Guérivière (Guérivière, 1993, p. 44).

Nowadays each nationality has its own groupings, perhaps a club or church, or more informally cafés or bars where they may encounter each other. These networks may not be confined to EU staff. The national diplomats of the Permanent Representations to the EU and the Delegations to NATO, together with the national embassies and the expatriate employees of multi-national companies, law firms, lobbyists, pressure groups and non-governmental organisations may all be involved. Liesbet Hooghe examined what she calls 'clubness' and hypothesised that it resulted from national socio-cultural cohesion, from organisational and financial resources, and from deliberate networking policy by national governments. It is not an equal feature of the social life of all the different nationalities. It seems to feature more highly in the life of the Irish and the Danes, for example, than of the Germans. Neither is it equally well tolerated. For instance, a celebration organised by the Irish will be much more tolerantly – even enthusiastically – accepted than one organised by the Germans because Irish nationalism is more acceptable than German nationalism (Abélès, Bellier and McDonald, 1993, p. 58). However, the social networks – churches, sports clubs – are not necessarily altogether mononational. When a 'Belgium–Luxembourg' branch of the important and elitist association of former students of the French École Nationale d'Administration (ENA) was launched in 1990 it included former students from the international programme of the ENA who were British, German and Italian, for example (Guérivière, 1993, p. 43).

The non-Belgian members of the EU staff find themselves, it seems, neither integrated within their country of residence, nor totally drawn into a new, multi-national milieu. 'Europe' may well demand lengthy and intensive working hours. As numbers grow, the missionary zeal dissipates and a career in the institutions of the Union becomes more of a career like any other; it does not constitute or absorb a social existence as well. Ambiguity persists, links with national networks continue and ease of communication means that physical separation may not imply a serious rupture with one's country of origin. One Greek senior official had found it impossible to meet her Belgian neighbours, but depended upon contact by telephone with her family who remained in Greece (Abélès, Bellier and McDonald, 1993, p. 27). Although the Staff Regulations require officials to reside within a reasonable distance of their place of employment, better and cheaper travel means that many senior staff follow the pattern exemplified by the first Secretary General of the Commission, Emile Noël, who worked very intensively in Brussels during the week, but returned each weekend to his home and family in Paris (Brigouleix, 1986, p. 23).

Maintaining links with 'home' is not necessarily a comfortable option, however. The role and identity of EU officials is now more generally contested. For Spence in the mid-1990s it was no surprise that Commission officials are little understood and little liked. Viewed from a British perspective:

> The Commission appears on the national horizon only when its President causes controversy (by visiting the British Trade Union Conference or expressing a view about the outcome of the Danish referendum), or a newspaper publishes an article critical of EU policy or when a national politician attributes blame to the Commission rather than to the Council. (Spence, 1997a, p. 97).

There has been no lessening of anti-EU feeling since 1994, and 'Eurocrats' are a visible target, criticised for their indifference to the socio-professional realities that their decisions affect (Bellier, 1994a, p. 254). They can be represented as physically and psychologically detached from the general public of the member states and can seem hard to hold to account for what they do or do not do (Spence, 1997a, p. 97). The sense of being isolated from the local community and misunderstood by the European public at large is a further factor in the delicate balance within the Commission between the forces of integration and disintegration.

Conclusion

EU officials operate within an environment in which nationality and language retain their salience despite supranational objectives. Their position is ambiguous. These factors contribute to the stereotyping and fragmentation which characterise the working practices of a world in which shared loyalty to an employing institution, and beyond that to a notion of a European project, contested though that may be, co-exists with a marked plurality of networks, languages and lifestyles. And this plurality is echoed in the range of tasks undertaken and the conflicts which arise, to which the next two chapters turn.

Chapter 7

Roles, Tasks and Functions

It is important to analyse the tasks and roles of the administrators of the European Union, not least because doing so reveals the ways in which their work differs from that undertaken by their counterparts in the member state bureaucracies. This chapter presents an analysis of their work, broken down into twelve types of activity within three broad functional categories:

Policy functions

- Policy formulation
- Preparation of legislation
- Negotiation
- Presentation and representation

Management functions

- Resource management
- Monitoring, supervision and enforcement
- Executive action
- Audit and financial control

Support functions

- Research
- Secretariat duties
- Linguistic duties
- Housekeeping and support

The categories are useful for analytical purposes, although the boundaries may blur. Thus in some cases a single official may undertake several activities (senior officials in particular may be expected to carry out a wide range of both policy and management functions); in other cases the activity is sufficiently specialised for it to form the major part of an individual's duties. The elements would be familiar to most administrations; it is the mix which makes the difference, as changes in both scale and balance present new challenges. For example, the Commission, which in Jean Monnet's conception was a small secretariat and policy-making institution, has grown into an administration with substantial management functions. One reason why the Commission has been slow to embrace the management reforms which have swept through most national administrations is probably due to the significance of this changing pattern not being recognised at the highest levels: for example, the six major functions identified by Commission President, Jacques Delors – innovation, law-making, policy management, monitoring of policy implementation, negotiation and diplomacy (Hay, 1989, p. 17) – were heavily orientated towards the more glamorous policy functions. The analysis carried out for the DECODE exercise in 1998 (Table 7.1) shows how important management and support functions have become.

Policy functions

The four tasks in this category, mainly the preserve of staff in category A, are the most prominent and sought after. Officials who formulate policy and prepare legislation, who negotiate and represent their institution in a variety of fora, are involved in activities which require them to interact frequently with external interests including governments, business lobbies, policy communities, interested parties among the public, the media and the academic community, as well as with their colleagues within the EU institutions, who may well represent divergent and even conflicting interests (see Chapter 9).

Policy formulation

This is frequently regarded as the key task of senior bureaucrats. Within the French system, for example, the somewhat rigid structures are designed to protect the independence of judgement of those assigned the task of 'conceiving' and formulating policy. Whilst the Whitehall system nowadays emphasises management values, the highest esteem and the fastest promotion is arguably

TABLE 7.1   *Breakdown of intramural Commission staff by task*

	Tasks	Person-years	% of total staff
01	Management	1 028.06	4.6
02	Co-ordination	937.67	4.2
03	Policy development	646.47	2.9
04	Representation, negotiation	451.97	2.0
05	Relations with institutions	384.54	1.7
06	New legislation	278.19	1.2
07	Current legislation	303.93	1.4
08	Case handling	831.31	3.7
09	Legal advice	147.65	0.7
10	Partnership member states	689.42	3.1
11	Commission programmes	532.67	2.4
12	Commission projects	742.21	3.3
13	Finance and budget	1 286.22	5.7
14	Economic analysis	216.51	1.0
15	Statistics	333.85	1.5
16	On-the-spot controls	341.27	1.5
17	Evaluation	230.85	1.0
18	Internal consultations	346.77	1.5
19	Informatics	1 268.01	5.6
20	Information and communication	935.15	4.2
21	Staff management	348.67	1.5
22	Administration and logistic support	6 910.41	30.7
23	Linguistic	1 767.00	7.9
24	Other	901.65	4.0
25	Vacant	635.71	2.8
	TOTAL	22 496.46	100.0

Source: European Commission (1999) Annex 4.

still reserved for those engaged in formulating policy advice for ministers. In the European Union the task is most especially one for the staff of the Commission, although the development of secretariats for the CFSP and the police and judicial co-operation policy pillars means that tasks of policy formulation may now also be found within the Council staff to a greater extent than before the 1990s. As Table 7.1 shows, a relatively narrow definition of the task of policy development (narrow because it evidently excludes relevant aspects of tasks 10 and 18) absorbs less than 3 per cent of Commission staff time, and even if senior members of the staff of the Council of Ministers can also be seen as having a policy formulation input, the total involved is small in relation to overall numbers.

Although the numbers of staff engaged in policy formulation may be small, they tend to enjoy the highest prestige within the organisation (Hooghe, 1997, p. 108; Nugent, 1997, p. 5), and policy formulation is the first role which springs to mind when politicians and senior managers want to explain what their staff do. Moreover, there is evidence that officials see themselves as having a particular duty to initiate and draft legislation and to promote integration. 'Commission officials are expected to "shake up" things' (Hooghe, 1997, p. 102). Cram observes that in social policy, when in the 1960s the Commission's ambitious formulation of a policy to harmonise social security systems ran headlong into the resistance of the member states, Commission staff shifted their policy formulation role to 'catalytic research activities' and the use of policy analysis as a means of persuasion, while always seeking as far as possible to extend the scope of the Commission's role (Cram, 1997, p. 37). Staff engaged in transport policy adopted a similar strategy for almost 20 years (Erdmenger, 1983, pp. 30–4).

Officials have no monopoly of agenda setting, but they do have an important influence upon it, together with considerable scope to define the problem and pursue their preferred solution. 'Access to cross national data places the Commission in the position of being able to identify common problems and thus potential areas conducive to future regulation' (Cram, 1994, p. 211). Examples include the development of policy for industrial support and information technology which led to the ESPRIT programme

(Cram, 1997, pp. 61–97), and the reform of the Structural Funds in 1988, when a small task force of officials, elevated for a short period into a Directorate General, produced new regulations for the funds (Hooghe, 1997, p. 92). In both cases the absence of a common approach within the Commission as well as between the member states meant that part of the policy formulation task was the creation of supportive networks and coalitions both inside and outside the institution. In the words of an official interviewed by Liesbet Hooghe (Hooghe, 1997, p. 103): 'This ... is a House where nobody can take the luxury of not answering a good argument and nobody gives orders and nobody takes orders. You have to convince, so you have to know your task.'

Sometimes officials may even have the opportunity to develop their own policies: for example, 'when the DG concerned finds itself stepping in to fill a policy vacuum' (Cini, 1996). A particularly striking example of this is the European Union's policy of equal opportunities between men and women. Although there were external trigger factors and events, much of the impetus for the rapid development of the policy came from a small group of determined officials with a strong commitment to the values and goals of equal opportunities (Hoskyns, 1996). Similarly, European Union environmental policy, which was formulated and codified into a large body of regulations in the 1980s, was for a long time the concern of a group of committed officials who gave their Directorate General the reputation of being 'dominated by ... "ecological freaks"' (Cini, 1997, p. 78). However, commitment, energy and competence cannot guarantee success, as may be seen from the Commission's failure as yet to persuade the member states to agree to a carbon tax.

The task of policy formulation may include the acquisition of detailed technical knowledge of the topic, research and policy analysis, liaison with interested parties, the creation of support groups and networks within and outside the Community institutions, the organisation and management of the procedures and timetable for the development of the policy proposals, the presentation and defence of the policy proposals through the marshalling of the arguments into detailed submissions and presentations, and eventually the drafting of the documents which will constitute the legal and public embodiment of the policy. These documents are not limited to the legal texts, to which the next section of this chapter turns: they may also take the form of speeches and articles by Commissioners and officials, more formal policy proposals such as white and green papers, or reports and work programmes. All these 'provide useful insights into Commission thinking' and serve 'to reduce the ... uncertainty that has plagued European policy formulation ... Such tools can compel change within a particular policy environment as much as any legally enforceable instrument can' (Cini, 1996, p. 146).

Preparation of legislation

Legislation is one of the major activities of the European Union, being the principal task of both the Council of Ministers and the European Parliament, and a key task for the Commission, which generates legislative proposals for the other two institutions to consider. Since its production constitutes the main and most visible part of the activity of the Commission, the successful preparation of a piece of legislation may play an important role in the career advancement of senior officials. Critics argue that this magnifies the EC's penchant for unnecessary regulation. Disentangling motivation is all but impossible. The personal ambition of individual officials is only one amongst a complex set of factors and not readily revealed by the statistics for legislative output. These show trends which clearly reflect political priorities although they cannot show the number of proposals mooted which never made it as far as the College of Commissioners. In so far as ambition is a factor it does have the effect of skewing the activity of the Commission staff and enhancing the role of the preparation of legislation within the spectrum of their activities.

European Union law, whether embodied in Regulations or Directives, does not require the pernickety phrasing that the literalistic habits of the English-speaking courts demand. General administrators in category A are thus expected to be able to write legal documents and this ability is seen as a skill which is central to the portfolio of a senior administrator. They are expected to prepare initial drafts in one or both of the Commission's two working languages (French and English), and to steer a proposal through the extensive process of consultation both inside the

Commission and externally (see Chapter 9). Although the preparation of legislation is a part of the tasks of most senior officials it constitutes the major element of the work of the Commission's legal service, and the specialised legal linguistic service who review the final texts.

Commission officials are not the only EU staff who may make an important contribution to the exact formulation of a legal instrument. The staff of the Council of Ministers may become closely involved not only in assisting the Presidency to steer it through the legislative process, but also in the production of forms of words to embody the Council's amendments. Equally the staff servicing the committees of the European Parliament, most of whom have a legal training and who acquire expertise through their familiarity with the papers handled by their committees, will use their expertise to draft amendments. Commission staff sometimes complain that their Parliamentary colleagues lack the expertise and depth to undertake such drafting properly. However, they are primarily a secretariat, and as such their drafting has to find an acceptable balance between the technical requirements of the subject and its legal context, and adherence to the political instructions of the MEP who has requested that the drafting be undertaken (Abélès, 1992, pp. 281–2).

Negotiation

Negotiation is integral to the delivery of policy outcomes which meet the objectives of the Union whilst respecting the limits of what the relevant policy community can be brought to accept. Before the Commission publishes a legislative proposal, negotiation will take place (though it may be called consultation) with interested parties such as the industry concerned, consumers, the representatives of the member states, and not least with other parts of the Commission. As the proposal makes its way through the legislative process there will be further negotiations in the Council of Ministers and the Parliament, which must be skilfully handled if the final text is to be a coherent and satisfactory piece of legislation.

In addition to these negotiations, the Commission as the executive arm of the EC conducts negotiations with third parties on the basis of mandates agreed within the Council of Ministers, notably under Article 133 (trade negotiations), but also under other Treaty articles (for example, Articles 71 and 80 for transport). The Council mandate lays down the parameters within which the Commission can negotiate, establishes a committee which the Commission must consult as it proceeds (another forum for negotiation), and a procedure for bringing the results back to the Council for endorsement before the agreements are signed.

Presentation and representation

Advocacy is another important policy function. Policy communities are often constructed around the status quo and those who want to bring about change must be prepared to argue their case at every appropriate level, both privately and in public. The official responsible for a policy has to 'sell' ideas both within the institution and to those outside it who will be affected by what is proposed, since their opposition, reflected within the decision-making processes of the EU, may have the capacity to defeat or at least deflect the proposal. Because of the special position of the Commission as the formal initiator of all legislative proposals within the European Communities, senior officials have always had to be willing and able to present and defend their ideas not only in the working groups which they convene to help them define their proposals, and in the negotiations which ensue within the EU institutions, but also in more open fora such as public conferences and academic seminars. Officials are also encouraged to contribute to public debate in writing. The staff report form routinely invites them to list their publications. This does allow for technical discussion and advocacy, but as one of the Commission's spokespeople complained to Christoph Meyer (1999, p. 628), 'here is a mindset which is overly inward-looking and technocratic ... We are too much geared towards magazines and specialised publications rather than focusing more on television.'

In addition to this general duty of presentation and representation which is shared by virtually all EU officials engaged in policy
work at a senior level, there are two more specialised forms of
presentation and representation. The first of these is relationships
with the media. All the institutions recognise the need to undertake political communication: information about the issues under
debate, about the nature of the decision-making procedures, and
about who is responsible for advocating or implementing a policy
(Meyer, 1999, pp. 622–3). The Council of Ministers and the
European Parliament are largely 'event-oriented' (Meyer, 1999,
footnote 1), and the Council is intrinsically rather secretive.
Their press and information services deal with the media interest
in meetings and sessions as they occur. The most prominent focus
of EU information activities is the Press and Communication
Service of the Commission. This service was constituted in 1999
by President Prodi from the former Spokesman's Service and
parts of the former Information and Communications DG (X),
including the Commission's information offices in each of the
member states. The service provides daily briefings and a weekly
press conference, working (since President Santer abolished the
previous practice requiring questions to be put only in French) in
French and English. It issues a steady stream of press material –
now available electronically and including audio, video and
photographic coverage – on the decisions of the Commission.
The daily press briefings provide a focal point for media interest
in the EU. Even after its reorganisation the service is likely still to
be inadequately staffed to cater for the 900 accredited journalists
in Brussels (Meyer, 1999, p. 628) although the reshaping is certainly intended to improve the service's performance, which was
widely perceived as inadequate during the crisis which led to the
Commission's resignation (*European Voice*, 11–17 February
1999; European Union, 2000, pp. 1107–9). The Commission suf-
fers from the disadvantage that 'when things go well for the EU,
member states take the credit and when things go badly they
blame us' (European Commission spokeswoman quoted in
European Voice, 4–10 March 1999). Nevertheless there had until
1999 been little attention paid to the public image of the
Commission, as distinct from the process of European integration
and the European Union as a whole.

Despite the existence of the service, within the Commission the task of disseminating information remains widely dispersed. Each Commissioner had his or her own staff member for press and public relations, with the consequence, as Commission President Prodi noted, that 'a large group of individual Commissioner's spokesmen compete with each other for media attention' (*European Voice*, 10–16 June 1999). He was not, however, fully successful in his fight to ensure that a strengthened and more centralised service would put an end to the appointment of personal spokespersons by individual commissioners (*European Voice*, 16–22 September 1999).

A similar dispersal of information responsibilities characterises the Commission as a whole. Each DG is responsible for specialised information in its own field, and in 1993 their collective publicity expenditure was more than double that of the central service (European Community, 1994). According to the DECODE report some 935 person-years (4.2 per cent of intramural staff) were in 1998 engaged in tasks of information and communication. Any proposed decision going to the College of Commissioners must, according to the formal procedures, be accompanied by an 'information plan'. These procedures work quite well for specific, often very technical, matters and the 'information plans' do require the originating Directorate General to have given some thought to probable reactions to the proposal amongst various sectors of the public, including journalists, politicians not directly involved, interest groups, academics and members of the public who, while not affected by the proposed measure, may form an opinion of the EU on the basis of what they learn about it. However, this dispersal of activity results in communications of varied quality, since the task is often a 'minor low-quality' addition to an official's principal activities (Meyer, 1999, p. 628).

The second specialised representational function is that of diplomacy. In May 1998, according to the DECODE report, the Commission's six external relations directorates employed some 2530 persons on Commission premises and the equivalent of 907 persons extramurally (3437 person-years in all). Another 2525 persons were employed at 126 missions overseas, a resource commitment broadly similar to that of a medium-sized EU member state; about three-quarters of these are locally engaged support staff (Bruter, 1999, Table 3), but senior posts are filled by EU officials, mostly from the External Affairs and Development directorates. Those who accept such appointments are bound by the terms of Annex X of the Staff Regulations, which requires them to be mobile between the central services and any overseas post. In addition to the Commission's external policy staff in Brussels and overseas, the CFSP, the second pillar of the EU under the (Maastricht) Treaty on European Union, has its own Secretary General and a supporting staff of some 50 officials attached to the European Council (Peterson and Bomberg, 1999, p. 247).

The institutional divide which separates the CFSP from the external relations of the Commission reflects an important functional distinction. The CFSP, which grew out of the Council's political co-operation machinery, which guided such initiatives as the Euro–Arab dialogue of the late 1970s, is expressed mainly in common declarations of policy (152 between October 1997 and October 1998) with a much smaller number of common actions (5) and common decisions (15) in the same period (Bruter, 1999, p. 186). The work of the Commission's external relations directorates by contrast is expressed in much more practical manifestations, particularly trade policy and development co-operation. The same distinction is reflected in the way work is undertaken overseas. The EU's own mission deals with the external dimension of Community policies, whereas it is the responsibility of the country holding the Presidency for the time being, forming a troika with its predecessor and its successor, to make appropriate representations through its own diplomatic staff, to the host state arising from the European Union's CFSP. Important as these institutional distinctions may appear in the capitals of Europe as a reflection of the inter-governmental nature of the CFSP, they tend to slip out of focus in more distant places, and in any case the boundaries are blurred because the Treaty itself requires the Commission and its overseas missions to be fully associated with all aspects of the CFSP (Articles 16 and 19).

The tasks of EU missions are similar to those of national embassies in the sense that they are expected to represent the EU and maintain good relations with the host government, but their officials do not fulfil the full range of diplomatic duties: for example, they have no consular or other functions in respect of EU citizens, such functions still being the responsibility of the citizen's nation state. The main difference between an EU mission and the national embassy probably lies in the balance between economic and political functions. Whereas political relations with the host state are normally the core function of a national embassy, even if in practice ambassadors have to spend more and more of their time on commercial and economic relations, the balance is reversed in an EU mission. Until 1988 all but six of the EU's then total of 70 missions were primarily concerned with development aid under the ACP Treaty which links African, Caribbean and Pacific countries with the EU. By 1998, the number of EU missions had grown to 126, of which 66 were in ACP countries and 60 elsewhere, but this reflected the growing importance of the EU's external trade and economic policy relations, especially with the countries of Eastern and Central Europe, rather than any significant increase in political work. Bruter (1999) sees this as a step towards a consumer-related diplomacy; it is evidence that EU missions are responsive to the demands of their constituency of business partners in the private sector, but it may have as much to do with the origins and traditions of the EU service and the predominant experience of its staff in work associated with trade and development rather than political relations.

Management functions

The institutions of the EU in general, most spectacularly but by no means only the Commission, have been slow to recognise the importance of management in the work of senior officials. As recently as 1997/98 the notion in some quarters that management was a tiresome distraction from the serious business of policy work resulted in unanticipated opposition to the Commission's MAP 2000 reform programme of such strength that it came close to failure. The reasons for this and the implications more generally are discussed in Chapter 8. Here we are concerned with specific management tasks. Within the EU the member states undertake most of the implementation both of the two largest expenditure programmes – agriculture and regional support – which together account for some 85 per cent of the EU budget, and of most of the regulations which give expression to other policies. Nevertheless the institutions of the EU and their staff have a key role to play in monitoring, supervising and enforcing the rules which govern all this activity. Management of the remaining 15 per cent of expenditure – at 14 billion euro still a large sum of money (European Parliament, 1999a, p. 32) – is the direct responsibility of the EU's own staff, and mainly of the Commission which together with its various agencies is the executive arm of the EU. Much of this money is spent under contracts which the staff have to draw up, oversee, evaluate and account for. Behind the line managers therefore, checking for regularity and propriety of expenditure (as well as, increasingly, value for money) stands a large supporting cast of financial controllers and auditors.

Resource management

Until very recently senior line managers with their responsibilities for the development of Community policies were not expected to bother themselves unduly with the chores of management. It was someone else's job to provide and manage the supporting services which a policy directorate might need. Within each Directorate General of the Commission, the Assistant to the Director General maintained liaison with the centralised personnel and administration service over the deployment and management of staff, as well as the provision of administrative services such as accommodation, messenger services, travel and subsistence payments, or the hiring of agency typists, but the budget for these things, and the responsibility for providing and managing them, was held and controlled centrally. As a result the personnel and administration service was, and still is, far and away the biggest Directorate General with nearly 3000 staff, some 10 per cent of the Commission total. A similar pattern can be observed in the other institutions. Many senior officials recruited to the EU before the public sector management revolution swept through Europe in the 1980s liked it that way, as did the unions who enjoyed a privileged relationship with a centralised administration.

This situation began to change under the Santer Commission (1995–99) which introduced programmes designed to decentralise both personnel administration and financial management (see Chapter 8). The reforms envisaged by Commissioner Kinnock are intended to move decisively towards a situation in which policy directorates carry full management responsibility within a framework of policies determined centrally. The tasks involved are consequently becoming a more prominent feature of the working days of senior officials.

Monitoring, supervision and enforcement

The European Union differs fundamentally from national governments because it delivers scarcely any services to the citizens of the Union. Even where the European Commission is charged with the implementation of policy it generally fulfils this obligation by the framing of secondary legislation, and the taking of regulatory and management decisions. Participation in the Committees which bring together representatives of the member states and staff of the Commission to undertake the management of certain policies (most notably agricultural policy) – the so-called 'comitology' committees (Wessels, 1998) – is an important task for EU staff in some policy areas. These committees are an arena in which Commission officials can play 'a decisive role' (Wessels, 1998, p. 228) and a mechanism with which they evince considerable satisfaction. The reasons for this satisfaction seem to be that they provide a business-like yet informal setting for largely technical and problem-solving interactions with officials from the member states from which politicians – whether national politicians or the College of Commissioners – can largely be excluded. Technical expertise and consensus are highly valued in this setting, and quite durable networks are created (Wessels, 1998, p. 225).

In almost every case the application of regulations and decisions falls to the persons or enterprises to whom they apply, and their enforcement to the policing and judicial services of the member states. At the heart of this deliberately dispersed system of legal supervision, the European Court of Justice is charged with ensuring 'that in the interpretation and application of this Treaty the law is observed (Article 220). Legal and natural persons, member states and the several institutions of the EU can all act to advance or defend their rights under the Treaties and subordinate EU legislation, and where such rights are disputed the Court has the last word. Nevertheless, the other institutions of the EU are charged with ensuring the application of the treaties. Some tasks of supervision and enforcement fall to them, and in addition the administration has in a number of areas been given the task of monitoring developments in the member states, of encouraging good practice and diffusing information.

In considering the implementation and enforcement tasks undertaken by the administration of the Union, the distinction made by Shaw between direct and indirect implementation is helpful. Shaw (1983, p. 58) points out that direct implementation by the EU essentially involves 'activities by the Commission aimed at protecting the legal fabric of the Community'. These include, first, the exercise by the Commission of its duty to take action against member states for failing to abide by their treaty obligations. For example, every Directive agreed by the Council of Ministers has to be implemented within a reasonable time by appropriate legislation within each of the member states, so the Commission checks to see both that such legislation has been put in place and that it is fully consistent with the intentions of the directive. A breach of the Treaty by a member state may be alleged by the Commission or by any natural or legal person who may consider that their rights have been infringed. Even where the case has not been brought by the Commission, the Commission as guardian of the Treaties will almost invariably intervene before the Court to give its opinion. When treaty breaches are identified, the first step is to try to persuade the government concerned to put the matter right. If informal persuasion fails, and the Commission judges that it must take more formal steps to enforce a Treaty obligation (Article 226), the member state must next be given 'the opportunity to submit its observations' on the matter complained of. If this procedure still fails to bring about a satisfactory settlement, the Commission must next resort to a 'reasoned opinion', and only if the member state fails to comply with the terms of that opinion can the Commission finally bring the matter before the European Court of Justice. Such procedures may be very long-drawn-out – in the case of Commission proceedings against several member states for negotiating bilateral air service agreements with the USA (judgment sought in Case 466/98), proceedings which had commenced informally in 1994 were still pending in 1999 – but the slow pace may be deliberate if the Commission is using the legal procedure, in part at least, to support the parallel negotiations conducted by the policy directorate.

The Commission also prepares reports on the implementation of community policies and programmes. Where the programmes are essentially regulatory, the purpose of such reports, for which provision is often made within the text of the relevant legislation, is to assess to what extent the objectives of the policy have been achieved. As such the report may very well provide the foundation for new proposals designed to carry forward successful policies or to correct the deficiencies of those which have not been so successful. In the case of expenditure programmes, which often take the form of successive multi-annual programmes, the purpose of the report is more often to assess the impact of the investment which has taken place, again as part of the foundation for the proposals which may be brought forward for any successor programme. Such reviews, carried out by management as part of the responsibility for the effective deployment of resources, are distinct from the formal procedures of financial control and audit (see below), though of course programmes which are well managed and closely supervised by those who are directly responsible for them are much less likely than those which are poorly managed to give rise to cases of fraud and corruption.

Executive action

If the bulk of Community expenditure occurs in agriculture and the structural funds and hence is administered by the member states, the substantial minority which remains engages the responsibility of almost twice as many staff (Table 7.1, items 10–12). The biggest programmes of direct EU expenditure are for overseas aid, such as the ACP programme for countries in Africa, the Caribbean and the Pacific, the programmes of aid to eastern and central Europe, and the humanitarian aid programme. But there are many smaller programmes as well, in support of policies as diverse as Trans European Networks, culture, tourism, education, and various branches of research, all of which have to be managed. Usually this requires the Commission as the budget-holder and executive arm of the EU to construct a framework programme and invite competitive bids from organisations with the expertise and resources to do the work. Contracts have to be negotiated and payments authorised when the work has been satisfactorily carried out. The management of such processes is demanding and time-consuming, and there is growing evidence that some parts of the Commission have not paid sufficient attention to these aspects of sound management, with disastrous consequences.

In addition to managing some expenditure programmes, the Commission also manages directly some regulatory responsibilities, notably in the field of competition policy. The Competition Policy Directorate General exercises the powers of the Commission to investigate suspected abuses of a dominant position, including undertaking raids on premises to secure documentation and evidence, and may make rulings and levy fines. As Lee McGowan has pointed out (McGowan, 1997, p. 155), this directorate, with a predominance of legally trained officials on its staff, enjoys a great deal of independence in the investigation of cartels and abusive monopolies, although draft decisions are submitted to the Commissioner's *cabinet*, and the Commission legal service, before they are finalised by the College of Commissioners. In addition there is an advisory Committee on Restrictive Practices and Monopolies (with national representatives) which must be consulted, although its opinions are not binding. Officials working within these areas of competition policy have a role which is unlike that of almost all other EU officials.

A number of other tasks which needed to be carried out by EU bodies, rather than by national administrations under EU oversight, have been delegated to a range of specialised agencies (Table 7.2). For most of them the primary function is to collect, analyse and disseminate information in their respective policy areas, but four are mandated to go beyond this to create and co-ordinate European expert networks to ensure that information is based on equivalent comparable data. Finally there are two agencies with executive functions: the Office for Harmonisation and

TABLE 7.2   *The EU Agencies*

Name	Date	Functions	Staff (1999)	Site
European Centre for the Development of Vocational Training	1975	Information Promotion	81	Berlin, then Thessaloniliki
European Foundation for the Improvement of Living and Working Conditions	1975	Information	84	Dublin
European Environment Agency	1994	Information Networking	63	Copenhagen
Office for Harmonisation in the Internal Market	1994	Information Networking Public Register	407	Alicante
European Agency for Safety and Health at Work	1994	Information	24	Bilbao
European Agency for the Evaluation of Medicinal Products	1995	Information Networking Advice	203	London
European Training Foundation	1995	Vocational training in central and eastern Europe	130	Turin
Community Plant Variety Office	1995	Information Networking Public Register	25	Brussels, then Angers
European Monitoring Centre for Drugs and Drug Addiction	1996	Information Networking	45	Lisbon
European Translation Centre	1997	Translation service for EU agencies	131	Luxembourg
European Monitoring Centre on Racism and Xenophobia	1997	Information	17	Vienna

Sources: Kreher (1997) and EU Budget (1999).

the Community Plant Variety Office maintain public registers of trade marks and plant varieties respectively. The staff are employed under the staff regulations, and funding is by means of block grants from the Commission budget, though the two executive agencies, as well as the European Agency for the Evaluation of Medicinal Products and the Translation Centre, are supposed to become self-supporting from fees and charges (Kreher, 1997).

It has been suggested that the work of the Commission's Competition directorate could be similarly delegated to an EU Competition Agency, perhaps on the model of the German *Bundeskartelamt*, but it remains to be seen whether the member states will be willing to separate from the Commission, where political pressures can sometimes be used to influence decisions, a function which involves decisions (for example, on major mergers or large injections of state aid) which are often of high political salience within the member states concerned. There would also be the problem of agreeing on a site; it was this wrangle which held up agreement on the 1993 group of eight agencies until everyone except Belgium and the Netherlands had a trophy (the Germans, who ceded the European Centre for the Development of Vocational Training to Greece, had earlier won the much larger prize of the European Central Bank).

Audit and financial control

The arrangements for audit and financial control, which are rooted in the Financial Regulation and therefore apply to all the EU institutions, were summarised in Chapter 3. Under the Financial Regulation checks have to be carried out before resources are committed, as well as at the time of payment, and when the accounts are audited afterwards. In the past many of these checks have been carried out centrally, and this is thought to have diluted the responsibility of policy directorates for the sound financial management of their programmes. This responsibility is likely to be emphasised in any reforms which may be carried forward under President Prodi, but the budget will continue to be drawn up, commitments will continue to be checked against it, payments made and accounts audited, even if some of the staff who perform these functions are moved from central departments to the directorates which manage the expenditure programmes.

Alongside these routine controls of propriety and regularity in the management of expenditure, there has in recent years been an increasing emphasis within the Commission on getting better value for money. The aim has been to shift the culture of financial management towards much greater attention to the effectiveness of expenditure, working closely with the budget DG to spread a 'culture of evaluation' and to link budget allocation, effectiveness and evaluation (Levy, 1996; Laffan, 1997, p. 190). By 1999, under the SEM 2000 reform programme, each operational DG had its own service dealing with evaluation and there was a network of evaluators to exchange ideas and expertise; these evaluators had proposed a set of good practice guidelines, though the external consultants who examined the implementation of SEM 2000 commented that [evaluation] was 'not yet mature enough to be used systematically for decision support'. Value for money is also the concern of another small group of financial control staff, the Inspectorate General, which carries out regular staff inspections in the Commission's services, including major screening exercises, to see where staff may be either overburdened or underemployed, and to make recommendations for the better distribution of resources to match requirements.

Further safeguards are provided by the external audit function which rests with the Court of Auditors. Until 1975 there was no regular or extensive external audit of the expenditure of the EU institutions. A committee of representatives of the national audit bodies of the member states – such as the French *Cour des Comptes* (Court of Accounts) and the British Comptroller and Auditor General – met occasionally to comment on the financial control practices of the institutions. A German MEP published a report calling for a European Audit Office in 1973, and following lengthy debates on the form which it should take, the Court of Auditors was established by the 1975 Treaty. The TEU of 1992 enhanced the institutional status of the Court and required it to provide to the Council and the Parliament an annual 'statement of assurance' as to the accuracy and reliability of the EU accounts.

The Court has 15 members, appointed by the Council acting unanimously after consultation with the European Parliament. While the Treaty does not require this, in fact each member state supplies one member, and the enlargement of the Court with each accession of new members underlines the convention that this should be so (Laffan, 1997, p. 193). The court has a staff of about 500, of whom about half are directly involved in the audit function. In common with other EU institutions a rather high proportion of the staff are involved in linguistic services: 90 out of the 500 are translators (Laffan, 1997, p. 195).

The Court has found it difficult to reconcile the rather different approaches to the audit function which stemmed from the different national traditions of the member states. 'North European audit practices are concerned with both aspects of financial management (regularity and value for money), whereas the Mediterranean countries place greater emphasis on regularity and legality. Once correct procedures have been followed and the paperwork is in order the auditors are satisfied' (Laffan, 1997, p. 196). The Court has attempted to ensure that it incorporates both aspects of audit in its work, and has attempted to tackle them by adopting an audit approach that pays special attention to the soundness of the systems for financial business (Laffan, 1997, p. 196). Finding the right balance in its workload between concentration upon regularity and legality and value for money considerations remains for the Court of Auditors, as for some national audit institutions, an area of difficulty. The need to establish and maintain appropriate working relationships not only with the other EU institutions but also with the national audit bodies, since so much of the expenditure of the EU budget takes place in the member states, is another important aspect of the work of the staff of the Court.

A key task for the Court is the production of its annual report, which is produced 'in an iterative fashion by the auditors, the *cabinets* and members of the Court, and the full Court, based on draft reports' (Laffan, 1997, p. 199). Since the passage of the TEU the Annual Report has been accompanied by a statement of assurance on the regularity of the accounts, the introduction of which has, according to Brigid Laffan, involved considerable rethinking of the Court's working methods. She notes that sampling techniques have had to be adopted, the number of tests required in order to gauge the accuracy of the accounts as a whole is much greater than previously, and the length of the audit trail has been extended to involve much more auditing within the member states.

The crisis which overtook the Santer Commission in 1999 resulted in large part from the failure of these control mechanisms to prevent corruption and fraud with its roots in mismanagement and financial irregularities. We have already noted (see Chapter 3) that five-sixths of EU expenditure is managed by national authorities in the member states, and that is where most of the fraud also takes place. An anti-fraud unit was established in 1988 to co-ordinate the fight against fraud throughout the Community. By 1998 when it became a task force it had 141 staff; in June 1999 it became an autonomous Fraud Prevention Office, and staff numbers are expected to increase to 300 (European Parliament, 1999b, Chapter 5). Under the Treaty on European Union the member states agreed to 'take such measures to counter fraud affecting the financial interests of the Community as they take to counter fraud affecting their own financial interests' (Article 280). The specific powers of UCLAF to investigate fraud in all the member states were spelled out in Council Regulation 2988/95, and strengthened for OLAF in Regulation 1073/99.

These developments bear witness to the growing importance attached to the fight against fraud by Parliament, the Council, the Commission and the Court of Auditors, but the results have not so far been impressive. According to figures provided by UCLAF to the Committee of Independent Experts, between January 1996 and May 1999:

> 298 criminal prosecutions have been opened in respect of cases where UCLAF was involved. 51 of these involved more than one national jurisdiction. Only 13 of the 298 prosecutions have so far produced any judgement. In internal cases, of the thirty inquiries carried out by UCLAF, twelve have so far led to criminal prosecutions, but none to a conviction. (European Parliament, 1999b, Volume 2, p. 25).

The CIE report therefore goes on to recommend further measures of a supranational nature, which would give OLAF, under the direction of a European Public Prosecutor, increased powers to pursue cases of fraud both within the EU institutions and in the member states, but it remains to be seen whether these will be adopted.

Support functions

The final group of functions provides support to either policy or management or both. Research is conducted in order to inform policy, but the oversight of the extensive programme in the Community's own institutions, as well as in the member states, is a substantial management responsibility. Secretariat functions are needed to give coherence to the operations of each of the larger EU institutions; the linguistic service enables a multilingual organisation to function; and housekeeping provides each of the institutions with accommodation, communications and office services. The importance of these functions should not be under-rated: President Santer's failure to exercise any meaningful oversight of the security services for which he was responsible (see below) contributed to the crisis which made his position as President untenable.

Research

The European Union utilises research to support the achievement of its various aims. The Commission carries out much of its own statistical and economic analysis, but many other research functions are contracted out to appropriate consultancies, research institutes, company research facilities, and academic departments. Such contracts are financed either through the programme budgets for the operation of the institutions and the projects they sponsor, or through budgets for the Commission's successive research frameworks (Peterson and Sharp, 1998).

However, the Commission also maintains a substantial in-house research facility – the Joint Research Centre – reflecting the research obligations of the Coal and Steel and Atomic Energy Communities. In the 1980s and 1990s, when these establishments came under increased pressure from restraints on spending and the growing emphasis on the need to demonstrate value for money, they shifted towards the areas prioritised in the framework programmes, and began to increase their work on health and safety and on environmental impacts.

The research staff have always constituted something of a group apart within the staffing of the Union. Their tasks – essentially laboratory research, and its management and support – are very different from those of most of the staff, and they are geographically separate from the other staff, being based in Ispra in Northern Italy, which is the largest of the facilities, and also in Geel and Petten (the Netherlands), Karlsruhe (Germany) and Culham (UK). Their terms and conditions of appointment are, however, subject to the same Staff Regulations, which are not necessarily well adapted to the management of staff in research positions: guaranteed employment and relatively rigid career prospects are not necessarily incentives either to strenuous effort or to adaptability as the research context changes, and the Joint Research Centre's establishments do not enjoy substantial international reputations.

Certain types of basic research require investment in facilities, infrastructure and running costs which may well be beyond the means of any individual government, and duplication would undoubtedly be wasteful. However, such facilities can be established outside the direct ambit of the EU institutions, as in the case of CERN which spans the Franco–Swiss border, and the appropriateness of the continued employment by the Commission of permanent research personnel in these areas remains open to question.

Secretariat duties

Any organisation which depends as heavily upon discussion, negotiation and meetings as does the European Union necessarily engenders a heavy burden of secretariat duties. This is of course, the classic role for bureaucracies which service international organisations. As we have seen (Chapter 2), the origins of the EU administration lay in the need for such services, and Monnet's initial inclination was that its role should be confined to their provision. While it proved impossible to confine the administration in this way it is inevitable, given the scope and nature of the EU institutions, that an important proportion of staff resources should still be deployed in fulfilling such duties. The secretariat role is essentially a role of support for a committee or meeting, for its chair, its rapporteur where it has one, and its members. The physical organisation of meetings, the preparation of timetables and agendas under the chair's direction, the assembly and distribution of Committee papers, the creation and maintenance of records of proceedings and decisions, and the communication of those decisions to the individuals or bodies who need to be informed of them, are the classic duties of a secretariat. Duties of this type constitute a substantial part of the work of the staff of the Council of Ministers. 'Over 100 ministerial meetings and more than 2000 meetings at sub-ministerial level take place every year within the Council hierarchy ... and the Council Secretariat is responsible for organising and documenting the work of each one' (Hayes-Renshaw and Wallace, 1997, p. 118). Hayes-Renshaw and Wallace estimate that about 90 per cent of Council Secretariat staff are involved in the process of organising meetings: convening them, setting out the rooms, and the time-consuming and labour-intensive task of reproducing, translating, distributing and archiving the documents. Some 10 per cent of the Council Secretariat is more directly involved in servicing the meetings, through assisting in the formulation of the agenda, providing guidance notes for the chair, assisting with drafting when required during the meetings, and taking and producing the draft record. This is a role demanding great precision and care (Hayes-Renshaw and Wallace, 1997, p. 118). The minute-taker has the assistance of a taped recording of what was said, but it is the minutes, not the tape, which may be used in legal proceedings if the Council is taken to court. Equally, the decisions taken within the Council machinery often represent difficult political compromises, usually in quite technical fields, and these too need to be very accurately recorded.

The Committee Secretariat staff of the European Parliament and the staff of the Economic and Social Committee and the Committee of the Regions are also predominantly engaged in such work (Abélès, 1992, pp. 277–8). It does require a considerable degree of a particular type of expertise in the composition of documents and in procedures, but at least in the European Parliament the lack of technical specialisation is not perceived as a handicap, since the main role is to assist Parliamentary business; where more specialised knowledge is needed, the staff may consult with Commission staff or the Committee may organise hearings.

Secretariat duties form a smaller part of the work of the staff of the Commission. Nevertheless, the plethora of consultative groups and all the various types of committee known collectively as comitology require services of this kind. And at the apex of the Commission there is a collective body, the College of Commissioners, which itself needs a secretariat. According to the first President of the Commission, the General Secretariat was initially meant to be no more than a technical body to assist the College of Commissioners. However, under Emile Noël it acquired a more important role (Hallstein, 1972, p. 61) and the part it now plays in management and co-ordination is discussed in Chapter 9.

Linguistic duties

The European Union is a multilingual organisation. There are now twelve official languages, including Irish Gaelic, in which the Treaties and their amendments are available, and eleven working languages in which all formal official documents are published. In the internal workings of the institutions language use can be flexible. In the Commission and the Council documents circulate and spoken communication occurs predominantly in French and English (McDonald, 1997, pp. 57–9) and sometimes German (Cini, 1996, p. 128; Hayes-Renshaw and Wallace, 1997, p. 125), if with a copious admixture of in-house jargon and idiosyncratic expression. Many officials will undertake some translation in the normal course of their duties (Cini, 1996, p. 128). However, the need for translation of the final drafts of documents into all the languages before official adoption and promulgation, and for interpretation at many meetings, means that the provision of these services is the sole occupation of a substantial fraction of the staff of the institutions (see Table 7.1). While the advent of machine translation is changing the way in which translators work, and the EU is financing research in the area of 'language engineering', no realistic substitutes for the highly technical and meticulous human skills required for such linguistic tasks are in sight. All the central institutions require such services. Translation and interpretation are rather different skills, requiring different mentalities and working methods, as the then director of the Joint Conference and Interpretation Service told the House of Lords in 1988 (House of Lords, 1988, p. q. 674–6) so that there is very little staff movement between the providers of these services. Interpretation is undertaken for many of the Community's central institutions (Council of Ministers, Commission, Economic and Social Council, Committee of the Regions, European Investment Bank) by the Joint Interpreting and Conference Service, while the European Parliament and the Court of Justice each have their own staff of interpreters. Each of the institutions maintains its own individual translation services.

Housekeeping and support

Underpinning all the administrative services of the European Union described above are extensive support services. The DECODE report estimated that administrative and logistic support accounted for over 30 per cent of Commission staff (Table 7.1). These services, which cover a wide range from secretarial duties to building maintenance, security and cleaning, are provided mainly by staff in categories B, C and D. As Helen Wallace and Fiona Hayes-Renshaw point out for the secretariat of the Council of Ministers, for example, in 1995 almost two-thirds of the entire staff were clerical staff, involved in tasks such as typing, printing, photocopying and distributing documents for meetings, while some 5 per cent were messengers, porters, chauffeurs and maintenance staff, whose tasks include, for example, the physical preparation of rooms for meetings.

Since the nature of such tasks is common to many large organisations, and is not particularly shaped by the purposes and objectives of the organisation which requires them, many administrative organisations have increasingly sought to contract out such duties to companies which may be able to provide them both better and more cheaply as a result of specialisation and economies of scale. The provision of security services to the Commission is a case in point. Such services were provided by IMS Group 4/Securitas between 1992 and 1997, and thereafter by Securis, another Belgian company. However, if contracting out is to be acceptable, correct procedures must be rigorously followed in the letting of such contracts and in their subsequent management, which was evidently not the case in respect of the Commission's security services (European Parliament, 1999a, Chapter 6). The letting of the contracts was open to serious criticism in both 1992 and 1997, and it would appear that the contract with IMS Group 4 at least was used to hire as many as 65 staff for the Security Office overseeing the contract, including some 'ghost personnel' who were paid but may never have existed, by means which were in contravention of both the recruitment rules and the Financial Regulation.

There was a peculiar complicity within the security system and between the Security Office and other circles in the Commission that created a kind of `regulation-free zone', where existing laws and regulations were regarded as cumbersome barriers to various forms of arbitrary action rather than as limitations to be respected. Bernard Connolly, disciplined and dismissed from the Commission staff for writing a book which fiercely criticised EU policies, complained vehemently about his treatment by the Security Service. The security system appears to have been undermined by a sub-culture which was characterised by personal relationships, a system of 'give-and-take' and a withdrawal from the overall system of control and surveillance (European Parliament, 1999a, para. 6.3.14). When allegations surfaced in the Belgian Press in August 1997, the Commission took prompt action to investigate them both internally and in co-operation with the police. However, previously no action had been taken when the Commission's internal auditors uncovered some of the irregularities in 1993. It is not clear whether a blind eye was turned to these activities then and subsequently as a result of negligence on the part of those responsible for overseeing the management of the Security Office, or because its Director, with his close links to the Belgian police, allegedly had the power to offer small favours to colleagues in the Commission, such as cancelling police fines for parking offences or drink-driving or providing the services of drivers and gardeners (European Parliament, 1999a, para. 6.3.15). Whatever the reason, the CIE described the situation as a 'state within a state' (European Parliament, 1999a, para. 9.2.8), and since the Security Office was under the direct supervision of the President of the Commission and his Private Office, his failure to manage it properly contributed to the conclusion that he and all his Commission must resign.

We repeat these allegations here at some length, not so much on account of their intrinsic importance (which is debatable), but rather because they illustrate so clearly that good management, mundane as it may appear, cannot be ignored. Commissioners would doubtless prefer to concentrate all their attention on the more glamorous policy-oriented aspects of their responsibilities, but they cannot escape responsibility for good management as well, down to and including the proper management by their staff of the contract which provides the guards at the front door.

Chapter 8

Organisation, Hierarchies and Management

Public administration, according to Peters (Peters, 1995, p. 135), was long dominated by concern over the structure and design of organisations and 'almost obsessed with constructing the best organisational structures for implementing public programmes'. However, as Chapter 2 argues, the emergence of administrative structures, even in a new and unprecedented set of institutions, is never the product of an abstract rationality, but rather of 'history and economic and social conditions ... as well as ... ideas about the purposes of government'. Chapter 7 identified and analysed the many administrative tasks performed by the institutions of the EU. This chapter turns to an examination of the hierarchies, structures and procedures which have evolved to give shape and purpose to a set of tasks which are in themselves purpose-neutral. The second part of the chapter charts the history of the administrative reform proposals, which since the mid-1970s have generally been better at identifying the problems, and even the solutions, than actually achieving change.

The machinery of government

Following Gulick (Gulick, 1937) many commentators discuss the organisation of administrative bodies into distinct departments or divisions in terms of four principles: such division may be based on the geographic area served, on processes, on clientele, or on functions.

Given the integrative ideology which underpinned the EU institutions, organisation by geographic area has largely been unacceptable, except in the field of foreign relations, including development aid. It is also the case that the purposes of the EU are too broad to be served effectively by an organisation based on client interests, though a functional organisation can provide a focus for client lobbies, which may in some circumstances even come close to capturing part of a functional organisation (see below). But two of Gulick's four principles – organisation by function or purpose and organisation by process – are widely reflected within the structures of the EU institutions.

Organisation by purpose

Although the beginnings of the European Coal and Steel Community saw an attempt to devise a relatively undifferentiated administration based largely upon a single process (the provision of secretariat services), such an organisation could not match the purposes for which the High Authority had been created, still less the European Commission which succeeded it. The administrative organisation of all the institutions has since the early days been based largely upon the functional principle: that is, on the purpose and nature of the subject area. The services of the Commission, the Council secretariat and the administration of the Parliament are all largely organised in this way, as may be seen from the organisation charts in Figures 1.3–1.5 and Table 1.1.

The general adoption of the functional principle has given rise to a number of problems and difficulties. First, in the Commission, some policy areas may seem to be fairly well defined and distinct – agricultural policy, for example – and the Directorates General which deal with them enjoy the prestige and standing which come from longevity and an entrenched position, but there are frequently ambiguities and overlaps. For example, state aids to industry generally are monitored by the Competition Directorate General (formerly DG IV), but aids to airlines are dealt with by the Transport Directorate General (DG VII: see Armstrong and Bulmer, 1998, p. 60). Where are the boundaries between work on research and development policy generally (Research DG, formerly DG XII) and research specifically on information technology (Information Society DG, formerly DG XIII: Cram, 1997, p. 78)? Overlaps and ambiguity provide a fertile ground for the growth of competition and conflict.

Second, the logic of the division of responsibilities between various Commission Directorates General may owe more to political infighting and bargaining between member state governments than to any concept of administrative rationality. The practice of ensuring that each Commissioner has a functional area over which to preside, and the need to ensure national and political balance, has resulted in the reshaping of the Commission's machinery of government to suit the needs of each new team of Commissioners.

Third, a positive effect of organisation by purpose is the development of a good deal of specialised knowledge of a particular sector and the establishment of good networks of contacts within that sector. From this point of view the organisation of the Council Secretariat into functional divisions probably facilitates the smooth conduct of business. The negative side of this approach, however, is the fragmentation which is liable to occur if functional divisions are allowed to proliferate for broadly political purposes. The existence within the Commission before 1999 of no fewer than 24 Directorates General as well as five horizontal services was a much-criticised example of such fragmentation. One consequence of this fragmentation has been a lack of 'fit' between the structures of the different institutions (see Figures 1.3–1.5 and Table 1.1). There is no clear correspondence between the organisation of the ten Directorates General of the Council Secretariat which reflects the councils which they serve, the committee structure of the European Parliament and the structure of the Commission, although all deal, sometimes in an iterative fashion, with the same legislative drafts.

Fourth, organisation by purpose raises the question of the provenance and nature of the 'purposes' which are served. As Peters points out, 'over time the goals pursued by an agency generally come to mean what the incumbents of the roles want them to mean' (Peters, 1995, p. 159). Such goals, theorists argue, are likely to become increasingly self-seeking and related to the preservation of the organisation. Cini argues that commitment to a 'European vocation' and a 'distinctive vision of European integration' has waned in the 1990s (1997, p. 75) and Hooghe's extensive interviewing found substantial variations amongst top Commission officials about how the process of integration should develop. The consequences of the fragmentation of purpose for co-ordination and conflict are discussed in the next chapter.

A fifth aspect of organisation by purpose is the relative inflexibility of the structures which result. Where a new task develops suddenly, or alternatively when a task disappears as a result of contextual change or altered political priorities, existing and well-established structures may have difficulties in accommodating it. Within the Commission there have been varied responses to this dilemma. One such response has been the creation of task forces, as in 1983 in the creation of the Task Force for Information and Communications Technologies, or in 1986 when the prospect of the advent of the Single European Market prompted the setting-up of a task force for small and medium sized businesses. Such a response always risks an accentuation of processes of fragmentation. Although the Information and Communications Technologies task force was merged with an existing Directorate General (DG XIII, Information Market and Innovation) in 1986 to become DG XIII (Telecommunications, Information Industry and Innovation, subsequently incorporated in the Information Society DG), the Small and Medium Sized Business task force became a new DG in its own right (DG XXIII), which by 1995 had grown to about 90 statutory staff and some 300 others, mostly contract staff. This in turn became part of the Enterprise DG after 1999.

Sixth, the distinction between organisation by purpose and organisation for a specific clientele is not always clear (Peters, 1995, p. 158). There is an easy perception that a Directorate General for Agriculture may in fact be a Directorate General for farmers. The nature of the relationship between various Directorates General and their client and lobby groups and interests has been much explored (Mazey and Richardson, 1993; Greenwood, 1997). Whilst the administrative services of the EU do not typically see themselves as in any sense directly involved in the provision of 'services' to clients, the increasing activity of lobbyists of various kinds clearly indicates that this perception is not shared by many groups. The provision of regulation is in itself a service to many client groups, and may result in key advantages for certain businesses or companies in their relationships with their competitors. A number of structures within the EU – most particularly within the Commission but also, for example, in the Economic and Social Committee and the Committee of the Regions – incorporate aspects and characteristics of organisation for clientele. Even if the complex nature of EU policy-making renders outright 'capture' by specific client groups rather more improbable in the EU than in some other organisations, a degree of 'mutuality and exchange' undoubtedly occurs.

Organisation by process

The distinction between organisation by purpose and organisation by process largely corresponds to that classically drawn between the functions of 'staff' and 'line' agencies. 'Line' agencies are those which are concerned with the execution and implementation of policy – essentially with the delivery of services to the public – while 'staff' agencies devise policy, provide advice, co-ordinate and plan, though these functions may be present in varying proportions. The discussion of the tasks of the EU administration in Chapter 7 reveals that line functions, confined to a restricted field of implementation and some tasks of monitoring, supervision and enforcement, have not been regarded as very important. As a result, the structures of the EU administration overall retain the features and characteristics of a predominantly 'staff' organisation, including its relatively small size. While the broadest concepts of 'staff' and 'line' are thus of limited use in describing the organisation of the EU administrative services, they do point towards rather finer categorisations which are more helpful (Sasse *et al.*, 1977, p. 152). These include the distinction between subject area divisions and co-ordinating or horizontal services. Within the European Commission the Secretariat General, and the *cellule de prospective* – the forward studies group – could both be regarded as quintessentially 'staff' organisations, and in the Council Secretariat the private office of the Deputy Secretary General plays a similar role.

At the level of the DGs in the Council Secretariat and the Commission this distinction is evident in the existence of staff directly attached to the Directors General (see the organisation chart in Figure 8.1). For example, until the appointment of Javier

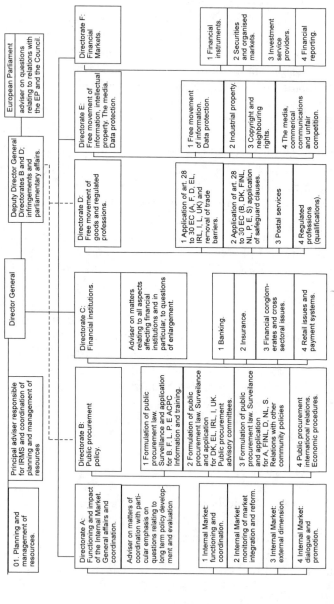

Figure 8.1 *Organisation chart of the Internal Market Directorate General*

Source: European Commission as at 3 February 2000

Key to Figure 8.1

A	Austria	F	France
ACPC	African, Caribbean and Pacific Countries	FINL	Finland
		I	Italy
		IRL	Ireland
B	Belgium	L	Luxembourg
D	Germany	NL	Netherlands
DK	Denmark	P	Portugal
E	Spain	S	Sweden
EL	Greece	UK	United Kingdom

Solana as both Secretary General of the Council of Ministers and High Representative of the EU on CFSP, the Secretary General's *cabinet*, comprising some 70 people (rather less than 20 of whom are A grade officials), undertook the 'staff' tasks of 'foster[ing] cohesion and continuity across the work of the Council' (Hayes-Renshaw and Wallace, 1997, p. 109) and preparing for the meetings of the European Council. It also covered the more 'line' functions of press and information, documentation and financial control. These functions are now undertaken by the staff of the Deputy Secretary General.

Within the structures of the Commission the Directors General have units directly attached to them. The increased emphasis on good management in the mid- to late 1990s resulted in the setting-up of resources units attached to the Directors General. Until then, at least in the smaller Directorates General, the Assistant to the Director General was also often responsible for the financial management of the Directorate. He or she still has key functions in the management of the Directorate General and the recruitment and deployment of personnel. Such posts are usually held by A4 grade officials (Sasse *et al.*, 1977, p. 153), although, in contrast to the pattern for other posts, typically for a relatively limited period, often about three years.

In addition one or more *Conseillers* – special advisers – may be attached to the Director General. Officials in such positions tend to be relatively senior people who for various reasons cannot be inserted into the normal hierarchy, but who are given a specific task or responsibility. The creation of such posts is a technique for dealing with the problems which arise when the number of relatively senior officials is expanded, perhaps because of enlargement or to ensure the promotion of able younger staff, beyond the capacity of the narrowing upper reaches of the hierarchical pyramid. Such *conseillers* were rare in the 1960s, when the organisation was new and small, but by 1972 there were some 12 such officials. The posts provided a temporary niche for *cabinet* staff displaced by changes in Commissioner, or for other senior officials displaced through the operation of the national quota. By 1974 all had disappeared, either absorbed into the hierarchical line management structures, or taking advantage of the generous redundancy terms then on offer (Sasse *et al.*, 1977, p. 153). But, for the same reasons as before, such posts have since reappeared, and in 1998 the DECODE team found 15 principal advisers and 167 advisers, 'a great many of them [with] only minor or poorly defined tasks to perform'. Increased attention to good management is uncovering similar situations in the other institutions, notably the Council Secretariat. There may, as the report recognised, be career development value in the adviser function for a limited period of three or four years, if real activities and responsibilities are involved, but 'cutting out any adviser tasks with no real political or technical added value ... would considerably reduce the number of advisers with no real tasks to perform' (European Commission, 1999, p. 44).

Hierarchy and management

The classic Weberian model of the internal structure of a bureaucratic organisation is pyramidal and hierarchical: at each level officials undertake certain tasks, subject to the direction and control of a smaller number of officials in the next grade up. In first-world English-speaking countries, as in Scandinavia and German-speaking countries, this model of hierarchical authority is assumed to underlie the structures of the administration, even if it is widely recognised that it is in fact never found in its 'pure' form (Peters, 1995, p. 162). Inter-personal relations and leadership matter and may be more important than the authority derived from position when it comes to ensuring the compliance of subordinates, and these are complicated by factors such as social status, age and gender. Moreover, the positions which confer authority may be awarded on the basis of different criteria: in some systems promotion depends importantly on on-the-job performance, whereas in others the level of initial qualification may be more important. Nevertheless, at a quite fundamental level the assumptions of the Weberian model are internalised throughout most bureaucratic organisations from these cultures. As McDonald says, speaking of 'those from the north' – she includes Britain, Ireland, the Netherlands, Denmark, Germany, Luxembourg, Sweden, Finland and Austria – 'the idiom of a rational ideal-type bureaucracy is theirs' (McDonald, 1997).

Within such systems it is assumed that hierarchical duty will override personal preference. Similarly, if such norms are deeply embedded, a veneer of informality may easily be applied to soften the harsher underlying realities. The lack of the trappings of deference does not mean that the constraints of obedience are absent. Maryon McDonald tells of a female French official in the European Commission who, finding her British superior rigid and unsympathetic, was all the more bewildered when he asked her to 'stop calling him "Monsieur" and call him "Jim"' (McDonald, 1997, p. 63).

This anecdote exemplifies what Maryon McDonald calls 'a meeting of incongruent systems' (1997, p. 62). Notions of politeness, of how to relate and speak to people in authority, of how a superior should act and how a junior member of staff may expect to be treated, all vary considerably between cultures (Bellier, 1994b). Languages such as French and German recognise both familiar and more distant forms of address – *tu* and *du*, *vous* and *Sie* – which carry with them a whole range of connotations, references and implications. The notion of hierarchy, indeed the word itself, does not mean the same in all languages. A Spaniard, as Bellier points out, has a different concept of what hierarchy means from a French person, being accustomed to relationships based more on personality and personal status, which certainly makes very little sense to the British (Bellier, 1994a, p. 258). Bellier adds that the hierarchical superior and the manager are two different entities, the one being a position and the other a function. To 'those from the north' such a distinction is largely meaningless; function determines position and position enables functions to be undertaken. To 'those from the south', however, position relates to personal connections within social groupings, 'often of a familial or patron–client kind' (McDonald, 1997, p. 66) and involves notions of deference and indebtedness, as opposed to more abstract virtues of loyalty, honesty or obedience. 'Indebtedness can be created as a matter of pride and honour and similarly debts [are] repaid with loyalty and support' (McDonald, 1997, p. 67). Position within the bureaucratic system will often derive from a combination of initial recruitment and seniority, and advancement up the positional hierarchy may be more or less automatic. Hence, for example, the distinction between grade and post found in the French system and echoed to some extent within the European Union's administrative structures.

The clash between these contrasting notions goes a long way, as the anthropological research of Abélès, Bellier and McDonald showed, towards explaining some of the features of the internal organisation of the European Union institutions, and most especially the largest, the Commission. The Directorates General are not organised pyramidally at their lower levels. Grade depends essentially on seniority, not on function. Even at grade A4 level there are a number of officials with no subordinates or managerial responsibilities, though since the reforms of the late 1980s there has been an increasing tendency to ensure the development of 'middle management' and to appoint A4 officials as heads of units with authority over more junior officials. Indeed, experience of this sort is now becoming seen as a prerequisite for promotion to the A3 grade. There is a more pyramidal structure to the senior levels of the Directorates General, though even this may be undermined by the interventions of 'staff' officials, whether from the *cabinets* or from the personal office of the Director General.

In the absence of strong pyramidal structures different hierarchies have space to establish themselves, such as the hierarchies of obligation, deference, and honour: 'honourable loyalties and alliances ... [with] their own precedence, reciprocities and proprieties' (McDonald, 1997, pp. 67–8). As one of McDonald's interviewees reported, 'It seems to be something to do with personal rank and honour, but precious little to do with management' (p. 64). 'Shame, naivety and stupidity' are ascribed to those who do not know how to work such a system (p. 68).

Parallel circuits of information, influence and action function rather readily in such a structure (Hooghe, forthcoming) This was a feature of the Commission's structure which Jacques Delors, utilising no doubt the knowledge gained in a not dissimilar structure in France, exploited to the full (Ross, 1995, p. 158). From a 'northern' perspective Charles Grant is categorical: 'His methods were often unorthodox, sometimes dubious and occasionally improper. By the end of his reign, Delors' personal system of command and control had begun to damage the Commission's internal organisation, sap the enthusiasm of its officials, and contribute to the tarnishing of its image' (1994, p. 91). Our interview evidence confirms this view. It is arguable that working in this way was the only possible means of ensuring the forward movement of very major projects.

> The Commission works only because it is able to put hierarchy aside ... The only way to make this thing work effectively within the deadlines that are fixed by politics is to do it fast and by relying on a certain key number of people ... You have to form allies in the cause of a particular advancement of the policy. (senior Commission official quoted in Hooghe, forthcoming).

Contacts, networks, deals, *pistonnage*, favours and fixes are all means of circumventing the rather rigid and relatively autonomous bureaucratic systems which are found, and accepted, to a greater or lesser degree, in many of the administrative systems from which EU staff come. And they are seen as useful.

To officials who understand, or learn to understand, such structures the Commission can seem open, exciting and 'democratic'. It may leave even relatively junior officials with a great deal of scope to make propositions, to 'do creative and exciting things' (McDonald, 1997, p. 65). To those to whom the norms of such a system are unfamiliar it can seem more like 'anarchy' (p. 63), a system without rules, without guidance, without a clear assignment of tasks. The unwritten understanding of what one can do oneself and what should be passed on, and to whom, acquired in different systems, comes to seem invalid, but since such understandings are by their very nature uncodified, unwritten, and deeply rooted in the culture within which they develop, there is no coherent or readily comprehensible alternative. The consequence can be that whether they come from structured or hierarchical backgrounds, Commission officials can experience their working environment as riven with internal politics, highly personalised, anarchic and insecure.

Process and procedure

In bureaucratic terms the European Union administration is a relatively young organisation. Its development has, moreover, coincided with extremely rapid development in office and information technology. It is perhaps not surprising that office processes and procedures are relatively undeveloped. Moreover, the working methods of the Commission are full of paradoxes: information is precious but leaks easily, and there is more openness to outsiders than, for example, in the notoriously uncommunicative British system. Working procedures and methods are rigid, juridical, hierarchical and compartmentalised, but can be circumvented and may provide scope for surprising levels of initiative and individual decision at low levels.

Within any bureaucratic organisation the nature of the flow of information is crucial to most operations. In most instances the bulk of the information is contained in paper documentation, although more and more written comments and exchanges now circulate electronically. The storage and accessibility of such papers reflects assumptions about the nature of bureaucratic work, and the relationships of those engaged in it. Some administrative systems maintain a registry at ministerial or divisional level to record, index and store files and papers so that files and documents are tracked, and can be retrieved, and the files show in an orderly way how any action was undertaken. Such systems imply a good deal of collegiality in working practices and facilitate public accountability for actions by enabling any colleague subsequently handling the file to see the state of play and allowing the formal history of a decision to be traced. Electronic communication may be overtaking and to some extent hollowing out such processes, but they remain the norm in some administrations.

Where such systems are not maintained, filing and document retention becomes a matter for the individual, or at most for a small group working together. File storage is much dispersed, and not necessarily orderly, and there are no general systems of classification or indexing. Hence it may be very difficult for any official to identify the existence of a particular file or to get to see it. The advantage of such systems is that the working files are closer to the individual official, and that the system is rapid and flexible. It is this latter system which prevails in the Commission.

This approach to documentation is underpinned by a number of features of the working practices of the Commission. Michelle Cini speaks of the 'dossier' approach. As she points out, the approach 'is an essentially juridical one, resting on the notion of individual responsibility for specific cases and on the technocratic expertise of officials who tend to become immersed in one small area of policy, becoming indeed experts in their own right' (Cini, 1996, p. 153). The physical as well as metaphorical possession of the file (*dossier*) becomes a key issue, especially where the issue with which the dossier is concerned is a new one. 'Questions such as where the files are kept ... are ... key political matters, affecting the relative importance and status of some DGs, directorates and units over others' (p. 154). Moreover, the different administrative cultures present among the Commission staff are marked in the way notes are written, and information conveyed or withheld. Submissions may be written in a classic French cartesian style or follow a more British sequential approach. French practice is that the official produces a *note de synthèse* in which he or she will bring together in a logical and orderly way the outcome of research and consultation. French dossiers tend in consequence to be rather slim. British, Irish and German officials put together proposals on the basis of check lists, of arguments for and against or of questions and answers with supporting evidence, so their dossiers are often thicker and more complete (Ziller, 1993, p. 465).

Information, and information flow, is thus a key resource in daily relationships within the Commission. Officials, or small groups of officials, develop their own expertise and may act as entrepreneurs or advocates for certain policies (see Chapter 7). What information is communicated and to whom becomes an important feature in an internal strategy, as well as being determined by cultural notions of loyalty and obligation. For officials used to a more centralised system of information storage and access, with a notion of it as a common good, to be shared quite widely amongst the team of insiders (though often jealously guarded against outsiders) and not kept as an individual resource, negotiating the more individualised tendencies of the Commission can be a nightmare; such officials can feel that their working lives are being blighted by an inability to tap into information flows or find out what is going on.

While information flows can act as a factor of exclusion for some officials, they can also be a device for incorporating colleagues or indeed useful external contacts within a personal or policy group, and for building support and alliances. The Commission has a well-deserved reputation for being an open organisation. The desk officer for any particular policy, engaged in formulating ideas or producing initial drafts, is likely to consult widely, not only with expert and consultative committees but also with member state officials (including those based in the permanent representations), with local government representatives, academics and firms, as well as with such interest groups and lobbyists as may present themselves. One of our informants said, 'Everybody leaks like mad. People show each other documents.'

A second paradox is that despite the proliferation of networks and alliances the one or two officials who alone will be fully *au fait* with the details of any proposal risk becoming so absorbed in the technicalities that they lose sight of the broader political context. This isolation is compounded by the hierarchical and compartmentalised rules which formally require officials to communicate only up and down the levels of their own unit, directorate and Directorate General. These formal rules stem in part from the notion of *délégation de signature*. Authority is vested with the College of Commissioners, and delegated downwards in a legally controlled manner. A signature on a document, whether an internal communication or a letter to an outsider, is a significant act, and the authority to undertake it is not widely dispersed. However, while Directors General may groan at the quantity of signatures they are daily required to append to the correspondence of their DG, they nevertheless find that it fulfils a useful purpose. The absence of a single political project within the College of Commissioners or even within many of the Directorates General means that EU policy is like an anthology of individual ideas, propositions and proposals. Directors General may have a clear view of what the policy line of their directorates should be, but they cannot necessarily be certain that their staff will stick closely to it. Personal signature is a method of monitoring the policy line that is emanating from their areas and maintaining its coherence.

Michelle Cini (1996, p. 152) highlights the iterative nature of vertical communication. Drafts may be returned from senior to junior for reworking several times. In practice a draft may have to pass through three or four hierarchical levels, but it is not likely that all the more senior officials will take a detailed interest in the subject. Cini points out that at the highest levels pressure of work may cause delays, but states that such vertical communication generally works quite well.

Horizontal consultation is also a formal requirement of the Commission's working practices. In straightforward cases this will involve the circulation of the dossier to other Directorates General and the Legal Services, in a procedure which mirrors the written procedure of the College of Commissioners, with failure to respond within a certain time limit implying consent. But, as Cini points out, this formal consultation happens only at a very late stage in the process of formulating proposals. Early consultation and preliminary clearance of drafts is much more difficult, because of the ruling that communication must pass through the vertical channels. Formally, therefore, an official who wishes to take the views of colleagues in six or seven other Directorates General is expected to pass a draft upwards to the Director General, who will pass it to the other Directors General, who will pass it downward to the appropriate member of their staff. Responses will take the same route in reverse. The process is very slow and rather discouraging. Incoming British officials, used to dispatching a draft around six or seven other ministries on their own initiative and getting it cleared within a day, are bemused by it. The same rules apply formally to contact with the Commissioner's *cabinets* which, if they are not alert and pro-active in circumventing them, risk discovering the detail of a proposal at a stage when their ability to influence it may be limited. Consequently, one informant told us, 'people tend to work on their own and not consult unless they have a friend whom they can trust not to rat on them to the Director General'.

Another consequence is that officials and *cabinet* staff find ways of circumventing the compartmentalisation and hierarchy. Telephone contact is a more informal and less traceable means of personal contact and consultation, although it is notable that until the early 1990s the EU did not have accurate and comprehensive staff telephone directories. In these circumstances personal contacts and networks become particularly crucial. As one interviewee said to us, a certain sense of relief is experienced when the person on the other end of the phone line turns out to share the same language or assumptions, so ease of communication may shape such interactions in particular directions. Amongst younger members of the staff in particular, electronic mail is now fulfilling the same functions. Drafts and comments can circulate quickly and discretely by this means. Describing the attempts of one Director General to maintain hierarchical control, one of our interviewees said 'it's actually fairly crazy. People leak and e-mail.'

Officials, then, may work in a fairly isolated and compartmentalised manner, or they may utilise personal networks and contacts to try to ensure that their work will enjoy a reasonably fair wind as it progresses through the system. Much of the time officials probably find that their working life is some combination of both aspects. Compartmentalisation and hierarchy can be an asset as well as a limitation. It encourages technical mastery, and may mean that relatively junior officials can take far-reaching decisions if their hard-pressed superiors fail to pay attention or even to read what they are signing. 'If you strip away the intervening levels which are just acting as a conduit quite junior people are taking decisions which are often not questioned', said one official.

The extent to which this is true may explain the perceptions noted above of the European Commission as a working environment with scope for creativity. It also helps to explain the permeability of the Commission and its openness to ideas and influence. If the Commission were less 'chaotic' it would be harder to influence, whether for member state governments or for outside groups.

Management: reports, reforms and resistance

Many of the features which we have noted about the organisation of the EU institutions are most evident in the Commission, where they pull in different directions. Its policy work is organised mainly on functional lines, but much of the management is still organised on the basis of process. The organisation of work is quite flexible, but the structure is strongly hierarchical. Many of the procedures are rigid, rule-based and bureaucratic, yet creative and imaginative officials constantly find ways around them. Many of these tensions and contradictions are the product of different national traditions which are not fully reconciled in a complex administrative culture.

In these difficult circumstances it is perhaps not surprising that the institutions have in general been markedly resistant to the impact of managerial ideas and priorities (Stevens and Stevens, 1997). This is in part a consequence of the range of expectations and presuppositions which the staff bring with them, the differing management styles of the cultures from which they come and the personalities of senior staff, but also of the structural factors discussed above. However, the esteem in which management is held and the efficiency and style in which it is carried out affect not merely the internal functioning of the institutions, but, given the role of leadership and management in ensuring the morale and self-confidence of all those involved in the enterprise, the ability of the institutions to achieve their purposes.

'Management' is a complex concept. Within the institutions 'the management' is often used to designate the upper echelons of the hierarchy, and the terms 'the management' and 'the hierarchy' are often used almost interchangeably, at least in French, although the connotations are far from identical (Bellier, 1994a, p. 257). As a concept and a function it may mean the 'rich and varied armoury of theories, concepts and techniques' which both facilitates the analysis of complex organisations and provides recipes for improving what they do. Within this broader concept, management at a mundane and practical level may be simply the organisation of those tasks which enable any institution to function effectively. Indeed Taylor, perhaps the most influential of all management theorists, claimed for his 'scientific' management principles that they would remedy 'inefficiency in almost all our daily acts' (Taylor, 1911, quoted in Pollitt, 1997, p. 329). Within any organisation it is the imparting of order and effectiveness to those daily acts which constitutes the function of management. Within the Commission, such management is still not seen as a task which is intellectually demanding or rewarding, and is consequently not held in much esteem. The culture change involved in the transition from an almost exclusive focus on the range of duties associated with policy formulation is a considerable one. One of our interviewees protested at the interest shown by his superior in controlling the process of the production of legislation. For him the content was all important, and whether it was produced smoothly and to a timetable was irrelevant. Another official drew a distinction between professional competence (*excellence professionnelle*) and management (*gestion*), and took the view that the former was more important than the latter for advancement at least to head of unit level (quoted in Bellier, 1994a, p. 261). At this practical level, management has two facets. The first is the organisation of the institution to achieve its purposes. This will involve decisions about the structure of the institution and of each individual section and sub-section of it, about the definition of procedures and the smooth performance of the tasks of the unit, and about the deployment of resources, as well as the motivation and leadership of the people who work within it. The second facet of management is ensuring that services are provided to those who need them. These services may be provided externally to clients of the institution, or they may be provided internally to the staff of the institution. It is thus a management function to ensure that a programme of humanitarian aid is appropriately designed and effectively delivered to meet the needs of those it aims to relieve, or equally to ensure that staff are recruited and paid, and, for example, that their waste-paper baskets are emptied.

While unable entirely to evade the necessity to undertake tasks related to the first facet of management – the organisation of the achievement of the purposes of the institution – many senior staff in the Commission have been very resistant to the notion that this was a function which required time, attention or priority, and it has not been accorded status or esteem. In consequence the tasks have often been done rather badly. For the Commission this was highlighted in the 1970s following the appointment by the Council of Ministers of a group of 'three wise men' (Edmund Dell, Robert Marjolin and Barend Biesheuvel) to consider the working of the institutions, and the more or less simultaneous appointment by the Commission of an Independent Review Group under Ambassador Dirk Spierenburg to examine the working processes of the Commission and to propose remedies.

The two reports were complementary, and their verdict was harsh. The Commission was not as effective as it should be. While to some extent this was due to a reluctance by the Council of Ministers to delegate responsibilities, it was also due to unwieldy, rigid structures within the Commission, to failures of administrative co-ordination, and to inadequate management. Amongst the consequences of these administrative failings was a degree of demotivation within the Commission which resulted in less satisfactory performance than might otherwise have occurred. Amongst the remedies proposed, the Three Wise Men suggested that to strengthen administrative co-ordination within the Commission the central services (personnel, budget and so on) should be brought together under the direct authority of the President of the Commission, who should be enabled to redeploy resources in accordance with policy priorities. Personnel management should be strengthened. The outcome should be a 'more compact and strongly-led Commission' (Biesheuvel, Dell and Marjolin, 1979, p. 70). These recommendations were accompanied by more detailed proposals within the Spierenburg Report. These addressed the role of the Directors General, who should take a prominent role in policy formulation, in internal co-ordination and in the active management of the Directorate General. The Report proposed, *inter alia,* a greatly increased emphasis on management qualities in senior staff (p. 24). Better staff discipline, greater staff mobility, clearer job descriptions, better staff reporting, and improved recruitment procedures were amongst the other reforms which the report advocated. The Council of Ministers rejected the proposals for a decrease in the number of Commissioners and a consequent slimming-down of the Commission. The College of Commissioners entrusted the follow-up of the detailed proposals for internal reform to a group under Commissioner Ortoli, accepting in particular the need to reconsider the number of basic administrative units within the Commission and the number of Directorates General. In due course the number of administrative units in the Commission was reduced from 339 to 291, and a number of other relatively minor reforms were implemented, but others ran into the sand or were opposed either by staff representatives or in the Council of Ministers, who would have had to agree increases in staff numbers or changes to the *statut*. Internal reform and management did not figure very highly in the Commission's priorities in a period which saw enlargement to include first Greece (1981), then Spain and Portugal (1986), a bitter dispute over the British contribution to the Community budget (not a good moment for the Commission to ask for more), and the beginning of the developments which were eventually to lead to the single market initiative.

Spierenburg's analysis is, however, generally acknowledged to have been remarkably clear-sighted and perceptive. The problems did not disappear; indeed the immense pressures placed upon the Commission by the expansion of its work, especially after the arrival of the Delors Commission in 1985, exacerbated some of them. In the member states Margaret Thatcher's government was actively pursuing new management strategies within the British administration, while in France in 1988 Prime Minister Rocard announced a programme of administrative modernisation. Change was in the air and Henning Christophersen, who held the portfolio for Personnel and Administration between 1985 and 1988, brought to the Commission an interest in administrative modernisation and reform. In Denmark, where he had been Minister for Finance and Deputy Prime Minister in the early 1980s, there had been government initiatives to simplify procedures and eliminate unnecessary legislation. From 1986 Christophersen was supported by Richard Hay as Director General, a British national with a Treasury background, who had served in the Commission since British accession.

Christophersen launched a high-profile modernisation programme which had three facets of particular importance. First, a
need for management training was recognised, and two-day seminars were organised for the entire staff of the Commission by
Directorate General, concentrating on team working, time management, good communications and related management themes.
At the same time an attitude survey of the staff was commissioned. Second, a 'screening' programme was undertaken. This
was intended to identify those areas of the Commission which
were severely underresourced and encourage the redeployment of
human resources into them. Linked to this was a crack-down on
the so-called 'mini-budgets' which had allowed the employment
of temporary staff financed from operational rather than administrative budget lines. The third strand of the modernisation was
the attempt to ensure the development of a 'middle management'
tier within the hierarchy, by appointing officials at grade A4 level
to posts as section heads (*chefs d'unité*) with management as well
as policy formulation roles. Hitherto no one below the rank of
A3 (Head of Division) had been expected, or even allowed, to
exercise any management responsibility.

In 1989 the portfolio for Personnel and Administration passed
to the Portuguese Commissioner, Antonio Cardoso e Cunha, and
in 1991 Richard Hay left the Commission and was replaced by a
Belgian Director General, Franz De Koster, who from 1993 to
1994 was supervised by a Belgian Commissioner, Karel van
Miert. These changes slowed the pace of modernisation, but they
did not reverse it. The problem of 'mini-budgets' had been identified and a start made on tackling it. The recruitment system,
especially at grades A7 and A8, had been opened up, through the
introduction from 1988 of more regular competitions, and, it was
hoped, fairer orientation (see Chapter 4). The Commission had
improved its own knowledge of how many staff were in fact
working for it and who they were. However, the extensive 1991
'screening' programme initiated by Hay (see above) had only a
minimal effect on the redistribution of resources, despite a report
which made detailed and well-judged diagnoses (Ross, 1995,
p. 164). A positive action plan for the improvement of equal
opportunities in the Commission was set up, and a special unit in
DG IX (Personnel and Administration) created to monitor and

promote action. The Commission's provisions for information technology were improved. The scope for reform was demonstrated when one new Director General made the management of his DG a major personal priority and brought to it experience from a multi-national company and a modernising national administration (Bellier, 1994a, p. 26).

These reforms were pursued during the early 1990s. As increasing importance was attached to the management of resources and personnel within DGs, specialised units for budgetary and administrative affairs began to appear. The 'middle management' role was further developed at A4 level, and more weight was given to management experience as a prerequisite for promotion to A3. The targets of the equal opportunities programmes were steadily raised, the use of information technology was encouraged and e-mail spread, especially among younger staff. Training programmes were improved, not just in the traditional areas of languages and information technology, but in management too (see Chapter 5).

Nevertheless, when Philippe Petit-Laurent, who was about to leave Brussels in 1994 for a Commission post elsewhere in the EU after acting allegedly as Jacques Delors' fixer in DG IX (Personnel), was asked to write a valedictory report on the state of the administration and its effectiveness, he found that many of the problems first identified by the Spierenburg Report fifteen years before had never been satisfactorily resolved, even if some progress had been made in fits and starts in the interim. However, a second report, completed in 1995, which concentrated on the 'image' of the Commission, suggested that the outgoing Delors Commission which commissioned it was still reluctant to believe that there was anything more fundamentally amiss.

The Santer Commission and administrative reform

The Santer Commission (1995–9) accorded a rather higher priority to administrative reform, though we shall see that their efforts fell short of what was required when faced with determined opposition from both management and the staff associations. Beginning with financial management in 1995, and extended in 1997 into personnel management and into questions of structure and organisation, from 1998 the Santer Commission was pursuing a wide programme of administrative reform for what they called *Tomorrow's Commission*. Each of the main programmes evolved over time, becoming more of an on-going process of change than a clearly defined programme of specific measures, but the reforms can be identified under their separate headings.

The programme of sound and efficient management (SEM 2000) was the first to be launched. Commissioner Liikanen who was responsible for the budget, and Commissioner Gradin, who was responsible for financial control, had the benefit of an incisive and critical analysis of the weaknesses in financial management prepared under the outgoing Commissioner. The first stage of SEM 2000, agreed in principle by the Commission in March 1995, was therefore ready for formal approval in June, and the second stage in November. These two stages concentrated on putting the Commission's own house in order. The third stage, which followed in 1997, focused on co-operation with the member states in the financial management of the major programmes accounting for 80–85 per cent of Community expenditure. Since these are resources which the member states administer themselves, stage three was drawn up under the aegis of the Personal Representatives' Group of the Council of Economic and Finance Ministers (ECOFIN). Exhibit 8.1 outlines the principal measures undertaken in all three stages.

The second component of the initiative is the programme for the modernisation of administration and personnel policy (MAP 2000: see Exhibit 8.2) which aims at decentralisation, simplification and rationalisation. Approved in principle by the Commission in April 1997, a programme of 25 main measures and 11 accompanying measures was endorsed in September of that year for implementation in 1998. The development of a second phase was put in hand immediately with the establishment of five groups of DGs to review the case for further reforms in cutting red tape, mobility, information technology, training and planning. However, in the face of opposition from many DGs, their adoption of many of the first stage measures was made voluntary, with the participation initially of only six DGs, and one key measure devolving to DGs the power to recruit auxiliary and

Exhibit 8.1   Sound and Efficient Management

Budgetary discipline

Since January 1996 (start of the budgetary procedure for 1997) the Commission has agreed priorities and set overall guidelines before DGs put in their bids. Directorates are also required to estimate financial and staffing implications whenever they put forward programme proposals.

Responsibilty of line managers

Staff and training have been provided to strengthen financial management to provide a 'counterweight' to the programme managers in each service. Following a competition for financial managers in 1997–98, six new staff were recruited at A5/A4 and 41 at A7/A6. However, central controls remain in place, so that responsibility is still shared and there are complaints of additional bureaucracy, which may partly be justified and partly be the natural consequence of creating a financial management 'counterweight'.

Central controls

Financial control advance checks on proposed expenditure have been reduced to a sample of 10 per cent, placing more reliance on the control exercised by line management. Internal audit visits all services every three to five years, and is moving towards greater emphasis on checking control systems rather than individual transactions.

Evaluation capacity

Evaluation is now an established function in most of the larger spending DGs, and there is a network of evaluators (Levy, 1996).

→

⟶

Evaluation of previous outcomes is not, however, used systematically to support decision-making.

Fraud prevention

The strengthening of OLAF (see Chapter 3) is the most significant development, but action has been taken under SEM 2000 to fraud-proof proposals in advance of implementation. For example, authorising officers are required to sign a declaration to the effect that they are not aware of any conflict of interest.

Reform of the Financial Regulation

A number of piecemeal reforms have been introduced since 1995, but it is recognised that if the primary focus of financial management and control is to be shifted from the central departments to line management, and the culture of the institutions transformed accordingly, the Financial Regulation will have to be completely rewritten.

Control of the Structural Funds

The Council Regulations governing structural fund expenditure, based on eligibility data sheets, were tightened up in 1997 and again in 1999.

Relations with the Court of Auditors

On the whole, the Commission now responds in a more constructive, less confrontational manner to the Court's comments, focusing on the substance of the observations rather than a narrow defence based on the rules and regulations.

Exhibit 8.2   MAP 2000: Modernisation of Administration and Personnel Policy

Internal organisation

DGs were given authority to implement reorganisation plans where no new management posts (A3/A4) were created, subject to the consent of their own Commissioner and following consultation with the Secretariat General and DG IX (Personnel). Simplified procedures involving only the President, the responsible Commissioner and the Commissioner for Personnel were also introduced for changes which would involve a net increase in management posts. The same simplified procedure was also to apply to appointments at the level of Adviser or Head of Unit (A3). These reforms were widely welcomed by all DGs.

Administrative budgets

Budget allocations for a wide range of administrative expenses, including the salaries of auxiliary and agency staff and detached national experts, travel and subsistence, entertainment, training, costs of meetings, and so on were all put into a single pot for each DG so that they would be able to transfer resources from one heading to another as required. Following union representations, the budget for training was ring-fenced within this allocation so that it could be increased but not reduced.

→

agency staff and detached national experts was deferred altogether. When the stage two measures were agreed at the end of 1998, they too were made voluntary, and in May 1999 when Steffen Smidt (Director General for Personnel and Administration) proposed that all DGs contribute to the preparation of a progress report for the new Commission, his request was refused and he was obliged to fall back on the preparation of an informal report based on discussions with 15 DGs. There was evidently still a serious gap between those managers who were

---

➡️

Personnel policies

Following strike action, most of the other more important personnel management reforms were deferred pending consideration of
the Williamson Report. Devolution of a number of more mechanical tasks associated with personnel management was agreed on a
voluntary basis, and B or C grade staff were transferred from the
Personnel DG to those DGs who volunteered for these tasks (about
one per DG). One of the measures which was made voluntary following a separate strike of messengers (*huissiers*) was the transfer
of their posts and management of their work from the Personnel
DG to the DGs they served, but in the event this change (affecting
approximately 200 staff) has become virtually universal.

Cost awareness measures

DGs were to be made aware of the costs of services still supplied
and paid for centrally, such as interpretation at meetings, translations, furniture and office supplies, postage, telephone and Internet
costs.

Information technology

Improvements in computer programmes for managing administrative tasks and greater use of e-mail is being encouraged for inter-
departmental consultation. The Personnel DG calculated that it had
saved 150 million pages of A4 paper by distributing a great deal of
administrative guidance and information on the Commission's
internal computer network.

---

willing to embrace management reform and those who were not,
but acceptance was growing. Whereas originally only six DGs
volunteered to take part in all the measures under stage one, by
December 1998 this number had risen to 27.

Many of these MAP 2000 reforms are relatively mechanical
and low-key, typical of the unrewarding management burdens
which a substantial group of senior managers was reluctant to
assume. However, their voluntary implementation by a growing
number of managers may have helped to prepare the ground for

the eventual adoption of more fundamental reforms which had to
be taken off the agenda in the face of determined opposition from
the unions.

In addition to SEM 2000 and MAP 2000 the Commission also
looked at another major screening programme (DECODE) as
well as the pension regime and the terms of the *statut* itself. At
the end of March 1998, following the advice of external consultants, the Commission had decided to bring all its reform plans
together under the umbrella of a broad programme called
'Tomorrow's Commission'. The plan was to pass the document to
the unions on 15 April for consultation, and to all staff on 16
April. There would be a first discussion by the full Commission
on 20 May and with the unions on 25 June. When the unions
were informed of these plans at the beginning of April they immediately made public their opposition both to any discussion by
the College of Commissioners before they had had their say, and
to the proposal being made available to all staff for their comments. What was already becoming a tense situation was further
inflamed when another report (the Caston Report) was leaked.
This made radical proposals for reform of the *statut* touching on
many sensitive areas of personnel management and career development. The management had made no attempt to prepare staff
for the reforms which seemed to be in prospect, and in calling for
strike action the unions were able to exploit widespread anxiety
and a sense that the management were being high-handed and
knuckling under to member states whose sole concern was to
reduce expenditure.

The strike, which had been wisely planned for Friday 30 April,
the day before a public holiday weekend, attracted very wide support from staff including some in management positions, and
many who did not actually take strike action chose to take a day's
leave. The Commission's offices were virtually deserted. As a
result Commissioner Liikanen felt obliged to disown the Caston
Report. Instead a group with equal staff and management
representation under David Williamson, who had recently
retired as Secretary General, was established to review a very
wide range of personnel issues. The Santer Commission left the
report which resulted (in November 1999) on the table for their
successors to handle. On recruitment it recommended more

regular competitions and a reduction in the size of the reserve lists to make success in the competition more nearly equivalent to a right to appointment. It did not propose the abolition of the A, B, C and D staff categories, but did envisage reversing the policy adopted by the Commission in 1996 and allowing the possibility of unlimited contracts for temporary staff. It advocated more training and greater mobility both within the Commission and between the Commission and the other EU institutions and member states.

The Williamson Group was successful in reopening the dialogue with the staff associations, but it seems to have conceded some ground to them (inevitably, no doubt, in a group which had equal representation from both sides): for example, there is no agreement on a better system of staff reporting, or on compulsory mobility for staff in certain sensitive posts (such as dealing with contracts). The Group formally rejected any notion of performance-related pay, preferring to rely on non-financial incentives such as promotion.

Meanwhile the third element in the Santer Commission's reform programme, *Designing Tomorrow's Commission* (DECODE), a review by the Inspectorate-General of the Commission's organisation and operation, appeared on 7 July 1999. Based on a very thorough 'screening' exercise of every DG and service, carried out between November 1997 and May 1999, it presented an authoritative analysis of the staffing, organisation and operation of the Commission at the close of the Santer Commission, followed by an extensive set of recommendations on structures, on activities and resources, and on working methods.

The Santer Commission undoubtedly took administrative reform more seriously than any of its predecessors. It made some real progress with financial management both internally and in tightening up the control of expenditure in programmes shared with the member states. By transferring tasks from the central departments to line managers it made a start in making the latter more fully responsible both for financial management and for personnel management. The planned modernisation of personnel management suffered a serious setback in 1998, partly as a result of poor communication with both unions and management, exacerbated by a lack of clear leadership from the top; when this led to strike action, the initiative was largely surrendered. Finally, of course, the crisis which overtook the Commission in March 1999 not only focused public attention on the mismanagement, corruption and favouritism which had been going on over many years, but prevented the discredited Commission from carrying its reform programmes forward. However, many of the reform proposals were picked up in the White Paper produced by Neil Kinnock on 1 March 2000. Chapter 9 reviews the means of co-ordination both within and among the EU institutions, and Chapter 10 turns to relations between the political and administrative levels. Both these factors have an important bearing on what can be achieved.

Conflict and Co-ordination

The complexity of the institutions and processes of policy-making and decision-making within the European Union (see Chapter 1) means that considerable co-ordination of the work undertaken is essential to the effectiveness of the whole structure. It is required within all the institutions, but particularly within the European Commission's administrative services since they are most prone to compartmentalisation and fragmentation, as the discussion of structure and hierarchy in Chapter 8 has shown. Such characteristics are much less prevalent in the other institutions, except to a limited extent in the European Parliament, since the range of functions undertaken is smaller. Co-ordination is also required between the various institutions, whose mutual relationships have to be managed in order to ensure a reasonably smooth flow of business. This chapter starts from the picture of fragmentation revealed in the previous chapters. In addition to underlying patterns of diverse linguistic, cultural, national and political allegiances and sympathies that condition personal and professional relationships within the bureaucratic structures, there are more institutionalised causes for conflict. In this respect the institutions of the European Union are not immune to internal politics such as may be found in any organisation even though these are shaped in particular ways by the unique and still undefined nature of the entity within which they operate (Radaelli, 1999, p. 38). This chapter looks at some of the forms which this type of conflict takes. It then discusses the formal structures through which such conflict is handled. The following chapter then turns to the nature, role and methods and impact of political control in seeking to impart direction and coherence to the administration.

Conflict

Laura Cram (1994) has rightly characterised the European Commission as a 'multi-organisation', but the epithet can equally be applied to the structures of the European Union as a whole. Conflict within and between the institutions occurs for a number of reasons, many of them structural (Page, 1997, p. 135). As Liesbet Hooghe's work on the development of cohesion policy in the European Commission showed, 'Actors were often motivated by a number of issues: more or less supranational control, more or less Europe of the Regions, the prevalence of one DG over another, the need for a mobilising idea for the Commission versus running things efficiently, public intervention versus free market, and career concerns' (Hooghe, 1997, p. 95). The complexity and intermingling of motives must not be forgotten, but for clarity it may be appropriate to distinguish a number of factors. These include:

- territorial conflict for influence and control within policy areas;
- ideological conflict over the policy approaches and solutions;
- conflict over the distribution of scarce resources.

'Turf wars'

The division of any organisation into functional units necessarily produces entities that have a vested interest in maintaining their own existence and beyond that in defending the scope of their responsibilities, and trying to acquire additional tasks and leadership within policy areas, especially if they are high-profile areas which bring increased influence or prestige. Moreover, the nature of the structural relationships within the Commission, which can trace their roots back to continental traditions of legally based administrative autonomy, has tended to encourage a possessive territorialism over particular policy areas. The need for senior officials to maintain managerial control over their directorates by procedural means, since they cannot take for granted a generalised loyalty, has enhanced this.

This relative isolation in organisational terms has been compounded by physical separation. As we have seen, the Berlaymont building, often represented as the home of the Commission, was never large enough to house all the Commission services, and since it was taken out of service on 1 January 1992 the Directorates General have become even more geographically scattered, reinforcing their tendency to act as if they were autonomous ministries. Moreover, location both reflects and influences status. For example, the relatively weak status of the Environment DG is reflected in its banishment, at that time, to the end of the metro line at Beaulieu (Peterson and Bomberg, 1999, p. 192). Romano Prodi's directive that the Commissioners of the College over which he presides are to have their offices located with those of their services, while intended to increase the Commissioner's direct contact with the services and decrease the role of his or her *cabinet*, may well exacerbate this tendency.

'Turf wars' arise because Directors General enjoy a good deal of status and prestige, and can be ambitious to increase this. This goal may be shared by their staff. In the Competition DG (IV), Cini and McGowan detected the aims of the extension of the DG's remit, enhancement of its prestige and the acquisition of wider powers (Cini and McGowan, 1998, p. 52). Moreover, many issues inherently fall across the boundaries of any division of responsibilities, especially when, as in the Commission, these divisions are determined by a combination of administrative rationality and political expediency. Food policy is such an area. It is bitterly contested between the Agriculture DG (VI) and the Trade DG (III) (Peterson and Bomberg, 1999, pp. 87 and 141). Agriculture may yet lose out if the plethora of scandals over food safety in the late 1990s leads to the creation of a European Food Safety Agency. Similarly, the formulation of a policy on energy use as a response to climate change involved as many as ten separate DGs, with the Environment DG (XI) fighting to hold on to it (Peterson and Bomberg 1999, p. 191).

Such competition can be exemplified by the history which Laura Cram (1997, p. 76) recounts of the development of European Community policy on Information and Communications Technology during the 1960s and 1970s, as various Directorates General struggled to impose their approach upon the sector. DG

III (then the Industrial Affairs DG) was taking initiatives to support mergers and concentration in this sector, in part to establish its position, for it was then a relatively new DG having been formed only in 1967. At the same time DG XII, responsible for research and development was staking its position through, for example, taking the initiative to issue in 1973 'a major blueprint for action in the ICT field' (Cram, 1997, p. 76). Meanwhile DG XIII, which eventually became the DG for Information Market and Innovation, was transforming itself from its previous role before the merger of the Communities in 1968 as the Euratom DG for the dissemination of information. In 1986 it was merged with an Information and Communications Technology task force that had been set up within DG III in 1983 to become a new DG XIII for Telecommunications, Information Industry and Innovation. But even within this one unit, Cram comments, 'relations are not always harmonious with each Directorate seeking a higher profile for its work' (1997, p. 78).

A not dissimilar picture can be traced in the Directorates responsible for policy related to the structural funds and cohesion (Hooghe, 1996). Between 1986 and 1992 the Directorate General for Regional Policy (DG XVI) fought (eventually successfully) to maintain and develop its position and role in the face of a rival which had been developed out of a small task force hived off from the Directorate General and attached to his personal office by the Commission President, Jacques Delors, at a time when he was anxious to ensure that the achievement of the single market was matched by compensating efforts in the areas of social and regional solidarity. In 1986 he established the task force as a separate Directorate General (DG XXII), with responsibility for the co-ordination of the structural funds and the integration of a regional dimension into policy across the Commission. While initially this seemed a real threat to DG XVI, in fact DG XXII was heavily dependent on the personal backing of the President, whose attention was by the end of the 1980s diverted to the negotiation of the Maastricht Treaty and the achievement of economic and monetary union, and moreover was answerable to a Commissioner (Henning Christopherson) who was not greatly interested in this area of his remit. Its mission required it to interfere in the policy of almost every other DG in the interests of the reduction of disparities between regions, an interference which was likely to be rejected, so its survival was always likely to be precarious. Moreover, it was faced with a longer-established DG with an active and ambitious Director General who was vigorously and successfully concerned with assuring his DG's leading position in cohesion policy, even above his concern for the substantive political goal of facilitating greater cohesion (Hooghe, 1996, p. 107). In 1992, DG XXII was abolished and by this time DG XVI had secured the leading position which it had been seeking.

Conflicting ideologies

As important as the struggle for position and leadership within policy areas is conflict over the approaches which policy should adopt. Directorates General are influenced by the nature of the sector in which they work, and by the beliefs, understandings and interpretations which they encounter in the various national government ministries, in the agencies, interest groups, lobbyists, academics and researchers, journalists and others who make up the 'community' which is concerned with and active in the policy area. These policy networks are crucial in the emergence of particular policy options and in the settling of policy details (Peterson and Bomberg, 1999, p. 21).

Liesbet Hooghe's detailed work has shown that even the 'sense of commitment to the European ideal' (Page, 1997, p. 136; Bulmer, 1998, p. 375), which is widely shared by top officials, may take contending forms (Hooghe, 1999b, p. 346). As a group, 'top officials of the Commission are slightly inclined to supranationalism' – that is, the promotion by the European Union of ever-closer union – 'but one out of four supports an intergovernmental design ... perceiv[ing] European integration as a means of reducing transaction costs of international co-operation' (Hooghe, 1999b, p. 346). But this in itself provides no guidance as to the precise course of action which will further that. During the period of the 1980s relaunch this general sense of commitment was supplemented by a more precise belief: that the way to move closer to the European ideal was through the rapid completion of the internal market. At least in the Directorates General most closely concerned, such as DG III (the Internal

Market), the positive value attached to the programme was important in inculcating a sense of common purpose: 'at long last and for the first time in many years ... [the staff] knew exactly what was expected of them' (Bulmer, 1998, p. 381).

Even this sense of common purpose, however, has not resolved disagreements over appropriate policy. For example, while the internal market was an early and central aim of the European Community, so too was economic and social cohesion. It was embedded within agricultural policy and underlay the 1970s development of regional policy and subsequently of the structural funds. Jacques Delors was intellectually (and, for a time, in practice) as firmly attached to it as to the internal market policy, though his attempts to impose the discourse of solidarity and cohesion throughout the Commission's senior officials foundered amongst their divergent national and ideological attitudes (Hooghe, 1999b). Indeed, within the Commission the two aims are far from reconciled. In the 1990s most of the top officials of the Commission felt that capitalism should be regulated (Hooghe, 1999b, p. 365), seeing the role of the Commission as to defend a 'conviction that European capitalist societies both were and ought to be different' (Ross, 1995, p. 46), with a particular model of culture and society which is neither 'Anglo-Saxon' nor Japanese and is shared across most of continental Western Europe. On the other hand, '20 per cent oppose the majority view' (Hooghe, 1999b, p. 365), and officials in the competition or internal market areas may see it as their mission to combat 'public interventionism, protectionism and overregulation' (interview with Commission official quoted by Hooghe, 1997, p. 97).

The situation is further complicated by the existence of a European Union environmental policy with which both the internal market and the cohesion policies are often in conflict; indeed, which they often contradict (Peterson and Bomberg, 1999, p. 199). The Environment DG has close contacts with various organisations lobbying for the protection of the environment. It 'is often depicted as a green colony' (Pollack, 1997b, p. 580), or even as being composed of 'ecological freaks' (DG XI official quoted by Cini in Cini, 1997, p. 78). In seeking to impose restrictions on trading or industrial activities in the name of environmental protection it finds itself confronting the very different views of the DGs for trade, and for the internal market and industry. Similar problems arise in relation to the environmental impact of agriculture. In a number of areas, including, for example, the proposals developed in the early 1990s for a carbon tax to restrain energy use and restrict its contribution to global warming, '[its] proposals are often watered down in negotiations with other DGs' (Pollack, 1997, p. 580). Similarly, the day to day work of the Competition DG leads it to be suspicious both of big business, whose anti-trust activities it polices, and of the interventionist tendencies of the nation states, which it acts to curb. But when those tendencies are directed towards transport, the sphere of the Transport DG (VII), they may be more indulgently treated, as the continued acquiescence in subsidies to national airlines suggests.

In a number of fields it scarcely seems too exaggerated to claim, in relation to the determination of policy (as did one official), 'quite simply, it's war' (Commission official interviewed by McLaughlin cited by Greenwood, 1997, p. 42). This 'war' can have deleterious effects. In the case of the regulation of media ownership (see Exhibit 9.1) the competition for power involved the various DGs concerned fighting to control the Commission's policy and their own policy areas, even though this meant that the extent of internal conflict in the institution was readily perceptible, and proved so paralysing that no proposal which could command the support of the full College of Commissioners could emerge (Radaelli, 1999, pp. 136–44). Battles occur over policy territory and over policy approaches and priorities. They also arise over resources.

Conflict for resources

Two types of resources exist around which conflict can occur. They are physical resources and intangible resources, especially salience and status. Staffing and money are the two crucial physical resources. In much of the Commission, though not the Council of Ministers and the Parliament, staff resources are inadequate. However, the tight limitations on the administrative budget and the rigidities of staff management inhibit conflict around the deployment of staffing. What results is not so much conflict as demoralisation and ineffectiveness.

Exhibit 9.1   Conflicting coalitions in the EU media ownership policy process

	Single market	*Pluralism*	*Convergence*
Pivotal actor	DG XV	European Parliament	DG XIII
Other members	■ Some German Länder ■ France (recently, for tactical reasons) ■ Commissioner for Competition Policy	■ DG X ■ Regions ■ Public interest groups ■ International Federation of Journalists ■ Public broadcasters ■ French Minister of Culture	■ DG III ■ DG IV ■ DG I ■ ECJ ■ OECD ■ WTO ■ USA ■ Large media groups ■ German federal government ■ UK
Approach to EU policy	■ Harmonisation of domestic laws around a single European rule ■ Audience share as main policy instrument	■ Limits to liberalisation ■ Opt-out for public broadcasters ■ Defence of pluralism and cultural diversity	■ Liberalisation ■ Policy convergence ■ Use of EU competition policy

WTO = World Trade Organisation.
Source: Radaelli (1999), p. 141.

Within national administrations conflicts around money are endemic and institutionalised. Ministries of finance struggle to contain spending. Spending ministries battle with each other and with the Ministry of Finance for the resources required to maintain, improve or extend the services they offer or to innovate. However, within the EU much of the conflict takes place between the two arms of the budgetary authority, the Council of Ministers and the Parliament. The constant battles between these two bodies led to the conclusion in 1988, 1993 and 1999 of multi-annual inter-institutional agreements on the programme for the evolution of Community finances. These have reduced, but not eliminated, conflict over appropriations between the institutions. As we have seen, the budgets of the institutions other than the Commission by and large finance only their own running costs, and these have in general been sufficient to supply their needs, though attempts were made in the early 1990s by the Parliament's Committee on budgets to keep staff numbers down (Corbett, Jacobs and Shackleton, 1995, p. 184). Within the Commission conflict over resourcing exists. As the Budget DG (XIX) starts each year to draw up the draft budget, 'inevitably it is subject to pressures from many sides: from other DGs, which forward their own estimates and bids, from national representatives ... from the EP... and from sectional interests' (Nugent, 1999, p. 402). Nevertheless in comparison with national governments conflict is limited not only by the multi-annual framework which sets the outlines of the appropriations for the medium term, but also because:

- much of the cost of new regulatory policy falls outside the EU budget;
- the financing of the Common Agricultural Policy, still the largest element of expenditure – even though it now accounts for only about half total annual expenditure – allows little discretion once the policy framework has been set, as it is designated as compulsory expenditure (of which category it constitutes almost all);
- conflict can be exported from the Commission to the Council of Ministers and the Parliament, since it is through the transactions between these three that the final shape of the distribution of funds is determined.

The distribution of other, less tangible resources also gives rise to conflict. For any individual, or group of individuals, wishing to advance actions which they favour (for whatever reasons), one crucial resource, as those analysts who study agenda setting in public policy remind us, is salience. The matter needs to be sufficiently visible and important for other groups and bodies, all of them with crowded programmes, to afford it time and attention.

Inclusion on the Commission's annual work programme, or at least incorporation into the flow of business going to the Commission, is vital for any project which requires a Commission decision. The importance of timing is recognised in the official Commission procedures which require the documentation attached to measures which the Commission is being asked to approve to include an annexe showing the proposed timetable. George Ross's vivid portrait of Jacques Delors in operation makes clear the frenetic pace at which he and the team around him worked and points out (Ross, 1995, p. 77) that, for example, in 1991 the Commission had eleven major priorities in its work programme. Each Presidency of the Council of Ministers has its own priorities which the Council Secretariat will endeavour to respect. And the Parliament also has its own timetable and agenda, which it sets with considerable autonomy. The Parliament's programme is set by the conference of the Presidents, consisting of the chairmen of the Parliament and the political groups.

The second crucial intangible resource around which conflict may occur is status and reputation. This is so hard to measure that discussion of it can only be based on subjective perception. With that warning, it can be suggested that amongst the factors which influence this within the Commission are the following.

- Responsibility for one of the EU's common policies. This assists the Agriculture and Competition Directorates General, for example.
- Longevity. This factor is clearly linked with the first, but tends to work against areas such as environment, consumer policy and enterprise. The exception is perhaps the RELEX group of directorates, which retains a relatively high status despite organisational change. This may, however, be linked to the next factor.
- The standing and reputation of the Commissioner(s) with responsibility in the area. Some areas are seen as more central than others, and while national interests in these matters may vary, the manoeuvring around the distribution of portfolios as new Commissions are formed illustrates the weight attached to such considerations.

- Useful and influential friends. Alliances shift and vary, but an 'advocacy coalition' centred on a particular Directorate General may be a powerful resource if its constituent parts are influential, or possess valuable expertise. Thus the Agriculture Directorate General used the farm lobby to consolidate its position in the 1960s and 1970s. As the political pressure for reform grew and it found itself under challenge from other coalitions, it remained strong, partly because it could draw on other resources such as longevity, but also because it could call upon a powerful ally, the government of France. Both political expediency and nationality (the Agriculture DG (VI) from 1958 to 1999 always had a French director general and, despite the appointment of a Spanish head in 1999, remains a very 'French' DG) have created a strong and valuable link (Peterson and Bomberg, 1999, pp. 140–1). Agriculture is a somewhat special case. But so, in some senses, are all the other cases. Part of the policy formulation task in most cases is the creation of supportive networks and coalitions both inside and outside the institution. Officials in the Commission want wherever possible to have links to large, co-ordinated groups representing all the interests involved in a particular policy area (Greenwood, 1997, p. 19).

Fragmentation and the more institutionalised conflict described above make co-ordination of activities all the more crucial. It is to the mechanics of co-ordination that this chapter now turns.

Co-ordination and management

In the interests of clarity two types of co-ordination may be distinguished although they are in practice intimately linked. Structural co-ordination is provided for by methods such as the establishment of horizontal units whose role is to draw together aspects of the functioning of the whole organisation, to provide common services, and to ensure a measure of smooth operation and uniformity. Prescribed procedures and regular patterns of meetings also produce structural co-ordination. It is essentially concerned with the *form* of the processes within an organisation. Political co-ordination, on the other hand, relates to *content* and is concerned, for instance, to mitigate or resolve the ideological differences and to impose direction and coherence upon the policy-making process. The role of political direction and co-ordination is an important feature of all bureaucratic systems, and is considered in the next chapter.

Structural co-ordination: horizontal Directorates General

The European Parliament, the Council of Ministers and the Commission all have horizontal Directorates General with the task of providing structural co-ordination. In the Parliament these are DG V (personnel, budget and finance) and DG VI (administration). In the Council Secretariat these functions are provided by DGA (personnel and administration). The Personnel and Administration (formerly IX), Budget (formerly XIX) and Financial Control (formerly XX) DGs are the horizontal Directorates General in the Commission. In the smaller institutions the work of these DGs is largely routine. In the Commission they must be consulted if any policy proposal being elaborated will have implications either for staffing and the Commission's organisation (Personnel and Administration), or for expenditure (Budget and Financial Control). In bringing together, as we have seen, the various bids and estimates of the services the budget DGs act as 'horizontal controllers' (Laffan, 1997, p. 88) within their institutions. The Personnel and Administration DGs are responsible for the organisation and operation of their institutions. Their ability to affect the detailed activities of the institutions has been limited, although some horizontal policies have emerged. One example is equal opportunities policy for the Commission and, more recently, the Council Secretariat.

Within the Commission the Personnel and Administration DG (IX) has some formal status. For example, it alone may respond to the Court of Auditors on questions relating to the actual organisation and operation of the Commission. But in a fragmented culture and in the face of more powerful bodies such as the *cabinet* of the President of the Commission, and the Secretariat General, it has been able to do little more than provide services. Influencing the way that the administration operated and facilitating institution-wide policies for change and development were beyond its reach, and largely beyond its aspirations. In the late 1980s the combination of British Director General Richard Hay and Danish Commissioner Henning Christopherson did attempt to improve management (see Chapter 8). Commissioner Erkki Liikanen, whose energetic incumbency from 1995 to 1999 entailed responsibilities for two horizontal Directorates General, Financial Control and Personnel and Administration, also succeeded in introducing initiatives to improve both financial procedures (SEM 2000) and management (MAP 2000: see Chapter 8). The former seems to have made better progress than the latter, but neither the Personnel and Administration DG's initiatives, nor its disciplinary policies, were sufficiently effective to avert the 1999 crisis. The public emphasis on reform under Commission Vice-President Neil Kinnock is, however, likely to enhance the Personnel and Administration DG's profile.

Structural co-ordination: the core services

In addition to the horizontal Directorates General there are important horizontal services with a role in co-ordination. These are the Legal Service, the Press and Communication Service, and the Secretariat General, which together 'provide an administrative, political, and public relations power base of enormous skill and intellectual ability' (Spence, 1994b, p. 110). All Commission legislation, as well as, for example, decisions in competition cases, must pass via the Legal Service of the Commission. The responsibilities of the Legal Service include ensuring that Community legislation is in accordance with the Treaties and does not conflict with or contradict itself, and to advise the Commission on its powers. This gives it a more than technical role, for it means that the Legal Service must take a line on what the legal basis of any proposed action is and what measures may be used to implement it. 'A favourable opinion from the Legal Service on ... [a] text ... is a clear political advantage' (Spence, 1997b, p. 114). The Press and Communication Service is the point at which the Commission presents a co-ordinated public relations face to the outside world (see Chapter 7).

In all the institutions the Secretariat General is by far the most important instrument of co-ordination in both the policy and organisational areas. The Secretary General is in each case the most senior administrator. In the major institutions the incumbents have mostly enjoyed long periods in office, so that hierarchical seniority is allied to long experience. Since 1958 the Parliament has had five, and in 2000 the post was occupied by Julian Priestley. The Council of Ministers has been served by only five Secretaries General since the establishment of the Coal and Steel Community in 1952. The first incumbent served an unbroken 21-year term from 1952 through the creation of the new Communities in 1958, the merger of the institutions, and the first enlargement, retiring in 1973. This 'element of continuity' is particularly important in an institution where the ministers who constitute the Council membership 'can change from month to month' (Hayes-Renshaw and Wallace, 1997, p. 107) and the Presidency rotates every six months. However, the nature of the office changed markedly in September 1999 when Javier Solana was appointed as not only the fifth Secretary General, but also as the EU's High Representative for Common Foreign and Security Policy. As a consequence, much of the work of co-ordination has since fallen upon the new Deputy Secretary General, Pierre de Boissieu.

The Commission has had four Secretaries General since 1958: from 1958 to 1987 Emile Noël, a formerly very senior French official, David Williamson from 1987 to 1997; Carlo Trojan, a Dutchman of mixed Dutch-Italian parentage, from 1998 to 2000 and then the Irishman David O'Sullivan. The Secretariat General of the Commission was modelled on the French *Secretariat Général du Gouvernement* (Spence, 1997b, p. 110), itself strongly influenced by the example of the British Cabinet Secretariat.

All the Secretariats General have, formally, a number of key functions:

- they organise the flow of papers and business through the decision-making bodies; the Conference of Presidents in the Parliament the European Council, the Council of Ministers and COREPER for the Council Secretariat, and the College of Commissioners;

- they act as the 'memory' of the decision-making body, classifying and registering documents, recording the outcomes of the decision-making process, maintaining precedents, procedures and archives;
- they oversee the publication of decisions and their application;
- they centralise relationships with other bodies, both the other institutions of the Union and outside bodies and individuals.

These formal functions provide the framework for a very much wider and very crucial range of activities. The Secretary General is the principal adviser on procedural and legal matters to the chair of the decision-making body (the legal service of the Commission reports to the Secretary General). In all the institutions, advice to the chair can and does go well beyond the merely technical to include both technical and strategic advice (Hayes-Renshaw and Wallace, 1997, p. 170). Similarly, the involvement of the Secretary General and his staff in drafting conclusions and minutes can be very important. Council Secretary General Niels Ersbøll 'was widely regarded as having played a central role in the drafting of the Luxembourg and Dutch documents which formed the basis of what became the TEU' (Hayes-Renshaw and Wallace, 1997, p. 109).

The nature and implications of secretariat work have been discussed above (see Chapter 7). Here the crucial point is that the Secretariats General have overall responsibility for the co-ordination and organisation of the administrative work of their institutions. Since the work of the Commission is particularly complex, it may serve as an example. The Code of Conduct on internal co-ordination issued in 1999 explicitly allocates the General Secretariat substantial responsibilities for co-ordination.

First, the Secretariat General, working with the office of the President of the Commission, plans the Commission's annual work programme. This is the central statement of policy priorities for the year, reviewed, in principle, every six months. No longer a matter of the collation of the projects of the various Directorates General, 'an annual opening of filing cabinets' (Ross, 1995, pp. 267–8, note 22), the programme now involves a 'top-down' process to identify political priorities, on the basis of which the detailed work can be done by the administration.

At a more detailed level Directorate C of the Secretariat General 'keeps a constant watch over ongoing activities, thereby contributing to the more efficient organisation and planning of work before the weekly Commission meetings. Planning is ... an effective internal coordination tool' (Secretariat).

Second, the Secretariat General monitors and co-ordinates the work of all the Directorates General. This work takes various forms. First, the Secretariat General sets the general working procedures. In the Commission there is a manual of working procedures, introduced initially in the mid-1970s when the then Secretary General, Emile Noël, recognised that the 'muddling through' that might have suited a small and rather more cohesive staff was inadequate for a larger, nine-nation body. These procedures contain, for example, formal requirements for the signature of all the DGs concerned to be appended to any proposal submitted to the College of Commissioners.

In addition the Secretariat General attempts to fulfil the requirement laid upon it by the Code of Conduct to 'develop a culture of co-operation' through inter-service groups and committees. These were first set up in the late 1980s, in the words of the then Secretary General quoted by David Spence, 'not to mould a technically perfect administration but one which will work' (1997b, p. 111). At administrative level the groups of Commissioners which were set up with the advent of the Santer Commission to improve co-ordination in certain vital areas were underpinned by networks of Directors General created in anticipation of the new Commission. They covered the internal market, industry and competitivity; environment, cohesion and Trans-European Networks; justice and home affairs; and external relations. The last three, arguably those in the most sensitive areas, are chaired by the Secretariat General. These networks have worked with varying degrees of success, though the External Relations group seems to have contributed to the lessening of the fierce rivalries between the Commissioners and Directorates General amongst whom responsibility for the area has been divided (Peterson, 1999b, p. 57). In addition, some task forces (see below) report to the Secretariat General.

The Commission Secretary General also plays a more political co-ordination role through his chairmanship of key weekly meetings. These are the Monday meeting of the heads of the Commissioners' personal offices (*chefs de cabinet*), which prepares the ground for the Wednesday meeting of the College, and the weekly meeting of Directors General.

Co-ordination is involved in the Commission Secretariat's General role in serving as the focus for the Commission's relations with the other institutions of the European Union. The Deputy Secretary General, in particular, plays a crucial role in ensuring continuity and coherence in the Commission's relationship with COREPER.

In all the institutions a final major aspect of the co-ordination work of the Secretariats General is responsibility for the organisation and management of the administrative services of the institution. This means that the Secretary General will be involved in appointments at the most senior levels. Even more importantly, this means that major reorganisation and management initiatives – in the Commission, the 'screening' process of the early 1990s and the 'Designing Tomorrow's Commission' exercise of 1998 – have been based in the Secretariat General.

Verdicts on the role and power of the Secretaries General vary. The task is an enormous one and the Secretariat General 'can only concentrate on things when it becomes a political priority that there be co-ordination ... it would be very much resented if they leaned too heavily on others' (senior official quoted by Hooghe, forthcoming). In the Commission the considerable influence and authority of Emile Noël is undisputed. If he rarely spoke at the meetings of the College of Commissioners, he had great influence behind the scenes, as a 'fixer', a brilliant drafter of formulae and minutes (Cockfield, 1997) in which '*mots justes* jostled with subjunctives' (Jenkins, 1997) and an important voice on internal appointments and promotions (Middlemas, 1995, p. 222), not least when the administration had to be reconfigured to accommodate the 1973 enlargement. Williamson is portrayed as having adopted a more low-key and cautious approach (Cini, 1996, p. 104), 'efficient, self-effacing and conscientious' (Grant, 1994, p. 102), but he is recognised as having introduced better co-ordination and information-sharing and better monitoring of progress in the Commission's priority areas. He was, however, deeply implicated in the methods by which Commission President

Jacques Delors operated (see below), working closely with him (Grant, 1994, p. 102; Ross, 1995, pp. 67 and 74; Endo, 1999, pp. 43–7). He thus attracts criticism for not having 'stood up to' Delors (Grant, 1994, p. 102), although for a former British civil servant loyalty to a political master would be axiomatic. His deputy, Carlo Trojan, succeeded him. He, too, had worked within the Delors system and perhaps perpetuated some of that approach: 'He likes to 'get around' rules and now he is at the top of a system to enforce them' (senior official quoted by Peterson and Bomberg, 1999, p. 43). In the context of the crisis of 1999 this trait perhaps exacerbated the criticism that he encountered as the official ultimately responsible for the performance of the Commission administration and in the middle of 2000 he was replaced by Prodi's former *chef de cabinet*, David O'Sullivan.

Structural co-ordination: task forces

From time to time issues arise within the Commission that do not fit easily or smoothly within the administrative framework. Policy and action in these areas has normally been consigned to a task force, composed of a few key officials. These task forces may be the forerunners of substantive Directorates General, they may be disbanded when the issue is resolved, or they may be retained in one form or another. Thus the task force set up to handle the first enlargement of the Community became a Directorate within the External Relations Directorate General and subsequently handled the Mediterranean enlargements of the 1980s. A new task force under the Commissioner for External Political Relations handled the 1995 enlargement. The task force set up for the 1996 inter-governmental conference continued as the Amsterdam Follow-up Unit.

Structural co-ordination: inter-service consultation

The hierarchy and compartmentalisation of the DGs described in Chapter 8 militates against inter-service co-ordination. However, the collegiate nature of the Commission makes co-ordination indispensable. This is recognised by the operating procedures issued by the Secretariat General. These insist on the principle that 'the administration is 'one and indivisible': although each sector is the responsibility of a different Member, the administration as a whole serves the Commission as a whole'. The weekly meeting of Directors General allows a general overview to be taken of the progress of work and the extent to which disputes or failures of co-ordination are causing specific projects to be hindered or delayed. The 1999 code of conduct emphasises the role of the 'competent' or 'lead department' for genuine and substantive co-ordination, and the procedures require the lead department to initiate 'a constructive dialogue' and that on-going consultation is to continue as work progresses. More formally, if decisions are to be taken through the College's written procedures, then all the DGs concerned must sign their approval. If the matter is to be debated in the Commission then a summary of the views of the DGs concerned must be provided. 'This applies especially to documents which have been discussed by any of the networks of Directors-General.' This formal requirement is underpinned by the existence of formal inter-service groups, set up with the authorisation of the Secretariat General which keeps a record of them. In 1993 there were 63 groups. The existence of these formal procedures and structures is a way of trying to induce consultative and co-operative behaviour within a structure whose organisations, norms and culture do not naturally encourage it.

A description of the formal provisions for inter-service consultation certainly 'understate[s] the extent of co-ordination through more informal means' (Spence, 1997b, p. 114) including the telephone and electronic mail. But this has to be set against the hierarchical structures which discourage horizontal consultation at relatively junior levels, against the depth and extent of the conflicts described above, against the weakness of the management process and against the problems posed by fragmentation at all levels, up to and including the level of political direction. The existence of official frameworks and requirements, combined with the need and willingness of Commission officials to consult widely at the policy formulation stage with national and interest group representatives, ensures that internal consultation and co-ordination probably occurs more widely in the

Commission's services than in many (not all) of the national administrations of the member states; but it remains an area of concern and difficulty.

Inter-institutional relations

The structure of the European Union makes inter-institutional relations an area where clear and rigorous procedures are particularly important. In the broadest sense the history of the institutional development of the European Union, and indeed of the process of the integration of the European Union, is the history of the changing relationships between the various institutions. Even on a more day to day basis conflict and disputes range 'from disagreements between officials to full-scale court cases' (Hayes-Renshaw and Wallace, 1997, p. 198). This study is concerned with the administrative underpinnings of those relationships. The EU policy-making process is indisputably cumbersome, and liable in consequence to be slow. 'Processes would be extremely inefficient if the Commission, the Council and the European Parliament did not co-operate with each other on legislative planning and timetabling' (Nugent, 1999, p. 381). Moreover, there is the tricky issue of the external representation of the European Union. Co-ordination in that area between Commission and Council is crucial and operating procedures and practices have to be found which accommodate the fluidity, complexity and tensions involved (Hayes-Renshaw and Wallace, 1997, pp. 190–1). Moreover, because the staff of all the institutions are subject to the Staff Regulations and the Financial Regulation, there must be co-operation among the institutions over any changes in management which require these regulations to be amended.

As with internal co-ordination in the Commission, there are two levels at which inter-institutional administrative co-ordination takes place. There is first of all a formal political and official level. 'Trialogue' meetings take place monthly between the Presidents of the Council of Ministers, the Commission and the Parliament. At the official level formal co-ordination between the three bodies takes place principally at the level of the officials of the Secretariats General charged with relationships with the other bodies. The 'trialogue' meetings are prepared by these officials.

These meetings are underpinned at official level by the 'Neunreither group' (named after the official who established it), which brings together officials of the Commission, Council of Ministers, Parliament, Economic and Social Committee and Committee of the Regions (Corbett, Jacobs and Shackleton 1995, p. 220). Initially intended to manage the Single European Act procedures smoothly, it now co-ordinates the management of the business for Parliamentary plenary agendas, and acts to ensure the smooth running of the co-decision procedures in the legislative process (Westlake, 1994, p. 245).

As we have already seen, the role of the Secretariats General is crucial. This is the channel through which papers pass from the Commission to the Council, and it is the Secretariat General of the Council which provides the consistent staff work to ensure the prioritising and programming of business through the Council procedures (Hayes-Renshaw and Wallace, 1997, p. 186). Officials from the Secretariat General of the Commission and the Commission legal service attend throughout all meetings of the Council of Ministers and of COREPER, while officials from the DG concerned support the relevant Commissioner at Council of Ministers' meetings for specific items of business. Provided they are sufficiently senior – it is customary for officials who speak at COREPER meetings to be at least of Director level (for COREPER II) or head of unit level (for COREPER I) – they take part, under the leadership of the Secretariat General, in COREPER meetings for the business of their DG. However, these mechanisms are not strictly reciprocal, reflecting the fact that the Commission is neither subject nor accountable to the Council, and their role is not so much co-ordination as to allow the Commission to act as a protagonist in the legislative stage of policy-making. Similarly, officials of the DGs and the Secretariat General attend Parliamentary sessions to support the Commissioner and to ensure liaison with the Parliament.

Internally within the Commission it is the Secretariat General that ensures that each DG has an official responsible for the smooth handling of the Parliamentary aspects of the DG's business, and arranges monthly meetings of this group. There is also a Parliamentary Affairs group of representatives of the Commissioners' *cabinets* which meets weekly.

Below this formal and structural level of co-ordination there is a second informal level of consultation and co-ordination. 'The continuous round of soundings, telephone calls, lunches, lobbying opportunities and pre-meetings that are such a part of EU life in Brussels, Strasbourg, Luxembourg and national capitals' (Nugent, 1999, p. 352) facilitates inter-institutional co-operation as much as, if not more than, it does consultation between officials and interest groups, lobbies, experts and other actors in the various 'policy Communities'. The structures of co-ordination provide the procedures and the framework for policy co-ordination and management, but are not in themselves sufficient to ensure that clear, coherent, prioritised policy in fact emerges; for that, political will and direction are required. It is to the relationships between the administrative services and the sources of political direction that the next chapter turns.

Chapter 10

Political-administrative Relationships

The discussion of administration in the previous chapters has, at least implicitly, treated it as a distinct activity, separate from other functions, and especially political ones. Herbert Simon (1957) assigned the notion that administration is distinct from politics the status of a proverb rather than a theory, but argues that it is functional for both politicians and administrators. Administrators enjoy a protected sphere in which they may take action under the cover of technicality and neutrality, while politicians also enjoy a certain freedom to distance themselves from technical constraints (McSwite, 1997, p. 149). More recently theorists have sought to extend the scope of their ideas in the search for explanations that extend across from economic to political and social spheres. Thus notions have developed to explain a number of relationships in terms of 'principal-agent' theory. The notion of separation implies that it is possible for the political principal to delegate to the administrative agent, without incurring excessive transaction costs or losing control, a wide sphere of support for decision-making (for example, handling the paperwork and procedures and devising appropriate wordings) and for designing and executing implementation.

Expressed too starkly this dichotomy is of course misleading: technical solutions to societal problems can never be entirely insulated from their ideological and political context. Even in the Whitehall model of political-administrative relations, which comes close to the Weberian model, it is apparent that 'the achievement of the ideal that civil servants should be just 'managers' or just concerned with 'means' is fraught with difficulty' (Hill, 1997b, p. 122).

217

Indeed, the European Union is often condemned for a too great insulation of precisely this kind. The notion of 'a Europe run by technocrats' gained a good deal of currency during the debates on the ratification of the Maastricht Treaty and on the Treaty of Amsterdam, when matters were further complicated by the discussion of the role to be played in the management of the common currency by 'independent' bodies such as the national central banks and the European Central Bank (Radaelli, 1999, pp. 1–3). It is certainly possible to argue that knowledge and expertise have become key resources in the decision-making process. It may be that political decisions influenced by competing pressures and public opinion may appear far from rational, but there are in fact competing rationalities. Economists, or natural scientists, have wide areas of disagreement amongst themselves. And in the end 'politics has to do with values, and no algorithm will ever provide an answer to the puzzle of confronting values' (Radaelli, 1999, p. 7).

In the context of the European Union, attention to the question of whether a distinction between politics and administration can be discerned and, if so, what the relationship between the two may be points towards some very specific (if sometimes puzzling) features, which are crucial both to an understanding of the nature of the EU bureaucracy, and more broadly of the European Union itself. This chapter considers first the problems of identifying the site and level of the political and administrative components, turns then to the constraints upon political controls over the administration, and finally looks at the mechanisms by which some political direction is imposed upon the activities of the administration.

Who is a politician? Who is an administrator?

Those accustomed to systems based broadly upon British models are likely to find this question banal. Politicians within such governance systems are usually elected persons owing their allegiance to a political party and the leader of that party. Administrators, on the other hand, are permanent, or at least likely to spend a substantial period of time as administrators; they may work under the direction of several different politicians. The two career paths are well separated, and there may be rather little social contact between the two groups. Officials have no programme of their own, and their own political opinions are irrelevant, or unknown or both.

Such responses are of course caricatures, but it is also worth remembering that even in a much more nuanced form they do not apply to many of the national systems within the European Union. First, ministers are not necessarily members of the legislature (indeed, in France the two roles may not legally be combined) and may not even be members of a political party. Several recent Prime Ministers of Italy have not had a party political background. In some countries (for example, the Netherlands), subject expertise may be as important as political allegiance in the appointment of ministers. In many countries coalition governments require the negotiation of a governmental programme in which substantial parts of the objectives of the individual parties may be diluted or abandoned. Administrators may be much less reticent than in the United Kingdom about their political opinions, though subject to a legal framework intended to constrain the impact of those views on working practices. Senior posts may be filled on the basis of these opinions, and there may be, to a greater or lesser extent, a spoils system so that while officials will not necessarily lose their status and salary as an official, a change in the identity of the political direction may result in substantial changes of post-holder at senior levels. In addition officials, especially senior officials, may well be active within political parties, may go on to careers as elected politicians or as ministers, and may return thence to official duties. There is in consequence much less social distance between the two groups who, in some countries (for example, France), tend to form part of a fairly small, tight and interconnected elite. The boundaries between 'politics' and 'administration' can thus fall in different places across the countries of the EU, and the relationships between the two spheres can take on quite varied forms.

Within the European Union itself the situation is very complex. This is perhaps unsurprising, since in some respects that complexity is intentional. Jean Monnet's design for the European Coal and Steel Community gave a High Authority of appointed expert administrators responsibility for both determining and implementing the policies of the ECSC. He saw it as a sphere that required expertise, not involving the conflicts of values that are the core of politics, or at least, no conflicts that could not be solved by the application of knowledge and expertise and the involvement in the search for the right answers of interest groups with relevant experience. Informed rational people presented with a problem will come to agree upon the solution. In other words, the objective was the 'depoliticisation' of the issues. It was the insistence of Belgium and the Netherlands that resulted in the creation of a Council of Ministers, and even then it is sometimes argued that this was conceived more as an upper chamber of a legislature, along the lines of the German Federal *Bundesrat,* which represents the constituent states of the Federation, rather than as a source of political oversight and control.

The scope and range of the activities envisaged for the European Economic Community at its creation made the notion of a depoliticised Community untenable. In the European Union the Council consequently exercises substantial political as well as legislative power, through its ability to set guidelines for the Commission, and through its role as a budgetary authority, so it is much more than a purely legislative body. One helpful way of thinking about its role has been developed through the application of 'principal-agent' theory to its relationship to the Commission (Pollack, 1997a). As the principal it delegates to its agent certain tasks, in the same way that a national government will delegate tasks to bureaucratic departments and agencies. These tasks include those of formulating the details of the legislation that will further the policies upon which the Council is broadly agreed; of policing compliance with and infringements of this legislation by member states and in some cases by companies; and, Hix (1999, p. 51) argues, of acting as the 'umbrella' under which national governments can shelter from the consequences of decisions they feel are necessary but know will be unpopular.

The Council of Ministers is not, however, a government comparable to those of European nation states. It has no platform and successive presidencies each bring their own programmes to their brief tenure of office. Hence it has minimal unity of purpose, while its capacity to undertake the detailed management either of policy formulation or policy implementation is limited both by the nature of its formal powers and by sheer practicalities. Principals need to have ways of ensuring that agents act in their interests, and the national governments can use their right to nominate Commissioners (see Chapter 1), working groups of the Council, the operation of the mixed (comitology) committees and the power to take the Commission to the Court (Pollack, 1997a, p. 113), as well as the ultimate weapon of renouncing or revising the treaties, and thereby threatening the Commission's survival. However, as long as they choose to work within the treaty framework of the EU the relationship is a relatively equal one, involving a substantial degree of mutual dependency and power-sharing as well as delegation.

For this reason, however, it is also somewhat misleading to describe the Commission as a government or a cabinet, even if it possesses many of the same features (Hix, 1999, p. 32). The College of Commissioners does share political leadership and the Treaty of Amsterdam has reinforced the powers of the President of the Commission, through the assignment of a general duty of political leadership. Many, but by no means all, Commissioners have previously been career politicians, although there has always been a quite deliberate policy on the part of the member states to ensure that the full range of the mainstream parties of national politics in Europe are represented in the College. It is hence a 'grand coalition'. The political status of the Commissioners appears to be confirmed by their monopoly of policy initiation. Under the direction of a determined President policy options can be pushed forward, and the Commission has a substantial role in driving the policy agenda, especially at the lowest level of policy decisions.

However, the College of Commissioners not only acts as the agent of the member states in a number of roles but also retains some of the 'depoliticised' technocratic features of the original High Authority of the ECSC with its essentially administrative role. The method of appointment of the Members of the College prior to the Amsterdam Treaty provisions suggests interesting parallels with the senior 'political' officials appointed by decision of the French Council of Ministers, or found at the top of German federal ministries. Indeed, the French government in two successive Commissions appointed as their two Commissioners a pairing of an ex-minister (Cresson, then Barnier) and an administrator (de Silguy, then Lamy). Their role of policy initiation looks not too dissimilar to the role of policy formulation played by such officials. The College of Commissioners is thus not a government in the sense in which that term is used in national states, but neither are its members solely the equivalents of British Permanent Secretaries or French *Hauts Fonctionnaires*. They are slightly uneasily balanced between the administrators of the Directorates General and the political impulsion of the European Council. Perhaps they are really rather like eighteenth-century British ministers. They are both politicians and administrators, but without pre-existing or ideologically defined loyalties to each other, subject to a degree of democratic accountability to the Parliament, but subject also to ultimate political direction and consent, not of the monarch but of the Council of Ministers and the European Council. Administrative theory tends to suggest that the position of the College of Commissioners is pre-bureaucratic and hence pre-modern.

The nature of political-administrative relationships within the administrative services is consequently a complex one. In some of the institutions the administration is small and has responsibilities primarily for the smooth operation of the institution. But within and between the Council of Ministers and the Commission the position is more complex. Equally, in the Commission the ambiguity of the role of the College of Commissioners makes the political oversight of their services a particularly difficult problem.

The degree of political control, whether by the College of Commissioners or, more remotely, the Council of Ministers, varies with different roles and tasks performed by officials (see Chapter 7). Where the task is one of developing a general policy programme and approach, the role of the *cabinets* (discussed below) is crucial. The secretariat role involves less policy input by officials. Nevertheless, many of the senior staff of the Council of Ministers are importantly involved in the processes of drafting and in the giving of advice on ways of achieving political solutions to difficulties. The enlargement of the scope of the Council Secretariat to incorporate the staff of the Schengen secretariat and those working on the Common Foreign and Security Policy is certainly increasing the areas where the staff will need political sensitivity and direction. In areas where there is a broadly agreed common ideological approach, political control can concentrate upon the performance of officials in handling the practical measures required. Examples include the implementation of the Single Market, or the development of economic and monetary union.

Some tasks, however, while equally highly technical (Matlary, 1997, p. 275) and demanding a sound mastery of procedures and policy instruments, arise from the more technocratic mode of policy formulation. The officials have no monopoly of agenda-setting in such circumstances, but they have an important influence upon it, and there is markedly more scope for them to define the problem and undertake the choice of the solution (Cram, 1994, p. 211; Peterson and Sharp, 1998, pp. 218–19). Examples of such policy-making include the development of policy for industrial support and information technology, and indeed technology policy in general. Political control in such areas is difficult. In technology policy, for example, assessing and directing policy requires the political leadership to make judgements on complex and rapidly changing technical issues. In some circumstances control is exercised, but frequently 'policy networks of like minded actors, often organised and led by the Commission, have considerable scope to set the agenda and influence outcomes' (Peterson and Sharp, 1998, p. 219). In general, as Laura Cram has demonstrated, the Commission and its staff have 'proved to be remarkably adaptable' (Cram, 1997, p. 57).

Constraints on political control

Power is both shared and delegated between the Council of Ministers and the Commission. It is also both shared and delegated between the College of Commissioners and their administrative services. This sharing of power in the institutions of the European Union constitutes one of the ways in which the mechanisms of political delegation and control and the inter-dependency between politicians and officials differ within the European Union from those found in most nation states. In the EU both the Council of Ministers and the Commission have an interest in monitoring and controlling the work that officials undertake. But there are features which render the operation of political control distinctive and difficult. These difficulties have contributed to the problems of management, accountability and legitimacy which the EU administration has faced.

The first feature is the lack of overall and unified political purpose by which administrative action can be oriented and guided. The inter-governmental levels of the EU and the Commission itself are grand coalitions, and consequently have no overarching ideological or partisan vision. While ever-closer union is enshrined as a primary goal by the EU constitution, and the treaties also specify subsidiary aims such as balanced and harmonious development, these objectives are all relatively content-free. The Commission is enjoined to serve the Community interest, but the definition of the nature of that interest is more procedural than political: it may not go very much further than ensuring that the voices of all the parties to the Union are heard. The political steers given by the European Council (such as those on the nature and speed of eastward enlargement) provide general guidance, but do not provide a yardstick against which any and every policy development can be assessed. Although the experience of an active political, indeed ministerial, career is the rationale for the appointment of many Commissioners, they do not come into the College with a specific political mandate or authority. As Page emphasises (1997, p. 119), 'Commissioners are not commissioned by anyone to do anything in particular.' The College of Commissioners, especially under determined leadership, can, does, and, it may be argued (Peterson, 1999b), should programme action and order priorities. It must, however, do so in ways that will avoid stirring up too much opposition and controversy, since this is likely to result not, as would be the case in nation states, in the installation of an alternative body with a different programme, but in a backlash against the whole process of Union. Its annual work programme is hence an exercise in prioritising and scheduling, not informed by a shared underlying ideology. Indeed, where such an ideology is an important factor in determining priorities, it is underplayed or concealed. It is readily accepted that Jacques Delors' determination and priorities were sustained by a personal commitment to a social democratic ideology with strong Catholic roots. It was not, however, on account of this commitment that he was appointed as President of the Commission, and too overt and specific a statement of an intention to 'organise Europe' (Ross, 1995) along such lines would have been unacceptable to some of his colleagues within the College as well as exacerbating conflict with the member states, against whose veto major progress could not be made. As a consequence other, more subterranean (and ultimately rather damaging) means were used to further his project within the administration.

Moreover, the Delors period was in a number of respects exceptional. His successor, lacking Delors' power base and legitimacy, eschewing some of his methods and leading a larger and less cohesive College, presided over a period where the Commission no longer enjoyed the legitimacy conferred by the energetic pursuit of one or two relatively clear-cut and consensual 'big ideas'. The issues for the second half of the 1990s – unemployment, eastward enlargement, bovine spongiform encephalopathy (BSE), even EMU – were in many cases largely beyond the competence of the EU, or intractable, or largely procedural, or controversial and widely unpopular, or some combination of these. Administrative performance cannot, for these reasons, readily be checked against an overall statement of purpose. The EU's administrative services consequently lack one of the most pervasive, if invisible, instruments of political control available to governments: the self-control that civil servants exercise by measuring their actions and ideas against the likely response of the political leader, which can be forecast from known ideological preference (Page, 1997, p. 160).

A second factor which renders political control difficult operates at the level of the College of Commissioners whose ability to exert political control over the administration is weakened by its structure. Directorates General do bear some resemblance to national ministries, and the similarities seem to be increasing (Conlon, 1998). However, individual members of the College may be assigned a portfolio covering several DGs, and conversely at times a single DG may answer to more than one Commissioner (Cini, 1996, p. 110). The complexity that resulted from this was one of the motives behind the reform of Commission structures initiated when Romano Prodi and his colleagues took office. The restructuring of DGs and revision of the portfolios that then took place was intended in part to give the Commissioners a more cohesive domain to manage and to encourage a sense of responsibility and accountability for the area under their purview.

The relationship of Commissioners to DGs and Directors General is not a straightforward one. Budgetary constraints, the rigidity of personnel procedures and behavioural conventions mean that Commissioners and their staff have little capacity or incentive to intervene in the operation of the DGs. Directors General frequently, though often unsuccessfully, discourage direct contact between desk officers and the Commissioner. As in the United Kingdom, though not in France or Germany, a Commissioner is usually obliged to work with the incumbent Director General, whose appointment will have resulted from a complex combination of organisational, political and nationality considerations. On rare occasions and with difficulty it has proved possible to displace senior officials with whom the Commissioner cannot work. The Greek Commissioner in the 1993–95 Commission succeeded in shifting three senior officials, all of them German, from his DG by redeployment or early retirement, but it took most of his term of office to achieve this (Page, 1997, p. 153). The departures of Dieter Frisch and Sigismundo Crespo by resignation in 1993, and of Peter Wilmott under the provisions of Article 50 of the Staff Regulations in 1995, have all been ascribed (Page, 1997, p. 152; *The Economist*, 4 November 1995) to the malevolence of the Commissioners concerned and their *cabinets*. Conversely, Jacques Delors and his *cabinet* attached a good deal of importance to the positioning of 'their' people as the heads of key DGs, particularly in the face of a College of Commissioners in his second term with whom, by and large, he had little rapport and sympathy (Ross, 1995, p. 15ff).

The Commissioners' obligation to work with the incumbent Director General is not counterbalanced, as it is in the United Kingdom, by an ethos of ultimate loyalty to the political orientation of the government of the day. The consequence has sometimes been an attempt to separate the roles of the two rather strictly in principle, along the lines of the separation between policy and administration that the discourse of the French administration has long sought to assert. This separation assumed a particular salience when the operation of parts of the services was shown to be seriously deficient. Neither the European Parliament nor the Committee of Independent Experts was prepared to endorse this view, and the Code of Conduct for Commissioners and their departments specified that the relationship should be based on 'loyalty and trust'. The thrust of the Committee of Independent Experts' argument was to urge Commissioners to accept both full political and managerial responsibility for their departments, while recognising that the longevity in office of some Directors General meant that they risked becoming 'excessively dominant in their spheres'. The Committee observed that:

> In the aftermath of the outgoing Commission's resignation, one commissioner was heard to complain that commissioners cannot in practice supervise the actions of their directorates-general. That complaint must be taken seriously. However, the Committee does not know of any legal, or other, provision which prohibits a commissioner from instructing or supervising their departments, provided that the competence to do so is clearly defined. (European Parliament, 1999b, para. 7.9.7).

Control by committees

One of the principal ways through which the member state governments, whether individually or acting collectively as the Council of Ministers, manage political control of the Commission and its services is through the use of Joint Committees. This relationship is a delicate and controversial one. The committees in which both institutions are involved fall into three categories: first, there are the expert groups which the Commission establishes and in which national civil servants take part, theoretically in their personal capacity as experts, and possibly alongside others such as academics, researchers, or pressure group representatives. The process is a two-way one, although the Commission largely controls its nature and timing. The Commission officials are seeking to engage the other participants in the policy making process, to receive from them early warning of likely hazards ahead, and to implicate them in the outcome.

The national officials, while in no way committing their governments, seek to influence the developing measures and shape them in ways that the governments they serve will find acceptable. The political-administrative relationships at work at this level are complex, and a matter of influence rather than control, since there is a great deal of mutual dependency (Kassim and Wright, 1991, p. 834; Rometsch and Wessels, 1996).

Second, there are those legislative Council Committees which Commission representatives attend as parties to the negotiating process. These are the crucial, and much neglected because very secretive, working groups that underpin the Council of Ministers, in which, it is estimated (Hayes-Renshaw and Wallace, 1997, p. 98), 70 per cent of EU legislation is 'decided'. Another estimate calculates that 'around 90 per cent of the final texts of legislation and action are decided at that level' (Rometsch and Wessels, 1997, p. 226). These groups, of which on any working day some 20 may be in session, involving perhaps 500–600 national officials, will be attended by the Commission officials concerned with the proposals under consideration, usually a representative from the DG involved, and one from the Secretariat General. At this level, too, the political-administrative relationships are complex and balanced. On the one hand, the Commission officials will have a mastery of the details of the proposal, at least as wide an overview as any of the national representatives, and the formal constitutional position as the sole proposer of any text. On the other hand, without the consent of the member states the measure will not proceed, and each member state will be seeking to protect and advance its own interests, so coalitions have to be built (Cini, 1997, p. 170; Rometsch and Wessels, 1997, p. 226). The networks that build up at this stage involve the Commission officials, the Council Secretariat, members of the Permanent Representation staffs, and desk officers and their superiors in the national capitals.

The third type of committee in which both the Council and the Commission are involved is the so-called 'comitology' committees which operate under Council decision 1999/468/EC of June 1999. These are committees which are essentially concerned with the implementation and execution of policy, and here the political-administrative balance may seem more clear cut, and the structures more amenable to an interpretation in terms of principal-agent relationships. They derive from the fact that the Commission has rather limited powers to take executive decisions under the Treaty. However, as the scope of EU action has grown, legislation has often been accompanied by the delegation of management or implementation powers, but in ways which preserve a substantial role for the member states in the procedures. The extent of political control which the member states can exercise over administrative decisions through these procedures depends upon the type of committee and the specific procedure, out of the three specified in the 1999 Council decision, involved. All the Committees are chaired by a Commission official. The complex structure provides a framework in which relatively expert and technical discussions are possible and may take place in a fairly 'non-hierarchical' way. Nevertheless, in situations of conflict or difficulty the formal structures can provide a channel which allows for the exercise of political control and, although 'preposterously arcane', they do allow national political influence 'to be wielded even in the "deepest" recesses' (Peterson and Bomberg, 1999, p. 43). The crisis provoked by the announcement of a possible link between BSE and human disease illustrates the point. The 'previously obscure' (Peterson and Bomberg, 1999, p. 126) Standing Committee of Veterinary Experts was made responsible for decisions on the consequent ban on exports of British beef, and national governments saw it as an arena for the exercise of national political pressure (Hix, 1999, p. 45; Peterson and Bomberg, 1999, p. 126).

The European Parliament's members are generally fiercely critical of the operation of this system: they see it not as an instance of normal political control of an administrative agent, but as a usurpation of Parliamentary rights to scrutinise the executive, and, since the procedures do not allow them a role, as a diminution of their right to be involved in legislative decisions. This controversy also serves to highlight the ambiguity and the complexity of the political-administrative relationships within which the EU's services operate.

Control by counterstaffs: the role of the cabinets

Some of the weaknesses of political control are counterbalanced by official or unofficial mechanisms to allow for the assertion of political control over the operation of the administrative hierarchy. The first of these is the attachment to each Commissioner of a personal staff – a *cabinet* – with the triple task of supervising, co-ordinating and on occasion substituting for the administrators. Structures which group a personal staff around the political head of an administrative department, as an extension and emanation of the political control of the leader, have been a feature of the systems of political-administrative organisation in several of the original member states of the European Union – Belgium, France and Italy – since the nineteenth century. In those systems the crucial reasons for their development were the needs of the political head of department for support, co-ordination and control. Support was required for leaders in their task of devising policies which conformed to their personal political stance, especially in the absence of strongly developed political party machinery for the initial formulation of policy. The administrative services were populated by staff who were immovable, who guarded their autonomy jealously, and whose criteria for policy formulation might not be those of their head; all the more so if they had been appointed, as was frequently the case before the advent of open competitive recruitment, by the patronage of predecessors of a different political orientation. Co-ordination was an administrative necessity in ministries and departments that lacked an internal mechanism for ensuring overall coherence. In some administrative systems (such as the British system, and including the Directorates General of the Commission and the Council Secretariat), the internal structure is a perfect pyramid with a single person – Permanent Secretary, Director General – at its apex. But in many systems government departments are confederations of divisions, with no single hierarchical superior. In such systems the minister's personal staff ensure the co-ordination and uniformity of the departmental output. Moreover, at all stages – both formulation and execution – the minister may need a personal staff to ensure that priorities are respected, action taken and progress chased.

When the European Economic Community was created in 1958 it was apparent that its Commission would be a larger and much more wide-ranging body than the High Authority of the European Coal and Steel Community, and its need for co-ordination and cohesion correspondingly greater. The first Secretary General of the Commission, Emile Noël, suggested that Commissioners should have a personal private office, based on the French model to which he was accustomed, 'as a general aid to both horizontal and vertical co-ordination' (Cini, 1996, p. 112). Commission President Walter Hallstein was wary, fearing – with good reason as it turned out – the impact of such a system, and he insisted that the size of the offices should be tightly limited. The French term for such a staff – *cabinet* – is almost invariably used, untranslated, to designate these offices.

Despite President Hallstein's initial caution, the *cabinets* grew rapidly: while initially comprising only two administrative staff (four for the President) plus a secretary and typist allocated to each Commissioner, they provided for little more than basic personal assistance, but they expanded rapidly (until the advent of the Prodi Commission: see below) as they acquired functions closely analogous to those of their counterparts in the national systems. In 1968 each had on average four staff, but by 1974 their average size had grown to 14, of whom some six were A grade officials. This remained throughout the 1990s, and continues to be, the number of A grade officials financed from the Commission budget in each *cabinet*. Officials from within the Commission are technically seconded to the Commissioner's *cabinet*, while those from outside but on the Commission's payroll are placed on temporary contracts. In the mid-1990s and until 1999, on average a further three administrative grade officials were attached to each *cabinet* on secondment from other organisations, such as the national government of the Commissioner's country of origin (Cini, 1996, p. 113).

The composition of the *cabinet* staff has been in general a matter for the personal choice of the Commissioner, subject to a number of unwritten conventions. It was, at least until the advent of the Prodi Commission, accepted that this is an area where nationality was likely to play an important role. The Commissioner's choice, whilst personal, has not in every case been entirely free, since national governments, who nominate Commissioners, have a crucial interest in the composition of the *cabinets*, so the mechanisms for its exercise vary 'dramatically' (Cini, 1996, p. 112). The Commissioner will have views about the profile of the staff members he or she is looking for, but at the same time the Permanent Representation, in liaison with the national central government department responsible for the co-ordination of relations with the EU (in the UK the Cabinet Office, in France the *Secrétariat général du Comité interministériel pour les questions de coopération économique européenne* (SGCI), for example), will have a list of suitable candidates to propose. As Ella Ritchie points out (Ritchie, 1992, pp. 103–4), in the early years of the EEC the very close contact that took place between the Commission and the member states' governments was 'co-ordinated and supervised' (Donnelly and Ritchie, 1997, p. 44) by the *cabinets* rather than channelled through the Permanent Representations which were not established until some years after the creation of the EEC. As a consequence *cabinets* came to be regarded, as they still are, as a privileged point of access both for the national government of that member state and, in some cases, for the officials of that nationality within the Commission.

The *cabinet* staff have tended to reflect a balance between persons with national experience and those with a background of service in the Commission. One of Page's informants estimated the balance as approximately two-thirds Commission insiders and one-third outsiders (1997, p. 127). Outsiders frequently included seconded national officials, but staff have come from other sources: 'academics, party officials and managers from the private sector' (Cini, 1996, p. 112). In the *cabinet* which Neil Kinnock set up in 1995 there were five ex-Commission career officials, and the other senior officials were from the British civil service, while in Sir Leon Brittan's *cabinet* four officials had come from the British civil service and three from Commission backgrounds. All *cabinets* traditionally contained at least one 'foreigner' with a nationality different from that of the Commissioner: the deputy head of the *cabinet* Kinnock set up was a Belgian, and it also contained a Dutchman. In Brittan's *cabinet* there was one official from Ireland and one from Spain. Officials may acquire extensive *cabinet* experience. Neil Kinnock's first *chef de cabinet*, Philip Lowe, had already served in two previous *cabinets*, and Romano Prodi's first *chef de cabinet*, David O'Sullivan, had belonged to the *cabinets* of two successive Irish Commissioners, Peter Sutherland and Padraig Flynn.

Cabinet staff from official backgrounds can expect to be re-absorbed into their administrations of origin when the term of office of their commissioner ceases.

Much criticised flurries of *parachutage* have tended to occur as each Commission's term of office nears its end. Such practices are not confined to the Commission. The President of the European Parliament has a *cabinet* and in 1999 the appointment of a former member of it to a Director General's post within the European Parliament's services gave rise to court cases by two European Parliament officials who felt that they had been unfairly passed over. Those who already have the status of European Union officials have looked to further their careers, sometimes by substantial promotions, while those from outside who do not wish to return home seek to find themselves a permanent niche in the Union's services.

The possibilities for favouritism and nepotism to which the *cabinet* structures can potentially give rise were highlighted as the crisis that led to the 1999 resignation of the Commission developed. The response to these concerns was a Code of Conduct, adopted by the Prodi Commission as it took office. This code, drafted initially within the Santer Commission and vocally opposed by some of the then *cabinet* members on the grounds that reduced numbers would increase workloads and multi-nationality would reduce cohesion (*European Voice* 25 February–3 March 1999), reaffirmed the previous limitations on staff numbers and made the presence in each *cabinet* of officials from at least three nationalities a requirement. However, the appointment of a *chef de cabinet* of a nationality other than that of the Commissioner is merely an aspiration, as is the achievement of a gender balance. President Prodi set an example by the appointment of a highly regarded Irish official, David O'Sullivan, as his *chef de cabinet* and by soliciting applications for a number of the remaining posts. Since the consequence, according to *European Voice* (8–14 July 1999), was some 13 000 applications, and appointments had to be made fast, the process was probably less than rigorous, but symbolically important.

It seems likely that in the immediate aftermath of the crisis and under the vigilant eye of the press and member state governments these various restrictions will, for the time being, be complied with. The ingenuity with which formal constraints have been evaded in the past suggests, however, that considerable political determination and vigilance from the President of the Commission will be required to ensure that they result in a long-term change in culture and expectations.

The central functions of the *cabinets* in the European Commission are broadly the same as the classic ones of their national counterparts (Donnelly and Ritchie, 1997, p. 43): to be the political eyes and ears of their boss; to provide an additional source of, and channel for, policy advice; to co-ordinate policy development, and to control the work of the administrative services attached to their boss. The public presentation of the Commissioner's approach and image and liaison with the member states are also important functions (Donnelly and Ritchie, 1997, p. 45). In the European Commission, but also in the *cabinets* of the President of the European Parliament and of the Economic and Social Committee and the Committee of the Regions, staff provide support, both through the provision of personal assistance and a 'hand-holding' service – diary management, secretarial functions, travel arrangements, bag-carrying (both literal and metaphorical), preparation of papers, drafting of speeches – and through policy advice and co-ordination. For the *cabinets* of Commissioners the collegial nature of the Commission means that their advice may be particularly important in assisting the Commissioner to keep abreast of, and formulate an opinion on, matters upon which the College will be deliberating and voting that fall outside the area of the service for which she or he is directly responsible. Hence each senior member of the *cabinet* staff will monitor and advise on a range of topics, between them covering the full gamut of EC activities.

Policy support for the Commissioner extends to the preparation of meetings and decisions. In much the same ways as Committees of the British Cabinet are shadowed by committees of officials, so the meetings of the Commission are prepared by meetings of the heads of the Commissioners' *cabinets*, the *chefs de cabinet*. The Wednesday meeting of the College of Commissioners is preceded by a regular *chefs'* meeting on Monday. This meeting, chaired by the Secretary General of the Commission, is an important element in the co-ordination of the work of the Commission services (see above, Chapter 9). But on specific topics, too, there are meetings of representatives of each *cabinet*, known as 'special *chefs*" meetings. These may be *ad hoc*, in relation to particular proposals under consideration, or programmed on a reasonably regular basis. For example, some four or five times a year *chefs* or their representatives from the *cabinets* meet to consider possible cases where the College of Commissioners, in their role as guardians of the Treaty, may wish to proceed against member states for infringements of the Treaty provisions. The meetings are chaired by a member of the staff of the President's *cabinet*. These various meetings at least expose the areas of conflict and disagreement, and frequently eventually result in a decision. In a whole range of detailed areas it is thus the *cabinet chefs* or staff, on behalf of their Commissioner, who actually settle the decisions that the College then formally endorses, or for which the College has given them delegated powers.

Although *cabinet* members necessarily act on behalf of their Commissioner, whose workload would otherwise be quite impossible, in the settling of non-controversial matters, the processing of routine business and the preparation of meetings and decisions within the Commission, they cannot and do not replace the Commissioner or the Directorates General in dealings with outside bodies. Commissioners' *cabinet* staff only attend meetings of COREPER, or of Council working groups, or of comitology committees, or of the Committees of the European Parliament to accompany their Commissioner, not as a substitute. When attendance at official level at such external meetings is required, it is the officials from the Directorates General who are present.

It is the underpinning which their activity provides for the collegial nature of the Commission, rather than very direct management of the policy-making process, which is the essence of the co-ordinating role of the *cabinets*. Unlike their national counterparts the *cabinets* have little scope for influencing the internal co-ordination and management of the DGs. This indeed may partly have underpinned the complaint of the Commissioner reported above that DGs could not in practice be controlled.

The 'political' input of the *cabinets* into the policy formulation process within the DG also constitutes a form of control. *Cabinet* members will attempt to ensure that the Commissioner's priorities are respected and that policy changes which the Commissioner wishes to see promoted are given due attention. This can cause tensions, especially when a new approach means that a policy area where the Directorate General has previously had a free hand is coming under closer scrutiny from the *cabinet*. The *cabinets* are the subject of rather contradictory criticism: first, that they meddle too much, and second, that they constitute too opaque a screen between the Commissioner and the staff of his or her DG(s).

'The distinction between policy guidance and interference is not always clear-cut' (Donnelly and Ritchie, 1997, p. 50). Directors General, Directors and Heads of Unit, who often have quite entrenched notions of what the 'right' policy approach is, have tended to seek to preserve the 'purity' of their policy formulation functions by discouraging contact between staff in the DGs and the *cabinet*. Staff may indeed be explicitly instructed not to contact or speak to the members of their Commissioner's *cabinet* so that all communication is channelled and controlled through the hierarchy. *Cabinet* members, on the other hand, seek to circumvent these restrictions as far as possible, to ensure that the policy line is in fact one that is acceptable, and to try to impose a broader coherence. The temptation is to take over the dossiers.

> Sometimes skilful *cabinets* became 'shadow *cabinets*' for their commissioner's administrations undercutting the autonomy of the appointed leaders of the Directorates General. *Cabinet* members, including the most junior of them, often re-worked and rewrote the work of the services – sometimes 'just for the fun of it' in the words of [then] Assistant Secretary-General Carlo Trojan. (Ross, 1995, p. 161).

Equally and paradoxically, however, the *cabinets* are perceived as an unhelpful barrier between the staff of the services and the Commissioner. For example, for British officials transferring to the service of the Community in Brussels in the 1970s with an ethos that downplayed the divide between administration and politics in favour of direct loyalty to the promotion of the policies of the politician at the top, the *cabinets* were a source of intense frustration. Accustomed to taking instructions from, and responding to, their minister directly, they resented the fact that their proposals would vanish into the *cabinet* and might emerge, if at all, delayed or much changed. Twenty-five years later the Committee of Independent Experts observed that '*Cabinets* often act as screens and fences, impeding direct communication between commissioner and departments', and result in a 'distant, needlessly hierarchical and bureaucratic approach' (European Parliament, 1999b, para. 7.12.2 and 7.12.3). However, as a means of political control over the administrative services, as well as of co-ordination, the *cabinets* have proved themselves indispensable. But they have also been a factor in fragmentation and conflict.

Control by networks

During his years as President of the Commission, Jacques Delors, in the interests of pushing rapidly forward with the priorities he regarded as crucial, supplemented the extremely energetic activities of his personal *cabinet* with less institutionalised methods of control. The Commission President and his *cabinet* sought as far as they could to mobilise and galvanise. Since the hierarchies were rigid and procedures cumbersome, this was essentially done through networks, contacts, personal acquaintanceship and obligation. In many ways the very French private office of a French President of the Commission was echoing the tightly knit world of the Parisian political-administrative-commercial elite. Administrators in very many large systems make extensive use of acquaintanceship, common interests, shared knowledge and trust to smooth paths and lubricate the working of the systems. Heclo and Wildavsky's characterisation of Whitehall as a 'village' contains a valid and important metaphor (Heclo and Wildavsky, 1974). But the Parisian elite is particularly small and tight, bound together by connection, by the *esprit de corps* of the small exclusive *corps* at the top, and by mutual obligation. In an echo of that system, networks (based, inevitably, partly on nationality, on language or on political affiliation) were cultivated across the services. In this way the Commission President and his staff could be informed of developments, could hope to shape and control them, and could urge along or hold back.

These networks were supplemented and extended by the second aspect of the Delors system, which was the placing into senior positions, 'down to head of unit level', wherever possible, of officials whom Delors and his *cabinet* felt they could trust and rely on: 'individuals who could be called on whenever needed without undue concern for institutional boundaries'. They were undoubtedly by and large very suitable for their posts, 'smart, knowledgeable, hard-working and independent (and many were French)' (Ross, 1995, p. 158). But they were also intended to be co-operative and 'flexible' towards the policies which Delors was pushing. This undoubtedly involved finding ways around the restrictions which established hierarchies and procedures imposed. It can be argued that Delors and Lamy, his *chef de cabinet*, intended a reconfiguration of the services, which was announced by the so-called 'screening' programme of the early 1990s. But the reconstruction of the machinery of the Commission implied by the outcome of that process never happened. In part, it was overwhelmed by the enormous difficulties of redeployment discussed above; in part it was overtaken by events, as Delors' attention was absorbed by the difficulties of the Maastricht ratification process and the drive to economic and monetary union; and in part it was in itself a rather superficial response to the very fundamental management problems which Delors and his team preferred to bypass rather than confront.

The success of the onward drive of the European programme in the Delors period was undeniable; but in the administrative area at least the price was high, for the effects of the Delors approach were almost entirely nefarious. Both at the time (Ross, 1995, p. 159) and after Delors' term in office was over, it was admitted within the Commission that the methods adopted were harmful to the long-term good management, morale and culture of the services. Flexibility shades all too easily into irregularity and contempt for procedure, in matters of personnel and money as well as policy, which are the first steps towards corruption and favouritism. The creation of alternative networks, alongside, through and across the formal hierarchies and structures, increased fragmentation and potential conflict and decreased the scope for good management. The use of appointments and *parachutage* to sustain personal loyalty and commitment increased resentment and decreased morale in those who felt ignored, passed over or excluded. Some of the harvest that was reaped in 1999 was sown under the Delors presidency.

Chapter 11

Conclusion

This study has described and analysed a complex administration, which draws upon many varied traditions and is organised within a complex institutional geometry. Its officials carry out a complex set of functions, without clear political guidance, and within institutions which lack a strong underpinning of democratic legitimacy. Bureaucracies are sometimes derided, but feared, for being remote, superior and oppressive, or ridiculed for being stuffy, rigid and pedantic; this tradition, found in the last century in Dickens and Courteline, continues in the urban myths about the bureaucratic imposition, from 'Brussels', of straight bananas or hairnets for fishermen (Meyer, 1999, p. 629). More frequently they are ignored, both by the press and, with a number of notable exceptions, by academic commentators, until something goes very wrong.

The achievements of the Brussels bureaucrats have in fact been very substantial. From the small beginnings of the European Coal and Steel Community they have built up, over half a century, and to a new and original design, an operational and active set of bodies. The design was not, by and large, the work of the administrators. But making the designs work has been the task of the administrators of the Council, the Parliament, the Court of Justice, the Court of Auditors, the Economic and Social Council, the Committee of the Regions, the Commission and its agencies. Seen in the light of the evolution of both the institutions and the policies of the EU, the achievements of its officials are remarkable. However, after half a century, there are signs of persistent weaknesses within the administration. This conclusion sums up the analysis of the previous chapters by discussing these weaknesses and their implications for the process of European integration. The emerging European polity will both shape and be shaped by its administrative infrastructure. Whatever form that polity may take, an effective administration is an essential part of its successful survival.

Administrative weaknesses

Any evaluation of an institution involves the comparison of the existing reality with a model or template of what is desirable. However well rationalised the choice of model may be, it is inevitable that it will, at least to some degree, reflect the culture and experiences of its advocate. Max Weber did not intend his model of bureaucracy to be a normative template, but rather a measure against which any system could be judged so that systems could be compared and categorised. Nevertheless he constructed his model on the basis of observation of society around him, and the features he described, although never and nowhere existing in complete or perfect form, could be identified because societies had found them legitimate and useful. So an assessment of the reforms needed in the European Union on the grounds that the administration is insufficiently bureaucratic in a Weberian sense seems defensible (Stevens, 1999).

The first test of the Weberian model which the EU administration fails is that the bureaucrats should be appointed in a defined, systematic and objective way on the basis of professional qualifications. Almost all European civil services conform, at least formally, to this pattern. However, selection and training have posed particular difficulties for the services of the European Commission. To find a selection mechanism which combines a sense, inherited from continental models, that a store of relevant knowledge is required, with the Anglo-Saxon insistence on personal qualities and breadth, has posed problems, as Chapter 4 shows. Despite the rigidity and formality of many of the recruitment procedures, the EU has departed from the model in ways which have allowed other considerations to outweigh merit. Co-option has been a significant element in the appointments made by a number of the institutions, and merit has not been the only factor in promotions.

Second, bureaucrats are supposed to be isolated from external influences. They have a career which constitutes their sole (or at least principal) occupation and is remunerated by a salary. Again, this characteristic is broadly found across all European civil services. Within the EU, apart from some flagrant exceptions, most officials do resist financial inducements (see Chapter 3). However, EU officials are not isolated from the pressures emanating from their home state. Hooghe (1999a, p. 398) characterises the administrative organisation of the Commission as 'consociational' – that is, as 'represent[ing] the diversity of the polity' – with officials distributed to reflect the proportion of their nationality within the EU population and hence, at least implicitly, ensuring an input that reflects their nationality. She contrasts this with a 'Weberian' principle of selection by merit. Her study showed that the majority of the 105 officials she considered were happy with the current position, and about a quarter felt that there was no cause for concern either about the dominance of certain Directorates General by certain nationalities, or about the possibility that officials' judgements might be influenced by their nationality. However, as she demonstrates, this does not in fact mean that officials are unduly subservient to their nation state's interest: rather, they tend to regard their nationality as one tool in the kit they utilise to ensure that their careers develop and that their contribution to policy-making – the most prestigious of activities – is effective (1999a, pp. 401 and 417). If the administration of the EU is not to be perceived as alien and incomprehensible by both politicians and public, there are obvious arguments in favour of the view expressed by an official who told Liesbet Hooghe (1999a, p. 417), 'I like my colleagues to reflect the diversity within the Community. There is a certain mystery as to how people with such different backgrounds can work together.' What is crucial is that both the extent and limits of external influence should be acknowledged and recognised and that good management should limit any likelihood that it will degenerate into capture or corruption.

A third feature of the Weberian model of bureaucracy is that the bureaucrats accumulate an institutional expertise. They acquire and stock files, archives, precedents and procedures. But in none of the EU institutions is induction into the institutional expertise well provided for. Few of the administrative systems from which the European Commission draws its officials have any tradition of in-service training and neither do many of the EU institutions have much sense of apprenticeship. The European Commission has been developing its provisions in this area, but only slowly (see Chapter 5). In Chapters 7 and 8 we argued that the retention and management of expertise is also poor. Information tends to be hoarded and prized: it is a precious and scarce resource but also very individual and personal. George Ross records his horror as a scholar at the destruction of the papers, dossiers and archives which occurred when in 1991 the office of Commission President Jacques Delors moved into more cramped and less robust accommodation in the Breydel building (Ross, 1995, p. 300). The Commission is riven with internal divisions and inclined to habits which prevent the free flow of information and ideas. And some attempts to counter the consequences of aspects of the culture, such as those employed in the era of Jacques Delors, with the emergence of informal, parallel personal networks and contacts through which projects could be driven forward (see Chapter 10), only exacerbated the situation.

Fourth, Weber made a clear distinction between the 'supreme head' of a system of legal authority and 'the type [i.e., model] of rational legal administrative staff [which] is capable of application in all kinds of situations and contexts. It is the most important mechanism for the administration of everyday profane affairs' (Weber, 1947). Theorists generally see political leaders as operating with a degree of autonomy. As 'principals' they will attempt to delegate to the administrative agent a wide sphere of support for decision-making (for example, handling the paperwork and procedures and devising appropriate wordings) and for designing and executing implementation without incurring excessive transaction costs or losing control. However, as we saw in Chapter 10, in the EU there are interconnecting patterns of control and a number of methods by which politicians endeavour to assert their control over officials. Chapter 10 discussed the difficulties of defining an identifiable 'supreme head'. In the European Parliament the bureau, and in particular the President, has a general oversight over the administration, but the administration of the Council of Ministers is subject to a collective head, embodied in short-term presidencies. The Council of Ministers at one level seeks to hold the College of Commissioners to an acceptable course and define the direction of development. It also seeks to exercise some control over Commission officials both through the presence of national experts on working parties and consultative committees and through 'comitology' decision-making. The College of Commissioners in its turn seeks to control its own officials.

Addressing weaknesses

Many of the weaknesses of the administrative services have long been recognised. Several interviewees remarked that the Spierenburg analysis was still very relevant 20 years later. The weaknesses were brought sharply into focus when the failure of the College of Commissioners to ensure that their services were honest and effective was a major factor in bringing about their forced resignation in 1999. The result was a commitment in the Commission to ensure rapid and radical reform, and some pressure on the other institutions, especially the Council Secretariat and the Parliament, to ensure that they too would not be found wanting. Part of the process has been an attempt, through seminars and presentations, to impress upon the staff of the Commission that a wave of reform, with accompanying cultural changes, has swept through the administrative services of member states. This is partially recognised. French EU officials say the Commission 'feels like the French administration of many years ago' (McDonald, 1998, p. 33). Continued adherence to more traditional mentalities will, it is implied, make the body that should be at the heart of political and public policy development in Europe seem marginalised and old fashioned. McDonald quotes the proponents of reform: it is 'necessary if the Commission wants to retain its independence' (McDonald, 1998, p. 30).

In the words of the advertisements for financial products, 'the past is no guide to the future'. If it were, there would be good grounds for pessimism about the future directions of the EU administration (see Chapter 8). Strong leadership from the top could be the key factor in breaking the patterns of the past. But it will have to reckon with the following elements.

- The unwillingness of staff in the Commission (and to some extent in the other institutions where there is some policy input) to abandon the model that accords prestige and priority to policy formulation and to devote time, attention and resources to management.

- The certainty that the staff associations will defend the entrenched rights of their members and the *statut* which embodies them and equally their own rights to shared management structures. Both these features inhibit flexible management.

- The certainty that the member states, through the Council of Ministers and their own Commissioners, will continue to constrain resources, not only money but also staffing. There is no proposal to abandon direct control of the Commission's staff numbers, which the British Treasury, for example, gave up at the beginning of the 1990s. Neither will the member states renounce the notions of proportionality and national influence in senior appointments to all the institutions.

- The attachment that officials have to the preservation of the status quo, or at least to their last big achievement, and their vested interest in blocking radical change, and in rendering their problems more manageable by limiting the number of options considered. This specifically bureaucratic version of the model known as 'path dependency' is discernible within the European Union and acts as a deterrent to change which is liable to upset established procedures. In practice, as a Swedish official interviewed by Peterson and Bomberg observed, 'it is more often a case of sticking a new procedure onto the old one, which of course is treated with reverence because so much blood was spilt to agree it' (Peterson and Bomberg, 1999, p. 257).

- The fact that the culture change required, which will be a very considerable one, will involve very different adjustments for different people, since the starting points vary so markedly depending upon the administrative and social culture from which an official originates. Moreover, however unjustifiably, since administrative reform of various types has been undertaken in many member states, it is perceived as a 'northern', or even 'Anglo-Saxon', project and is consequently harder for 'southerners' to accept. 'It's the British and the Danes again, always criticising the Commission', McDonald was told (1998, pp. 26 and 79).

The potential balance sheet of a major shift in culture and practices in the EU, and especially the Commission, is hard to draw up. Other factors, including the evolution of public opinion, the progress of the euro, and the speed and shape of further enlargement will have an effect which it is unlikely to be possible to disentangle from the effects of administrative change. And the story will be told in different ways. For some it may be a rather overdue process of catching up and conforming to best practice in management, whether public or private. The administration will become honest, accountable, 'mature' (McDonald, 1998, p. 27) and effective. For others it may be a story of loss and sell-out. What will have disappeared will be the autonomous, rational, expert European public service, where staff could argue, as officials everywhere may (Peters, 1995, p. 225) that 'they are likely to do a better job (technically) of making policy in a certain issue area than the relatively ignorant political executive', with an added implication that the official possesses superior information about the nature of the general interest in the EU. In this story 'we are being moved away from the European ideal to something resembling Coca Cola' (McDonald, 1998, p. 35).

Administration and the process of integration

Administration matters to the process of European integration for three interlinked reasons: its effect on the EU's capabilities, its effect on the EU's legitimacy and its implications for the nature of the integration process. First, despite the nostalgia of some for administrative attitudes and practices which are steadily less acceptable at nation state level in an ever more consumer-oriented era, and better-founded fears that the baby of appropriate ethical values will be thrown out with the bathwater of inefficiency and corruption, the EU's administration will change over the first decade of the twenty-first century. But 'redesign, or changing institutions may be even more difficult than the initial design' (Peters, 1998, p. 10). Some of the reasons why this is so in the member states scarcely fit the European Union infrastructure. Rather, officials have brought into the administrative services the assumptions with which their national counterparts defend their status in their countries of origin. This has tended to give it a somewhat purposeless rigidity, something that the theorists who come at these issues from the different perspective of rational choice theory, and view the relationship between the political leadership – the principals – and the bureaucracy – its agents – in more adversarial terms, would certainly understand and expect. However, in the European Union there are multiple principals and 'it is not always clear who is principal and who is agent' (Peters, 1998, p. 14: see also Chapter 10 above). Finding a solution which enables the administrative services of the Union to avoid being bureaucratic in the pejorative sense and to acquire more of those bureaucratic characteristics which are desirable, indeed essential, is very far from simple. Inter-cultural differences will not readily disappear, even if more explicit understandings develop about acceptable practice in some areas.

While the functions of the officials of the other institutions may not change greatly in the near future, the role of the Commission will evolve. Nevertheless it is worth recalling how deeply embedded are the preferences for centralised capacities and for affording priority to policy invention above innovation in governance. These characteristics are scarcely surprising if the Commission is guided only by the notion that it must 'build Europe' and that this is likely to mean expanding its own policy-making role (Mazey and Richardson, 1994, p. 11). They clearly derive from the administrative traditions out of which many of the EU staff have come. There is, of course, a possibility that if the evolution of the Commission is towards greater effectiveness and less vulnerability to attack on the grounds that it is wasteful, corrupt and inefficient, these characteristics could be enhanced. It is notable that Hooghe found that Commission officials from 'weak, incohesive, highly permeable and politicized administrations' (Hooghe, 1999a, p. 410) were likely to support the idea of EU services built on Weberian principles. If the administration becomes more 'bureaucratic' in a desirable sense, it might also risk turning into a 'bureaucrat's paradise'. Given the rather weak and diffuse controls (see Chapter 9) the proponents of rational choice theories of administration (see Exhibit 11.1) might expect a more effective administration to be better able to pursue the maximisation of the welfare of its officials, whether by budget maximisation or bureau-shaping. Many analysts point out that it 'has an interest in trying to acquire greater competencies than the Council of Ministers intends to delegate' (Dowding, 2000, p. 135). Experience under Jacques Delors (Endo, 1999) gave some indication of how this could be done, even with the less than perfect instrument at his disposal.

Theories based upon the rational choice model all contain within them the implication of conflict which is a necessary outcome of the derivation from economic models where competition is an indispensable underlying premise. Budget maximisers assume the existence of a sponsor who provides the budget. Bureau-shapers, if to a lesser degree, also posit a bureaucracy which is defined in relation to an external entity – the politicians, the legislators – which distributes competences.

There are, however, alternative visions of future development. One interesting solution has been advanced by Les Metcalfe. He proposes a radical re-invention of the Commission as a 'network organisation' which would 'develop expertise in ensuring the coherence and reliability of European management networks' (Metcalfe, 1996, p. 5). However, he underestimates the extent to which such an approach would be alien to the administrative ethos which non-Anglo-Saxon officials bring to the work of the Commission (see Chapters 6 and 7).

The second reason why the administration of the EU matters is the impact which it has upon the legitimacy of the EU. Legitimacy is a complex concept but, in the European countries which make up the European Union, the exercise of authority by bodies which govern is regarded as legitimate if they fulfil certain criteria both in the ways in which they are chosen and accountable, and in relation to their performance in the production and implementation of legislation and policies (Beetham and Lord, 1998; Banchoff and Smith, 1999; Meyer, 1999, pp. 619–20). For the administration of the European Union the latter criteria are crucial. If the administrative infrastructure is not capable of providing for the political institutions a level of effective and honest service which will enable legitimacy to be gained and sustained through satisfactory performance, the structures of integration as a whole will suffer. This performance must encompass not only standards of conduct that are acceptable to all parts of the EU, but technical effectiveness and expertise, political sensitivity and transparency. The administration of the European Union has in its first five decades been defective in all these areas. Change will be a slow, hard process, but it is as central to the overcoming of the EU's democratic deficit as are constitutional arrangements.

The third reason why administration matters is the light which it may throw upon the possible evolution of the EU as a polity. The pioneers of integration saw the creation of a European public service as a key element in the development of what might become in some senses a federal entity (see Chapter 2). The ever-closer union that is now the goal of the EU is usually portrayed as a process, but it is one which the existence of a substantial, and by now well-founded, administration will influence. Administrative theorists agree that a level of bureaucracy is an essential condition of a modern state. But, given the wide variety of stances and approaches within theories of public organisations, they do not provide us with a single convincing answer to the question of whether the nature of the EU bureaucracy points definitively towards the EU as a polity of a particular type or at a particular level of state-formation. Indeed, this study has pointed up a number of puzzles and paradoxes, many of them already quite familiar. The first is the necessity (and difficulty) of establishing the contours of the institutional separation of politics and administration. This is an aspect which is sometimes ignored. While theories of governance, such as the those of Rod Rhodes and others, which emphasise the possession and exchange of resources of various kinds as the key feature of policy-making and implementation, do not disregard the role of political resources in these exchanges, some formulations, including in particular those which regard and advocate governance as essentially a process of steering by networks (and see the EU as actually or potentially a prime example of this), fail to pay adequate attention to the nature and problems of political direction. As Fred Ridley pointed out nearly four decades ago in relation to technocracy, the mere possession of expertise does not provide an in-built guidance as to where and how it is to be applied. Bureau-

---

Exhibit 11.1   Institutional rational choice theory and the EU administration

Rational choice theorists of bureaucracy assume that bureaucrats 'will make most (not all) [of] their decisions in terms of what benefits them, not society as a whole' (Tullock, 1976, reprinted in Hill, 1997a, p. 87). Downs, for example, assumes both 'that every official acts at least partly in his [*sic*] own self-interest, and some officials are motivated solely by their own self-interest' (Downs, 1967, p. 83) and that bureaux and the officials within them enjoy significant scope to pursue their own goals. His 'law of control duplication' assumes that at the highest level a separate group or individual (legislators or political leaders) will struggle to control the activities of separate and self interested bureaux (1967, p. 252). Another major rational choice theorist of bureaucracy, Niskanen, also separates bureaux from their sponsors who provide the budget in return for the bureau's output and postulates a constant struggle between bureau and sponsor. What benefits officials may be to expand the size of the bureaucracy in which they work (Tullock and Niskanen) or to maximise its budget. Patrick Dunleavy, while retaining the fundamental assumptions of the public choice model: that is,

a. that every individual and group is interested in the maximisation of benefits/welfare and the minimisation of costs;
b. that every individual/group is fairly self-interested;

rejects the budget maximising model. He argues that self-interested officials seek to 'improve their welfare by providing themselves with

→

---

shaping theory equally ignores questions of political direction, and takes a monolithic view of the EU as a single bureau, which is unsustainable in the face of evidence of fragmentation of many types.

A second dilemma which these theories highlight is the conflict between the desirability of a thoroughly subservient bureaucracy, speedily responsive to the political whims of its masters but perhaps in consequence unduly subject to ephemeral

→

congenial work and a valued work environment' (Dunleavy, 1991, p. 200). They value 'individually innovative work with a developmental rhythm, a broad scope of concerns, low exposure to public criticism, collegial and elite work units, restricted hierarchy, congenial personal relations, high status organisational and social contacts ... and proximity to political power centres'. They do not want to deliver high expenditure in-out budgets and hard to deliver programmes (Dunleavy, 1991, p. 237). Within the European Union this approach gives rise to assumptions about the Commission as a competence-maximising rational actor (Pollack, 1997a, p. 128), seeking to increase both the Union's and its own competences. Dunleavy (1997) argues that the administrative services of the European Union are the most perfectly bureau-shaped bureaucracy in the Western world. They have a small policy-making elite, a rather small operational expenditure budget, considerable insulation from budget cuts, and the ability to delegate almost all implementation of programmes back to the member states. For Dunleavy, the structure of the EU is both cause and consequence of its function. As an analysis of some of the key factors in administrative choices (see Chapters 6 and 7), Dunleavy's argument is illuminating; as an explanation of the overall political dynamics of the EU it is less plausible. It lacks supporting empirical data (Dowding, 2000, p. 136) and fails adequately to specify the location of the boundary between the politicians and the administration of the EU, doing inadequate justice to the complex relationships which exist between the two.

partisan influence or special interests, and a reasonably autonomous bureaucracy, with an ethos and to some extent an ideology of its own. This ideology may in part be directed towards self-preservation. It may need checking and controlling: but it may nevertheless act as the guardian of certain important objectives. This is the role assigned by the structures and constitution of the EU to their services, and is one of the essential characteristics which distinguishes the administrative from the merely secretariat functions. But the exact balance between sub-servience and autonomy is difficult to establish.

There is a similar difficulty in establishing the balance between bureaucracy, in the strict sense, with the accompanying possibilities of rigidity and closure in the system, and the 'pre-modern' characteristics of the EU's administrative services, which have the advantage, however, of making the structures rather open and receptive. And this balance is linked to one of the other major themes of administrative theory, which is the nature of the link between accountability and democracy and expertise. Here, too, the current balance seems to be inappropriate, and the legitimacy of the policy-formulation and implementation role of the EU is consequently under attack. Whatever the eventual nature of the EU polity, administrative questions seem likely to remain at its heart.

Further Reading

The theories of Max Weber (Weber, 1947) are an indispensable starting point for any consideration of bureaucrats and bureaucracy. Martin Albrow (Albrow, 1970) provides a useful introduction to the concept, while Edward Page (1992) applies Weber's categories to comparisons between Western European bureaucracies. B. Guy Peters also takes a broad view in a very readable and stimulating book (Peters, 1995) while Aberbach, Putnam and Rockman's work (1981) is a now classic study of officials.

On the institutional context of the Brussels bureaucrats, Nugent's work (1999) is authoritative. Hayes-Renshaw and Wallace (Hayes-Renshaw and Wallace, 1997) and Westlake (1995) provide valuable information on the Council of Ministers. There is an increasing amount of work on the Commission. The pioneering study by David Coombes (Coombes, 1970) stood alone for a long time; many of its reflections and observations are still very pertinent. The collection edited by Edwards and Spence (1994) contains much insider information on its internal workings, as does Cini's book (Cini, 1996), and Neil Nugent's collected work, *At the Heart of the Union: Studies of the European Commission* (Nugent, 1997) also reflects considerable in-depth work. The Union at work is well portrayed by Laura Cram (Cram, 1997) and by John Peterson and Elizabeth Bomberg (Peterson and Bomberg, 1999), while Claudio Radaelli's thoughtful essay considers whether the EU is indeed technocratic (Radaelli, 1999). George Ross's fascinating participant observer study (Ross, 1995) puts a great deal of flesh on the bones. The two reports by the Committee of Independent Experts appointed by the European Parliament in 1999 are a gripping and revealing study of administrative pathology (European Parliament, 1999a, 1999b). Spierenburg proved remarkably prescient (Spierenburg, 1979) while Nicolas chronicles the scandals in detail (Nicolas, 1999). Brigid Laffan had already shed much light upon the finances of the Union and the challenges involved (Laffan, 1997).

European officials themselves have been the subject of socio-logical study by Edward Page (Page, 1997) and anthropological study by Marc Abélès, Irène Bellier and Maryon McDonald, reported in a number of articles and chapters (including Bellier, 1994a, 1994b; McDonald, 1995, 1997; Abélès and Bellier, 1996). Liesbet Hooghe undertook intensive interviewing in 1995 and 1997 and some of the results of her exploration of the atti-tudes of officials can be found in a series of articles (Hooghe, 1997, 1999a, 1999b, 1999c).

Much of the administrative history of the European union is still to be written. It has begun with the 1992 issue of the *Jahrbuch für Europäische Verwaltungsgeschichte* edited by Erk Volkmar Heyen and Vincent Wright ('Early European Community Administration', 1992). Glimpses of the administra-tion at a particular historical moment can be found in Virginia Willis's study of the arrival of the British in Brussels (Willis, 1982) and in George Ross's work (Ross, 1995).

References

Abélès, Marc (1992), *La Vie Quotidienne au Parlement Européen* (Paris: Hachette).

Abélès, Marc (1996), *En Attente d'Europe* (Paris: Hachette: Questions de Politique).

Abélès, Marc and Irène Bellier (1996), 'La Commission Européenne, Du Compromis Culturel à la Culture Du Compromis', *Revue Française de Science Politique*, Vol. 46, No. 3 (June), pp. 431–56.

Abélès, Marc, Irène Bellier and Maryon McDonald (1993), 'Approche Anthropologique de la Commission Européenne' (Brussels: unpublished report to the European Commission; cyclostyled).

Aberbach, Joel D., Robert Putnam and Bert Rockman (1981), *Bureaucrats and Politicians in Western Democracies* (Cambridge Mass.: Harvard University Press).

Albrow, Martin (1970), *Bureaucracy* (London: Macmillan).

Armstrong, Kenneth and Simon Bulmer (1998), *The Governance of the Single European Market* (Manchester: Manchester University Press).

Banchoff, Thomas and Mitchell P. Smith (eds) (1999), *Legitimacy and the European Union: The Contested Polity* (London: Routledge).

Beetham, David and Christopher Lord (1998), *Legitimacy and the European Union* (London: Longman).

Bellier, Irène (1994a), 'La Commission Européenne: Hauts Fonctionnaires et "Culture Du Management"', *Revue Française d'Administration Publique*, No. 70, pp. 253–62.

Bellier, Irène (1994b), 'The Commission as an Actor: An Anthropologist's View', in Helen Wallace and Alasdair Young (eds), *Participation and Policy-Making in the European Union* (Oxford: Oxford University Press and Clarendon Press), pp. 91–115.

Biesheuvel, Barend, Edmund Dell and Robert Marjolin (1979), *The Three Wise Men Report: Report on the Operation of the Community Institutions* (Brussels: Official Publications Office of the European Community).

Bodiguel, Jean-Luc (1994), *Les Fonctions Publiques dans l'Europe Des Douze* (Paris: Librairie Générale de Droit et de Jurisprudence).

Bodiguel, Jean-Luc and Jean-Louis Quermonne (1983), *La Haute Fonction Publique* (Paris: Presses Universitaires de France).

Bossuat, Gérard (1995), 'The French Administrative Elite and the Unification of Western Europe 1947–58', in Anne Deighton (ed.), *Building Post-War Europe: National Decision Makers and European Institutions 1948–63* (London: Macmillan).

Bottomore, Tom (1964), *Elites and Society* (Harmondsworth: Penguin Books).

Brigouleix, Bernard (1986), *C.E.E. Voyage en Eurocratie* (Paris: Editions Alain Moreau).

Bruter, Michael (1999), 'Diplomacy Without a State: The External Delegations of the European Commission', *Journal of European Public Policy*, Vol. 6, No. 2 (June), pp. 183–205.

Bulmer, Simon (1998), 'New Institutionalism and the Governance of the Single European Market', *Journal of European Public Policy*, Vol. 5, No. 3, pp. 365–86.

Cassanmagnago-Cerretti, M.-L. (1993), *The Role of National Experts and the Commission's Right of Initiative*, Report of the Committee on Institutional Affairs (European Parliament, 1993).

Cassese, Sabino (1987), 'Divided Powers: European Administration and National Administrations', in Sabino Cassese (ed.), *The European Administration* (Brussels: International Institute of Administrative Sciences), pp. 8–20.

Cassese, Sabino and Giacinto della Cananea (1992), 'The Commission of the European Community: The Administrative Ramifications of its Political Development (1957–1967)', *Jahrbuch Für Europäische Verwaltungsgeschichte*, Vol. 4 (Die Anfänge der Verwaltung der Europäischen Gemeinschaft), pp. 75–94.

Chalude, Monique, Robin Chater and Jacqueline Laufer (1986), *Equal Opportunities in the Commission of the European Communities*, COPEC (87) 256 1987 (Brussels: Editions Michel Chalude & Assoc.).

Church, Clive and David Phinnemore (1994), *European Union and European Community: A Handbook and Commentary on the Post-Maastricht Treaties* (London: Harvester Wheatsheaf).

Cini, Michelle (1996), *The European Commission; Leadership, Organisation and Culture in the EU Administration* (Manchester: Manchester University Press).

Cini, Michelle (1997), 'Administrative Culture in the European Commission: The Cases of Competition and Enviroment', in Neill Nugent (ed.), *At the Heart of the Union: Studies of the European Commission* (London: Macmillan), pp. 71–89.

Cini, Michelle and Lee McGowan (1998), *Competition Policy in the European Union* (London: Macmillan).

Cockfield, Arthur (1997), 'Communication to the Conference "A Tribute to Emile Noël"' (London: London Office of the European Commission), 24 October.

Conlon, Bernard (1998), 'Commission Navel-Gazing', *Public Service*, Vol. 1, No. 5 (July), p. 26.

Conrad, Yves (1989), *Jean Monnet et les Débuts de la Fonction Publique Européenne: La Haute Autorité de la CECA (1952–1953)* (Louvain-la-neuve: CIACO éditeur et GEHEC).

Conrad, Yves (1992), 'La Communauté Européenne du Charbon et de l'Acier et la Situation de ses Agents. Du Régime Contractuel au Régime Statutaire (1952–1958)', *Jahrbuch Für Europäische Verwaltungsgeschichte*, Vol. 4 (Die Anfänge der Verwaltung der Europäischen Gemeinschaft), pp. 59–74.

Coombes, David (1970), *Politics and Bureaucracy in the European Community* (London: Allen & Unwin).

Coombes, David (1975), 'Special Problems of Educating and Training Officials of the European Communities', in Y. Chapel (ed.), *Education and In-Service Training of International and European Civil Servants* (Bruges: de Tempel).

Corbett, Richard, Francis Jacobs and Michael Shackleton (1995), *The European Parliament*, 3rd edn (London: Cartermill Publishing).

Coudurier, Michèle (1994), 'Impressions d'un Voyage au Coeur de l'Europe; Janvier À Juin de l'an de Grace 1994', Unpublished typescript, June.

Cram, Laura (1994), 'The European Commission as a Multi-Organization: Social Policy and IT Policy in the EU', *Journal of European Public Policy*, Vol. 1, pp. 195–218.

Cram, Laura (1997), *Policy-Making in the EU* (London: Routledge).

Crozier, Michel (1964), *Le Phénomène Bureaucratique* (Paris: Le Seuil).

Dehousse, Renaud (1998), *The European Court of Justice* (London: Macmillan).

Dellis, George (1994), 'Le Regime Disciplinaire des Communautés Européennes: introduction générale', unpublished paper.

Dellis, George (undated), 'L'Application des Codes de Conduite – Regles Disciplinaires dans les Services Publics des Etats Membres des Communautés Européennes', unpublished paper.

Dondelinger, Jacques (1985), 'Relations avec les Administrations Nationales', in J. Jamar and Wolfgang Wessels (eds), *Community Bureaucracy at the Crossroads – L'Administration Communautaire à l'Heure du Choix*, Actes du Colloque Organisé par le Collège d'Europe (Brussels: de Tempel).

Donnelly, Martin and Ella Ritchie (1997), 'The College of Commissioners and their *Cabinets*', in Geoffrey Edwards and David Spence (eds), *The European Commission*, 2nd edn (London: Longman), pp. 31–49.

Dowding, Keith (2000), 'Institutionalist Research on the European Union: A Critical Review', *European Union Politics*, Vol. 1, No. 1 (February), pp. 125–44.

Downs, Anthony (1967), *Inside Bureaucracy* (Boston, Mass.: Little, Brown).

Dubouis, Louis (1984), 'L'Évolution de la Fonction Publique Communautaire Concorde-t-elle avec celle des Communautés

Européennes?', in *Etudes de Droit des Communautés Européennes, Mélanges Offerts à Pierre-Henri Teitgen* (Paris: Pedone).

Dubouis, Louis (1994), 'Fonctionnaires et Agents des Communautés Européennes – Commentaire des Décisions Rendues par le Tribunal de Première Instance et par la Cour de Justice des Communautés Européennes de Septembre 1989 à Juillet 1993', *Revue Trimestrielle de Droit Européen*, No. 2, pp. 171–373.

Duchêne, François (1994), *Jean Monnet: The First Statesman of Interdependence* (New York and London: W.W. Norton).

Dunleavy, Patrick (1991), *Democracy, Bureaucracy and Public Choice* (Hemel Hempstead: Harvester Wheatsheaf).

Dunleavy, Patrick (1997), 'Explaining the Centralization of the European Union', *Aussenwirtschaft*, Vol. 52, pp. 183–212.

Dupuy, Francois and Jean Claude Thoenig (1983), *Sociologie de l'Administration Française* (Paris: A. Colin).

'Early European Community Administration' (1992), *Jahrbuch Für Europäische Verwaltungsgeschichte*, Vol. 4.

Edwards, Geoffrey and David Spence (eds) (1997), *The European Commission*, 2nd edn (London: Longman).

Elles, James (1992), *The Staff Policy of the Community Institutions*, Report of the Committee of Budgets (European Parliament).

Endo, Ken (1999), *The Presidency of the European Commission under Jacques Delors* (London: Macmillan).

Erdmenger, Jurgen (1983), *The European Community Transport Policy*, translated and updated from *EG Unterwegs – Wege zur Gemeinsamen Verkehrspolitik* (Aldershot: Gower).

European Commission (1999), *Designing Tomorrow's Commission (DECODE)* (Brussels: European Commission Inspectorate General); available at http://europa.eu.int/comm/reform/decode/screening_en.pdf.

European Community (1994), *Information, Communication, Transparency* (Luxembourg: Office for Official Publications of the European Community).

European Parliament (1999a), 'Committee of Independent Experts: First Report', http://www.europarl.eu.int/experts/en.

European Parliament (1999b), 'Committee of Independent Experts: Second Report', http://www.europarl.eu.int/experts/en.

European Parliament: Committee on Institutional Affairs (1999), *Report of M. Herman on improvements in the functioning of the Institutions without modification of the Treaties* (Brussels: European Parliament Doc PE229072).

European Union Budget (1999), Budget of the European Union 1999, *Official Journal of the European Union L series*, No. 39, 12 February 1999.

European Union (2000), *General Report on the Activities of the European Union 1999* (Luxembourg: Office for Official

Publications of the EU), available at http//europa.eu.int/abc/doc/off/rg/en/welcome.htm.

Grant, Charles (1994), *Delors: Inside the House that Jacques Built* (London: Nicholas Brealey).

Greenwood, Justin (1997), *Representing Interests in the European Community* (London: Macmillan).

Guérivière, Jean de la (1993), *Voyage à l'Intérieure de l'Eurocratie*, nouvelle édition (Paris: Le Monde-éditions).

Gulick, Luther (1937), 'Science, Values and Public Administration', in Luther Gulick and L. Urwick (eds), *Papers in the Science of Administration* (New York: Institute of Public Administration).

Hallstein, Walter (1972), *Europe in the Making*, translation of *Der unvollendete Bundesstaat* (1969: Charles Roetter, trans.) (London: George Allen & Unwin).

Hay, Richard (1989), *The European Commission and the Administration of the Community*, European Documents Series (Luxembourg: Official Publications Office of the European Community).

Hayes-Renshaw, Fiona and Helen Wallace (1997), *The Council of Ministers* (London: Macmillan).

Heclo, Hugh and Aaron Wildavsky (1974), *The Private Government of Public Money* (London: Macmillan).

Hill, Michael (1997a), *The Policy Process: A Reader*, 2nd edn (London: Prentice-Hall/Harvester Wheatsheaf).

Hill, Michael (1997b), *The Policy Process in the Modern State* (London: Prentice Hall/Harvester Wheatsheaf).

Hix, Simon (1999), *The Political System of the European Union* (London: Macmillan).

Hooghe, Liesbet (1996), 'Building a Europe with the Regions: The Changing Role of the European Commission', in Liesbet Hooghe (ed.), *Cohesion Policy and European Integration* (Oxford: Clarendon Press/Oxford University Press), pp. 89–126.

Hooghe, Liesbet (1997), 'A House with Differing Views: The European Commission and Cohesion Policy', in Neill Nugent (ed.), *At the Heart of the Union: Studies of the European Commission* (London: Macmillan), pp. 89–108.

Hooghe, Liesbet (1999a), 'Consociationalists or Weberians? Top Commission Officials on Nationality', *Governance*, Vol. 12, No. 4 (October), pp. 397–424.

Hooghe, Liesbet (1999b), 'Images of Europe: Orientations to European Integration among Senior Officials of the Commission', *British Journal of Political Science*, Vol. 29, pp. 345–67.

Hooghe, Liesbet (1999c), 'Supranational Activists or Intergovernmental Agents? Explaining Orientations of Senior Commission Officials Towards European Integration', *Comparative Political Studies*, Vol. 32, No. 4, pp. 435–63.

Hooghe, Liesbet (forthcoming), *Images of Europe: Political Orientations of Senior Commission Officials.*

Hoskyns, Catherine (1996), *Integrating Gender: Women, Law and Politics in the European Union* (London: Verso).

House of Lords (1988), *Staffing of Community Institutions: 11th Report of the Select Committee on the European Communities*, HLP 66 (London: HMSO, 1987–88).

Jenkins, Roy (1997), 'Communication to the Conference "A Tribute to Emile Noël"' (London: London Office of the European Commission), 24 October.

Kassim, Hussein and Vincent Wright (1991), 'The Role of National Administrations in the Decision-Making Processes of the European Community', *Rivista Trimestrale Di Diritto Publico*, No. 3, pp. 832–50.

Kreher, Alexander (1997), 'Agencies in the European Community – A Step Towards Administrative Integration in Europe', *Journal of European Public Policy*, Vol. 4, No. 2 (June), pp. 225–45.

Laffan, Brigid (1997), *The Finances of the European Union* (London: Macmillan).

Levy, Roger (1996), 'Managing Value-for-Money Audit in the European Union: The Challenge of Diversity', *Journal of Common Market Studies*, Vol. 34, No. 4 (December), pp. 509–29.

Lintner, Val and Clive Church (forthcoming), *The European Union: Economic and Political Aspects* (London: McGraw-Hill).

Mango, Anthony (1988), 'The Role of Secretariats of International Institutions', in Paul Taylor and A.J.R. Groom (eds), *International Institutions at Work* (London: Frances Pinter), pp. 39–49.

Maor, Moshe and Handley Stevens (1996), *Converging Administrative Systems: Recruitment and Training in the European Commission* (London: The European Insititue of the London School of Economics and Political Science).

Martin, D. (1995), *What Future for the European Commission?* (London: Philip Morris Institute for Public Policy Research).

Matlary, Janne Haaland (1997), 'The Role of the Commission: A Theoretical Discussion', in Neill Nugent (ed.), *At the Heart of the Union: Studies of the European Commission* (London: Macmillan), pp. 265–82.

Mazey, Sonia (1992), 'Conception and Evolution of the High Authority's Administrative Services (1952–1956): From Supranational Principles to Multinational Practices', *Jahrbuch Für Europäische Verwaltungsgeschichte*, Vol. 4 (Die Anfänge der Verwaltung der Europäischen Gemeinschaft), pp. 31–47.

Mazey, Sonia and Jeremy Richardson (1993), *Lobbying in the European Community* (London: Routledge).

Mazey, Sonia and Jeremy Richardson (1994), *Promiscuous Policy Making: The European Policy Style*, Occasional papers in European

Public Policy, No. 6 (Warwick: European Public Policy Institute, University of Warwick).

McDonald, Maryon (1995), '"Unity in Diversity": Some Tensions in the Construction of Europe', *Social Anthropology*, Vol. 4, No. 1, pp. 47–60.

McDonald, Maryon (1997), 'Identities in the European Commission', in Neill Nugent (ed.), *At the Heart of the Union: Studies of the European Commission* (London: Macmillan), pp. 49–70.

McDonald, Maryon (1998), 'Anthropological Study of the European Commission' (Brussels: unpublished report for The European Commission).

McGowan, Lee (1997), 'The Commission and Competition Policy', in Neill Nugent (ed.), *At the Heart of the Union: Studies of the European Commission* (London: Macmillan), pp. 145–66.

McSwite, O.C. (1997), *Legitimacy in Public Administration* (Thousand Oaks, California, and London: Sage).

Mendrinou, Maria (1994), 'European Community Fraud and the Politics of Institutional Development', *European Journal of Political Research*, Vol. 26, pp. 81–101.

Metcalfe, Les (1992), 'After 1992: Can the Commission Manage Europe?', *Australian Journal of Public Administration*, Vol. 51, No. 1, pp. 17–130.

Metcalfe, Les (1996), 'Building Capacities for Integration: The Future Role of the Commission', *Eipascope*, No. 2, pp. 2–8.

Meyer, Christoph (1999), 'Political Legitimacy and the Invisibility of Politics: Exploring the EU's Communication Deficit', *Journal of Common Market Studies*, Vol. 37, No. 4 (December), pp. 617–39.

Michelmann, Hans (1978), 'Multinational Staffing and Organisational Functioning in the Commission of the EEC', *International Affairs*, Vol. 32, No. 2, pp. 477–96.

Middlemas, Keith (1995), *Orchestrating Europe: The Informal Politics of the European Union* (London: Fontana/HarperCollins).

Miliband, Ralph (1969), *The State in Capitalist Society* (London: Weidenfeld & Nicolson).

Monnet, Jean (1976), *Mémoires* (Paris: Fayard).

Morgan, Roger (1992), 'Jean Monnet and the ECSC Administration: Challenges, Functions and the Inheritance of Ideas', *Jahrbuch Für Europäische Verwaltungsgeschichte*, Vol. 4 (Die Anfänge der Verwaltung der Europäischen Gemeinschaft), pp. 1–9.

Nicolas, Jean (1999), *L'Europe des Fraudes* (Brussels: Editions PNA).

Noël, Emile (1992), 'Témoignage: L'Administration de la Communauté Européenne dans la Rétrospection d'un Ancien Haut Fonctionnaire', *Jahrbuch Für Europäische Verwaltungsgeschichte*, Vol. 4 (Die Anfänge der Verwaltung der Europäischen Gemeinschaft), pp. 145–58.

Nugent, Neill (1994), *The Government and Politics of the European Union*, 3rd edn (London: Macmillan).

Nugent, Neill (1997), 'At the Heart of the Union', in Neill Nugent (ed.), *At the Heart of the Union: Studies of the European Commission* (London: Macmillan), pp. 1–26.

Nugent, Neill (1999), *The Government and Politics of the European Union*, 4th edn (London: Macmillan).

Page, Edward (1992), *Political Authority and Bureaucratic Power: A Comparative Analysis*, 2nd edn (Hemel Hempstead: Harvester Wheatsheaf).

Page, Edward (1997), *People Who Run Europe* (Oxford: Oxford University Press).

Page, Edward (undated), 'The Problem of Nationality in the Administration of the European Union', *Insight: Newsletter of the Centre for European Studies*, University of Hull.

Page, Edward and Linda Wouters (1994), 'Paying the Top People in Europe', in B. Guy Peters and Christopher Hood (eds), *Rewards at the Top* (London: Sage), pp. 201–14.

Penaud, Jeanne, (ed.) (1989), *La Fonction Publique Des Communautés Européennes* (Paris: Documentation Française: Problèmes Politiques et Sociaux, Vol. 617).

Penaud, Jeanne, (ed.) (1993), *La Fonction Publique Des Communautés Européennes* (Paris: Documentation Française: Problèmes Politiques et Sociaux, Vols 713–14).

Peters, B. Guy (1995), *The Politics of Bureaucracy*, 4th edn (London: Longman).

Peters, B. Guy (1998), *The New Institutionalism and Administrative Reform: Examining Alternative Models* (Madrid: Instituto Juan March de Estudios e Investigationes, Centro de Estudios en Ciencias Sociales Estudio/Working Paper 1998/113).

Peterson, John (1999a), 'Jacques Santer: The EU's Gorbachev', *ECSA Review*, Vol. 12, No. 4, pp. 4–6.

Peterson, John (1999b), 'The Santer Era: The European Commission in Normative, Historical and Theoretical Perspective', *Journal of European Public Policy*, Vol. 6, No. 1 (March), pp. 46–65.

Peterson, John and Elisabeth Bomberg (1999), *Decision-Making in the European Union* (London: Macmillan).

Peterson, John and Margaret Sharp (1998), *Technology Policy in the European Union* (London: Macmillan).

Petit-Laurent, Philippe (1994), 'Réflexions sur l'Éfficacité de l'Institution et de Son Administration' (Report submitted to the European Commission), November.

Pierre, Jon (1995), 'Comparative Public Administration: The State of the Art', in Jon Pierre (ed.), *Bureaucracy in the Modern State: An Introduction to Comparative Public Administration* (Aldershot: Edward Elgar), pp. 1–17.

Pollack, Mark A (1997a), 'The Commission as an Agent', in Neill Nugent (ed.), *At the Heart of the Union: Studies of the European Commission* (London: Macmillan), pp. 109–28.

Pollack, Mark A (1997b), 'Representing Diffuse Interests in EC Policy-Making', *Journal of European Public Policy*, Vol. 4, No. 4 (December), pp. 572–90.

Pollitt, Chris (1997), 'The Development of Management Thought', in Michael Hill (ed.), *The Policy Process: A Reader* (London: Prentice-Hall/Harvester Wheatsheaf).

Radaelli, Claudio (1999), *Technocracy in the European Union* (London: Longman).

Ritchie, Ella (1992), 'The Model of French Ministerial Cabinets in the Early European Commission', *Jahrbuch Für Europäische Verwaltungsgeschichte*, Vol. 4 (Die Anfänge der Verwaltung der Europäischen Gemeinschaft), pp. 95–106.

Rometsch, Dieter and Wolfgang Wessels (1996), *The European Union and Member States, Towards Institutional Fusion?* (Manchester: Manchester University Press).

Rometsch, Dieter and Wolfgang Wessels (1997), 'The Commission and the Council of Ministers', in David Spence and Geoffrey Edwards (eds), *The European Commission*, 2nd edn (London: Cartermill).

Ross, George (1995), *Jacques Delors and European Integration* (Cambridge: Polity Press).

Rouban, Luc (1998), *The French Civil Service* (translated by Mary and Anne Stevens) (Paris: La Documentation Française).

Sasse, Christoph, Edouard Poullet, David Coombes and Gérard Deprez (1977), *Decision Making in the European Community* (London and New York: Praeger).

Simon, Herbert (1957), *Administrative Behaviour*, 2nd edn (New York: Macmillan).

Shaw, Jo (1983), *European Community Law* (London: Macmillan).

Siotis, Jean (1964), 'Some Problems of European Secretariats', *Journal of Common Market Studies*, Vol. II, No. 3, pp. 222–50.

Spence, David (1997a), 'Staff and Personnel Policy in the Commission', in Geoffrey Edwards and David Spence (eds), *The European Commission*, 2nd edn (London: Longman), pp. 62–96.

Spence, David (1997b), 'Structure, Functions and Procedures in the Commission', in Geoffrey Edwards and David Spence (eds), *The European Commission*, 2nd edn (London: Longman), pp. 97–114.

Spierenburg, Dirk, chairman (1979), *Proposals for Reform of the Commission of the European Communities and its Services. Report by an Independent Review Body under the Chairmanship of Mr Dirk Spierenburg* (Brussels: Official Publication of the European Union).

Stevens, Anne (1999), 'Bureaucrats in Brussels and Beyond', *International Relations*, Vol. XIV, No. 4 (April), pp. 33–45.

Stevens, Anne and Handley Stevens (1997), 'Le Non-Management de l'Europe', *Politiques et Management Public*, Vol. 15, No. 1 (March), pp. 33–52.

Taylor, Frederick Winslow (1911), *The Principles of Scientific Management* (New York: Harper & Row).

Tullock, Gordon (1976), *The Vote Motive* (London: Institute of Economic Affairs).

Weber, Max (1947), *The Theory of Social and Economic Organization* (A.M. Henderson and Talcott Parsons, trans.) (New York: Free Press).

Wessels, Wolfgang (1998), 'Comitology – Fusion in Action. Politico-Administrative Trends in the EU System', *Journal of European Public Policy*, Vol. 5, No. 2 (June), pp. 209–34.

Westlake, Martin (1994), 'The Commission and the Parliament', in Geoffrey Edwards and David Spence (eds), *The European Commission* (London: Longman), pp. 237–63.

Westlake, Martin (1995), *The Council of the European Union* (London: Cartermill).

Williamson, David, chair (1998), *Reflection Group on Personnel Policy*, European Commission (Brussels), November.

Willis, Virginia (1982), *Britons in Brussels: Officials in the European Commission and Council Secretariat*, Studies in European Policy, vol. 7 (London: Policy Studies Institute (European Centre for Political Studies) and the Royal Institute for Public Administration).

Women at the European Commission 1984–1994 (1994) (Brussels–Luxembourg: Commission of the European Communities).

Wright, Vincent (1994), 'The Administrative Machine: Old Problems and New Dilemmas', in Peter A. Hall, Jack Hayward and Howard Machin (eds), *Developments in French Politics*, 2nd edn (London: Macmillan), pp. 114–32.

Ziller, Jacques (1988), *Egalité et Mérite – L'Accès à la Fonction Publique dans les États de la Communauté Européenne* (Brussels: Institut International d'Administration Publique).

Ziller, Jacques (1993), *Administrations Comparées* (Paris: Montchrestien).

Zito, U. (1992), 'Recruiting and Training of Civil Servants in the EC', *Europäische Integration und Öffentliche Verwaltung* (Vienna: Orac: Verwaltungswissenschaftliche Studien).

Index